Targeted Advertising Technologies in the ICT Space

T0184663

Christian Schlee

Targeted Advertising Technologies in the ICT Space

A Use Case Driven Analysis

Christian Schlee
Darmstadt, Germany

ISBN 978-3-8348-2395-3   ISBN 978-3-8348-2396-0 (eBook)
DOI 10.1007/978-3-8348-2396-0

The Deutsche Nationalbibliothek lists this publication in the Deutsche Nationalbibliografie; detailed bibliographic data are available in the Internet at http://dnb.d-nb.de.

Library of Congress Control Number: 2013948610

Springer Vieweg

Printed on acid-free paper

Springer Vieweg is a brand of Springer DE.
Springer DE is part of Springer Science+Business Media.
www.springer-vieweg.de

Preface

Targeted advertising is one of the hottest new media buzzwords. Target group specific advertisments are ubiquitous in the Web and big players like Google owe their enormous growth to profits realized through advertising services based on sophisticated targeting technologies. However, the potential of targeted advertising reaches beyond the Web across the entire ICT space including IPTV, mobile and convergent environments.

This book provides a broad overview of trends and developments in targeted advertising covering all relevant ICT channels and gives a comprehensive introduction to underlying technologies. Basic chapters on targeting, ad formats and technological backgrounds allow the reader to quickly dive into the topic. The core of the book consists of a use case driven analysis of existing and upcoming targeted advertising scenarios across all ICT channels followed by technological deep dives. Supplemental sections covering business and legal aspects complete the picture. This approach likewise addresses readers with academic background and those coming from the ICT industry.

The book is based on my diploma thesis written at Darmstadt University of Technology and in cooperation with Detecon International GmbH. Research and analyzes I performed in this context allowed me to significantly improve both my methodogical knowledge as well as my professional expertise, which I am very grateful for. The reception of my work among my tutors and the feedback of experts and colleagues at Detecon International GmbH who read the thesis motivated me to share the knowledge I gained with others potentially interested in the topic. Due to the time that has passed since my graduation the work has been slightly modified and updated.

I would like to address some words of gratitude to everyone supporting me in writing this book. I want to thank my tutors at Darmstadt University of Technology Dr. Nicolas Repp and Dr. Julian Eckert for guiding me through the creation of my diploma thesis. I specially wish to thank my colleague at Detecon International GmbH Holger Diekmann for sharing his expertise and excellent methodical knowledge. I would further like to thank all interview partners, experts and colleagues at Detecon International GmbH providing me with their valuable inputs. Finally, special thanks to my family and friends who put up with me while I was writing this book, I thank you for your good wishes and your patience.

Christian Schlee

Abstract

In recent years the Information and Communication Technology (ICT) space started to change dramatically. Web services are significantly gaining importance creating new business models and revenue opportunities for Internet companies, while steadily increasing the demand for bandwidth. At the same time they expand their business towards the telecommunications domain degrading traditional telecommunication operators to "bit pipes". Carriers are hence increasingly threatened by high revenue losses requiring them to open up new business opportunities beyond their network core business. Targeted advertising is one of these opportunities basically following the "Telco 2.0" paradigm providing a service platform for the interaction of 3rd parties, in this case advertisers and consumers. The concept of targeted advertising includes the compilation of detailed information about consumers and their preferences in using the Internet or consuming other media for the purpose of providing them with individualized advertisements (ads).

This book deals with targeted advertising technologies in the ICT space as well as their strategic business implications, and provides a comprehensive overview of market trends. Since the whole ICT space is transforming to an all-IP world, Web advertising formats are a strong driver in targeted advertising. Most of today's Web portals already use targeting technology to identify the users, track their usage behavior and finally provide them with personalized Web offerings. The two-way architecture of IP networks potentially enables very promising targeting scenarios in Internet Protocol Television (IPTV). However, IPTV is still in early stages and operators will need to acquire more subscribers before being able to bring programmers and advertisers on board at a large scale. The most interesting IPTV use cases include network- and STB-based display advertising, interactive advertising, ad insertion in linear television (TV) and Video on Demand (VoD) scenarios, Electronic Program Guide (EPG) portal advertising and advertising in the context of personal TV channels. In the mobile environment, targeted advertising currently starts gaining traction, driven by recent technology developments in terms of devices and network infrastructure. The most significant use cases are mobile Web advertising, message advertising, on-device advertising, and mobile TV and video advertising. In future, next-generation advertising technologies for converged scenarios, allowing for targeted advertising campaigns across multiple ICT channels at the same time, will become more and more important. Certainly, such complex cross-channel advertising scenarios in triple-play environments pose particular challenges that have to be tackled.

The goal of this work is to perform a comprehensive but also practice-oriented analysis of targeted advertising technologies in the ICT space, therefore following a use-case driven approach. Based on information derived from expert interviews and literature research, the most interesting use cases in the Web, IPTV, in the mobile environment, and in converged scenarios are identified and described from a user perspective. Crucial points emerging from these descriptions are further deepened in a technological analysis resulting in elaborate models depicting underlying technology units and their interworking. This allows identifying technological opportunities and challenges of the respective scenarios. Resulting from these analyses important technological key building blocks are identified and examined more closely. This includes the generic description of a targeted advertising framework with functional components like profiling, targeting and recommendation units as well as technological deep dives into the subjects of Identity Management (IdM) and recommendation technologies. In order to achieve a comprehensive overview, business and legal aspects of targeted advertising are covered supplemental.

Table of Contents

Preface V

Abstract VII

Table of Contents IX

List of Figures XV

List of Tables XIX

List of Abbreviations XXI

1   Introduction 1

   1.1   Motivation and Problem Definition 1

   1.2   Methodology 2

      1.2.1   Structure of the Book 3

      1.2.2   Interview Proceeding 4

2   Definitions and Related Work 9

   2.1   Foundations of Targeted Advertising 9

      2.1.1   Targeted Advertising as Part of the Personalization Process 10

      2.1.2   Definition and Types of Targeting 11

      2.1.3   The Business Environment of Targeted Advertising 16

         2.1.3.1   Classification of the Targeted Advertising Business Model 16

         2.1.3.2   The TV Advertising Environment 17

         2.1.3.3   The Mobile Advertising Environment 20

   2.2   Use Case Basics 22

   2.3   Basic Technology 24

      2.3.1   IPTV Basics 24

      2.3.2   Mobile Communication Basics 28

      2.3.3   Implications for the Use Case Development 37

   2.4   Standardization Efforts in the Environment of Targeted Advertising 38

   2.5   Definition of Ad Formats 42

      2.5.1   Web Advertising Formats 42

2.5.1.1   Interactive Advertising Bureau 43

2.5.1.2   Online-Vermarkterkreis (Circle of Online Marketers) 45

2.5.1.3   Vendor Specific Advertising Formats.......................................47

2.5.2   IPTV Advertising Formats 47

2.5.2.1   Classic TV Ad Formats..47

2.5.2.2   Web TV/IAB In-Stream Video Advertising Formats 49

2.5.2.3   Interactive Advertising Formats..52

2.5.2.4   Summary of IPTV Relevant Ad Formats...................................54

2.5.3   Mobile Advertising Formats 55

2.5.3.1   Mobile Web...55

2.5.3.2   Text Messaging (SMS) 56

2.5.3.3   Multimedia Messaging (MMS)..57

2.5.3.4   Mobile Video and TV 58

2.5.3.5   Mobile Applications..58

3   Use Case Identification and Description...61

3.1   Targeted Web Advertising 61

3.2   Targeted Advertising in the IPTV Environment.......................................63

3.2.1   IPTV Display Advertising..68

3.2.1.1   Network-Based Banner Ad Insertion 68

3.2.1.2   Set-Top-Box-Based Overlay Ad Insertion.................................69

3.2.1.3   Interactive Advertising..70

3.2.2   IPTV Ad Insertion..71

3.2.2.1   Linear TV Ad Insertion..72

3.2.2.2   Dynamic VoD Ad Insertion 73

3.2.3   EPG Advertising 74

3.2.4   Personal TV Channel Advertising 75

3.2.4.1   Personal TV Channels..75

3.2.4.2   Personalized Barker Channel 76

3.3   Targeted Advertising in the Mobile Environment 77

3.3.1   Mobile Web Advertising..82

3.3.1.1   On-Portal Advertising 82

3.3.1.2   Off-Portal Advertising 83

3.3.2   Message Advertising 84

3.3.2.1   In-Message Advertising 84

3.3.2.2   Direct Message Marketing 86

3.3.3   On-Device Advertising 87

3.3.4   Mobile TV and Video Advertising 89

3.4   Targeted Advertising in Converged Scenarios 90

3.4.1   Targeted Advertising in a Triple-Play Environment 91

3.4.2   Dynamic Ad Replacement in Pre-Recorded Content 92

4   Technological Use Case Analysis 95

4.1   Targeted Web Advertising 95

4.1.1   Players in the Web Advertising Environment 96

4.1.2   Use Case Actors in the Targeted Web Advertising Platform 97

4.1.3   Targeted Advertising on an Operator Web Portal 98

4.2   Targeted Advertising in the IPTV Environment 104

4.2.1   Players in the IPTV Advertising Environment 104

4.2.2   Use Case Actors in the IPTV Targeted Advertising Process 105

4.2.3   IPTV Display Advertising 107

4.2.3.1   Network-Based Banner Ad Insertion 107

4.2.3.2   Set-Top Box Based Overlay Ad Insertion 112

4.2.3.3   Interactive Advertising 119

4.2.4   IPTV Ad Insertion 126

4.2.4.1   Linear TV Ad Insertion 126

4.2.4.2   Dynamic VoD Ad Insertion 136

4.2.5   EPG Advertising 142

4.2.6   Personal TV Channel Advertising 149

4.2.6.1   Personal TV Channels 149

4.2.6.2   Personalized Barker Channel 156

4.3   Targeted Advertising in the Mobile Environment 157

4.3.1   Players in the Mobile Advertising Environment............................157

4.3.2   Use Case Actors in the Targeted Mobile Advertising Process 159

4.3.3   Mobile Web Advertising...160

4.3.4   Message Advertising..169

    4.3.4.1   In-Message Advertising 169

    4.3.4.2   Direct Message Marketing 177

4.3.5   On-Device Advertising 180

4.3.6   Mobile TV and Video Advertising 183

4.4   Targeted Advertising in Converged Scenarios 190

4.4.1   Targeted Advertising in a Triple-Play Environment......................190

4.4.2   Dynamic Ad Replacement in Pre-Recorded Content.....................198

5   Analysis of Key Building Blocks in Targeted Advertising Technologies...217

5.1   Generic Description of a Targeted Advertising Platform 217

5.1.1   Content Categorization and Tracking 218

5.1.2   Profile Generation and Enrichment..219

5.1.3   Targeting and Recommendation 220

5.1.4   Campaign Management and Ad Selection.......................................221

5.1.5   Reporting and Feedback...221

5.1.6   General Implications for Targeted Advertising
          Implementations..222

5.2   Identity Management Issues...224

5.2.1   Identity and Related Concepts 225

5.2.2   Description of Identity Management Models 227

    5.2.2.1   Isolated Silo Identity Management Model...............................227

    5.2.2.2   Centralized Identity Management Model.................................228

    5.2.2.3   Federated Identity Management Model 230

    5.2.2.4   User-Centric Identity Management Model 231

5.2.3   Identity Management in the Telco Domain 233

    5.2.3.1   Identity Management Enabled AAA Services 234

    5.2.3.2   IdM/AAA Bridging in Next Generation Networks.................235

5.2.4   Identity Management in the Context of Targeted Advertising 239

5.3   Recommendation Technologies 242

    5.3.1   Terminology and Business Scenarios..242

    5.3.2   Overview and Definition of Recommender Systems 243

    5.3.3   Basic Types of Recommender Systems 244

        5.3.3.1   Content-Based Filtering 244

        5.3.3.2   Collaborative Filtering 246

        5.3.3.3   Other Recommendation Methods and Further Reading..........251

    5.3.4   Hybrid Recommender Systems 251

        5.3.4.1   A Stereotype-Based Hybrid Recommender System................252

        5.3.4.2   Evaluation of the Stereotype-Based Approach......................257

    5.3.5   Context-Aware Recommender Systems...257

6   Business and Legal Aspects of Targeted Advertising....................................263

  6.1   Business Aspects of Targeted Advertising...263

    6.1.1   Developments in Web Advertising 264

    6.1.2   IPTV Environment 264

    6.1.3   Mobile Environment...266

    6.1.4   Converged Scenarios 268

  6.2   Legal Aspects of Targeted Advertising...268

    6.2.1   General Principles of the Legal Framework..................................269

    6.2.2   Privacy Aspects of Targeted Web Advertising 271

        6.2.2.1   Legitimacy of Personal Data Collection and Usage...............271

        6.2.2.2   Legitimacy of User Profile Creation and Usage.....................272

    6.2.3   Privacy Matters in the Wunderloop Targeting Platform 274

    6.2.4   Limitations for Stream Manipulation through Targeted
        Advertising in IPTV 276

7   Conclusion and Outlook..279

Bibliography..285

Appendix 309

  Vendor Interviews...309

  Interview Targeting Platform Operator..327

  Interview IPTV Operator 333

List of Figures

Figure 1:	Generic personalization process	10
Figure 2:	Aspects of dynamic changes in the user environment	13
Figure 3:	The TV advertising value chain	18
Figure 4:	The mobile advertising value chain	20
Figure 5:	"Waterfall" model of software engineering	23
Figure 6:	Simple UML use case diagram mobile call initiation	24
Figure 7:	IPTV network architecture	25
Figure 8:	Simplified IPTV architecture	27
Figure 9:	Architecture of the GSM system	29
Figure 10:	Basic SMS network architecture	31
Figure 11:	Circuit- and packet-switched GSM subsystems	32
Figure 12:	GSM/UMTS based mobile TV service with vs. without MBMS	35
Figure 13:	Non-Linear Overlay/Non-Linear Non-Overlay Invitation Ads	51
Figure 14:	Linear Pre-Roll Video Ad with Companion Ads	52
Figure 15:	Examples for Red Button advertising	53
Figure 16:	DAL advertising example	54
Figure 17:	Mobile Web Banner Ad units in 6:1 and 4:1 aspect ratio	56
Figure 18:	MMS Pre-Roll Ad example	57
Figure 19:	Mobile Application/Game example	59
Figure 20:	Targeted online advertising on T-Online Web portal	62
Figure 21:	Option space: IPTV targeted advertising opportunities	64
Figure 22:	Use case diagram: IPTV targeted advertising	67
Figure 23:	Network-based banner ad insertion	68
Figure 24:	Local/STB-based overlay ad insertion	69
Figure 25:	Interactive IPTV advertising	70
Figure 26:	Interactive IPTV advertising flow	71
Figure 27:	Linear TV ad insertion	72

Figure 28: Dynamic VoD ad insertion..73

Figure 29: Targeted EPG banner advertising 74

Figure 30: APRICO personal TV channel..75

Figure 31: Personalized barker channel on ITV Digital (UK) 76

Figure 32: Option space: mobile targeted advertising opportunities.................78

Figure 33: Use case diagram: mobile targeted advertising................................81

Figure 34: On-portal advertising on T-Mobile Web'n'Walk 82

Figure 35: Off-portal advertising on FUSSBALL.DE 83

Figure 36: In-message advertising...84

Figure 37: Blyk ad funded mobile communication 86

Figure 38: AdMob iPhone in-app advertising 87

Figure 39: Deutsche Telekom Mobile TV on iPhone..89

Figure 40: Targeted advertising in a triple-play environment 91

Figure 41: Dynamic ad replacement in pre-recorded content 92

Figure 42: Players in the environment of a targeted Web advertising platform 96

Figure 43: Targeted Web portal advertising..99

Figure 44: Players in the environment of a targeted advertising platform in IPTV 104

Figure 45: Network-based banner ad insertion..108

Figure 46: STB-based overlay ad insertion 113

Figure 47: Interactive Red Button advertising, Request-For-Information 120

Figure 48: Linear TV ad insertion 127

Figure 49: Zone-based linear TV ad insertion..132

Figure 50: Linear TV ad insertion enhanced by overlay ads...........................134

Figure 51: Dynamic VoD ad insertion..137

Figure 52: Targeted advertising in a Web-based EPG 143

Figure 53: Personal TV channel advertising 150

Figure 54: Players in the environment of a targeted advertising platform in mobile networks...158

Figure 55: On-portal mobile Web advertising...161

Figure 56: In-message advertising in a news push scenario 170

Figure 57: Targeted advertising in a triple-play environment 191

Figure 58: Device authentication and AAA/IdM bridging 196

Figure 59: Overview dynamic ad replacement in pre-recorded content..........204

Figure 60: Detailed view on recording/transcoding/ad detection part............210

Figure 61: MobAd architecture diagram enhanced with C&PR.....................212

Figure 62: Use case model and corresponding MobAd functions/interfaces ..215

Figure 63: Generic targeted advertising platform 218

Figure 64: Relationship of entities, identities, and attributes..........................226

Figure 65: Silo IdM model and legend 228

Figure 66: Centralized user identity model...229

Figure 67: Federated user identity model 231

Figure 68: User-centric identity model with silo domains...............................232

Figure 69: AAA/IdM bridging in IMS based NGN networks 237

Figure 70: Circle of trust in an IPTV environment...239

Figure 71: Collaborative Filtering matrix of user-recommendation item
relations 246

Figure 72: Collaborative Filtering: user-based concept, item-based concept..249

Figure 73: Stereotype and item profile creation...253

Figure 74: Dynamic questionnaire for initial profile generation 254

Figure 75: User profile and media item representation....................................255

Figure 76: Creation of user recommendation lists...256

Figure 77: Architectural models for context-aware recommender systems 261

Figure 78: Multidimensional recommendation space......................................262

Figure 79: Order of application of legal regulations.......................................270

Figure 80: Data flow in the Wunderloop targeting platform 276

List of Tables

Table 1: Overview of interview partners...6

Table 2: Standards organizations in the context of targeted advertising..........38

Table 3: UAP specifications...44

Table 4: OVK standard forms of advertising 46

Table 5: Ad formats in linear TV 48

Table 6: Overview of special ad formats in linear TV 49

Table 7: Legal consequences of Web usage profiling......................................274

List of Abbreviations

3GPP	3rd Generation Partnership Project
A2P	Application-to-Person
AAA	Authentication, Authorization, and Accounting
ad	advertisement
ADS	Microsoft Active Directory Services
AHP	Analytic Hierarchy Process
AIS	Active Idle Screen
AKA	Authentication and Key Agreement
ANSI	American National Standards Institute
API	Application Programming Interface
app	application
ASP	Active Server Pages
AUC	Authentication Center
BBC	British Broadcasting Corporation
BCAST	OMA Mobile Broadcast Services Enabler Suite
BSC	Base Station Controller
BSF	Bootstrapping Server Function
BSS	Business Support System, in GSM context also: Base Station Subsystem
BT	British Telecom
BTS	Base Transceiver Station
BVDW	Bundesverband Digitale Wirtschaft e.V. (German Association for the Digital Economy)
C&PR	Contextualization and Personalization Resources
CATV	Cable Television
CB	Content-Based Filtering
CEPT	European Conference of Postal and Telecommunications Administrations
CF	Collaborative Filtering
CMS	Content Management System
CoD	Content on Demand
CPA	Cost Per Action
CPC	Cost Per Click
CPM	Cost Per Mille
cPVR	Client PVR, similar to home PVR
CRM	Customer Relationship Management

CSP	Communication Service Provider
DAL	Dedicated Advertiser Location
DHTML	Dynamic HTML
DMB	Digital Multimedia Broadcasting
DPI	Deep Packet Inspection
DRM	Digital Rights Management
DRTV	Direct Response TV
DSL	Digital Subscriber Line
DSLAM	Digital Subscriber Line Access Multiplexers
DTMF	Dual-Tone Multi Frequency
DVB	Digital Video Broadcasting Project
DVB-H	Digital Video Broadcasting – Handheld
DVB-T	Digital Video Broadcasting – Terrestrial
DVR	Digital Video Recorder
DVS	Digital Video Subcommittee of the SCTE
DWH	Data Warehouse
E-CRM	Electronic Customer Relationship Management
e.g.	exempli gratia, for example
EBIF	Enhanced TV Binary Interchange Format
EDGE	Enhanced Data Rates for Global/GSM Evolution
EIR	Equipment Identity Register
EPG	Electronic Program Guide
ESG	Electronic Service Guide
ESME	External Short Message Entity
et sqq.	et sequens, and the following
etc.	et cetera
ETSI	European Telecommunications Standards Institute
ETV	Enhanced TV
FG	Focus Group
GAA	Generic Authentication Architecture
GBA	Generic Bootstrapping Architecture
GEM	Globally Executable MHP
GEMA	Gesellschaft für musikalische Aufführungs- und mechanische Vervielfältigungsrechte
GGSN	Gateway GPRS Support Node
GIF	Graphics Interchange Format
GMSC	Gateway Mobile Services Switching Center
GPRS	General Packet Radio Service
GPS	Global Positioning System
GSM	Global System for Mobile Communications, originally Groupe Spécial Mobile

GSMA	GSM Association
GUI	Graphical User Interface
GUP	Generic User Profile
HDTV	High Definition Television
HLR	Home Location Register
HSDPA	High-Speed Downlink Packet Access
HSS	Home Subscriber Serve
HTML	Hypertext Markup Language
i.e.	id est, that is
IAB	Interactive Advertising Bureau
IAM	Identity and Access Management
ICT	Information and Communication Technology
ID	Identity
ID-FF	Identity Federation Framework
IdM	Identity Management
IdP	Identity Provider
IEEE	Institute of Electrical and Electronics Engineers
IMEI	International Mobile Equipment Identity
IMPI	IP Multimedia Private Identity
IMS	IP Multimedia Subsystem
IMSI	International Mobile Subscriber Identity
IP	Internet Protocol
IPC	Incomplete Pair-wise Comparison algorithm
IPTV	Internet Protocol Television
ISDN	Integrated Services Digital Network
ISIM	IP Multimedia SIM
ITU	International Telecommunication Union
ITU-T	International Telecommunication Union, Telecommunication Standardization Sector
iTV	Interactive TV
J2ME	Java 2 Platform, Micro Edition
JPG	Joint Photographic Experts Group, graphics format
JSP	Java Server Pages
kbit	kilo bit
LAN	Local Area Network
LBS	Location-Based Services
LDAP	Lightweight Directory Access Protocol
Mbit	Mega bit
MBMS	Multimedia Broadcast Multicast Service
MD5	Message-Digest algorithm 5
MHP	Multimedia Home Platform

MMA	Multimedia Marketing Association
MMS	Multimedia Messaging Service
MO	Mobile-Originated (SMS)
MobAd	Mobile Advertising enabler
MPEG	Moving Picture Experts Group
MPEG-4 AVC/H.264	MPEG-4 Part 10 (Advanced Video Coding), standard for video compression
MS	Mobile Station or Microsoft
MSC	Mobile Services Switching Center
MSISDN	Mobile Subscriber ISDN Number
MT	Mobile-Terminated (SMS)
MVNO	Mobile Virtual Network Operator
NAF	Network Application Function
NAL	Network Abstraction Layer
NAS	Network Access Server
NGN	Next Generation Network
nPVR	Network PVR
NSS	Network and Switching Subsystem
OCAP	OpenCable Application Platform
ODP	On-Device Portal
OMA	Open Mobile Alliance
OMC	Operation and Maintenance Center
OoH	Out of Home
OS	Operating System
OSS	Operations and Support System, Operations Support System
OVK	Online-Vermarkter Kreis (Circle of Online Marketers)
P2P	Here: Person-to-Person, also Peer-to-Peer
PAD	Personal Authentication Device
PAL	Phase Alternation Line
Par.	Paragraph
PCU	Packet Control Unit
PDN	Packet Data Networks
PNG	Portable Network Graphics, graphics format
POTS	Plain Old Telephone Service
PSTN	Public Switched Telephone Network
PVR	Personal Video Recorder
RADIUS	Remote Authentication Dial In User Service
RAN	Radio Access Network
RC	Remote Control
RFI	Request For Information
ROI	Return Of Investment

RSS	Radio Subsystem
SAML	Security Assertion Markup Language
SCTE	Society of Cable Telecommunications Engineers
Sec.	Section
SGSN	Serving GPRS Support Node
SIM	Subscriber Identity Module
SME	Short Message Entity
SMS	Short Message Service
SP	Service Provider
SS7	Signaling System #7
SSO	Single Sign-On
STB	Set-Top-Box
STP	Signal Transfer Point
TA	Targeted Advertising
TCP	Transmission Control Protocol
TDOA	Time Difference Of Arrival
Telco	Telecommunication operator
TISPAN	Telecoms & Internet converged Services & Protocols for Advanced Networks
TV	Television
TVoW	TV over Web
U.S.	United States of America
UAP	Universal Ad Package
UE	User Entity
UICC	Universal Integrated Circuit Card
UK	United Kingdom
UML	Unified Modeling Language
UMTS	Universal Mobile Telecommunication System
URI	Uniform Resource Identifier
URL	Uniform Resource Locator
USP	Unique Selling Proposition
VG Media	Gesellschaft zur Verwertung der Urheber- und Leistungsschutzrechte von Medienunternehmen
VLR	Visitor Location Register
VoD	Video on Demand
VoIP	Voice over Internet Protocol
WAP	Wireless Application Protocol
Webco	Web companies entering the Telco space, compare Telco
Wi-Fi	Trademark of the Wi-Fi Alliance, denotes class of wireless local area network (WLAN) devices based on the IEEE 802.11 standards

WLAN   Wireless LAN
WMV   Windows Media Video
WWW   World Wide Web
ZIP   Zone Improvement Plan, ZIP code = system of postal codes
                    used by the United States Postal Service (USPS)

1 Introduction

In recent years the advertising industry has undergone substantial changes that can be characterized by two major developments. First, traditional advertising channels like television (TV), radio, newspapers, and out of home (OoH) media lose importance while online advertising has been growing significantly in the last six years, experiencing an average growth rate of more than 40% year-on-year across 16 countries in Europe [209]. Online advertisements (ads) are gradually replacing traditional formats. Second, advertisers are increasingly facing problems in reaching distinct audiences across the diversity of emerging advertising channels. In addition, advertisers have to deal with an inability to accurately identify and target potential customer segments due to the broadcasting nature of traditional advertising channels leading to suboptimal campaigns and lower return on investments (ROI). In consequence, the growing popularity of non-traditional channels in combination with the capability to identify customers and track their behavior have led to a major interest and increasing investments in targeted advertising [46].

1.1 Motivation and Problem Definition

Since the beginning of the new millennium online advertising has become omnipresent on websites and more recently on Web TV and in the mobile environment. Being the major driver of online advertising technology Google has actually reinvented online advertising with their targeting framework AdSense/AdWords[1]. Large Internet players like Google and Yahoo! are aggressively exploiting the shift of advertising money from traditional media to the Web now also moving their targeting capabilities to other screens [19, 108].

The concept of targeted advertising basically includes the compilation of detailed information about consumers and their preferences in using the Internet or consuming other media for the purpose of providing them with individualized advertisements. Hence, the key asset for targeted advertising is the ability to identify single users and collect data about their consumption behavior. This ability to evaluate feedback and reporting information is made possible by IP technologies opening up potential business opportunities for targeted advertising in other ICT channels like IPTV and mobile and also in converged environments. As advertis-

---

[1] https://www.google.com/adsense and http://adwords.google.de/

ers are continuously seeking the most efficient way to reach their customers, they turn their interest to IPTV and mobile screens challenging telecom operators (Telcos) to provide attractive business models. Hence, advertising via telecom delivery channels is about to take off, and its importance will increase substantially over the next few years [16]. Now that Telcos have established a solid footing in IPTV their suppliers are introducing the means by which carriers can leverage their IP advantage to become significant players in next-generation advertising [52]. Mobile advertising is expected to become a standard feature across the tier one mobile operators worldwide [209].

The goal of this work is to analyze targeted advertising technologies in the ICT space and their strategic business implications. Therefore, current market trends and recent technological developments must be analyzed in order to identify the most interesting use cases. The major input for this market and technology assessment is delivered from interviews with 14 Telco experts. The next step is to take a closer look at underlying technologies in the relevant ICT network channels, i.e. Web, IPTV, mobile, and converged scenarios. This includes aspects in the context of network architectures, service delivery, and also end devices. A special focus will be laid on the analysis of use case models and the functional elements building up a targeted advertising framework. The goal of this analysis is to identify the most promising targeted advertising scenarios in future Telco business showing up potential revenue opportunities. Attention must be paid to the fact that besides the pure technology aspects, there may also be social, legal, and business concerns potentially holding up the development of targeted advertising. This can for example include differing levels of receptiveness among consumers in different markets as well as concerns about privacy and not at least scalability issues if the subscriber base is too small to be interesting for advertisers [19]. Below the methodical approach of this work will be explained in more detail.

1.2 Methodology

In the following, first a short overview on the structure of this book shall be given and the methodical approach will be described in order to introduce the reader to the proceeding in the subsequent sections. In a second section, the interview approach chosen to collect input for use case selection is explained and all interview partners are listed.

1.2.1 Structure of the Book

As a start, section 2 will give some basic definitions and explanations around targeted advertising. This includes a classification of targeted advertising in the context of personalization, the definition of targeting types, and a description of the business environment, in which targeted advertising typically takes place. As the title further suggests the book follows a use case-driven approach to analyze targeted advertising in the ICT space. Hence, the next steps are to introduce some use case terminology and techniques before relevant ICT network technologies will be roughly explained as is necessary to understand the use cases. The section closes with a state of affairs overview on standardization efforts in the environment of targeted advertising in the ICT space and a description of typical ad formats in the different ICT channels.

The description of common and innovative ad formats in Web, IPTV, and the mobile space serves as a starting point and leads over to section 1 whose purpose is the identification and description of the most interesting use cases. In addition to current advertising scenarios derived from the ad formats, major input was generated from questionnaire guided interviews covering general aspects of targeted advertising in the ICT space and also informal interviews conducted in the context of specific topics. A more detailed overview on the applied interview methodology and the interview partners is given in the next subsection. Based on the outcome of the interviews the most interesting use cases are selected. As Internet technology is a major driver of developments in targeted advertising, a Web use case is described at the beginning. However, the main focus lies on scenarios taking place in IPTV, mobile and converged environments. Potential use case scenarios in IPTV and mobile are depicted in form of an option space in order to provide a comprehensive overview. Then the most interesting ones are selected and aggregated in form of use case diagrams. In the following the use cases chosen for a deeper analysis are each basically described from a user perspective and motivated concerning their particular relevance in the context of the book.

Section 1 deals with the underlying technology of the use cases and therefore can be considered as the actual core of the book. The analysis follows a structured approach in order to provide a consistent overview across the different ICT channels (Web, IPTV, mobile, converged scenarios). In a first step, the major players involved in the targeted advertising process are described. Basic players recurring in each of the cases are for example users, publishers, ad marketers, and the operator. Next, the analysis steps one level down describing the technology units acting in the domains of these players. After this introduction, each of the use cases is examined closely. For this purpose the scenarios are depicted in form of a functional diagram, which subsequently is described in form of a flow description. Finally, the background of each scenario is analyzed especially focusing on technological issues and challenges. The goal of this section is to provide the reader with a comprehensive understanding of major concerns and key developments within the respective area of focus.

As will become obvious during the use case analyses, targeted advertising platforms are generally made up of some core elements recurring across all of the surveyed ICT channels. Therefore, in section 0 these key building blocks are examined closer. First, an attempt is made to generically describe the key functionalities of targeted advertising platforms deriving adequate insights from a concrete Web-based implementation. Another focal point of this section is the complex of Identity Management (IdM) concerns, which are especially important in the context of converged scenarios. However, the ability to identify users and/or devices is a critical factor for targeting in general. Eventually, the role of recommender systems in the context of targeted advertising is explained and a comprehensive overview on common as well as state-of-the-art and future recommendation technologies is given.

While the main focus of the book is set on the technology behind targeted advertising, the subject certainly covers business and legal aspects as well. Therefore, section 6 aims at providing an overview of business opportunities and legal issues arising in the context of targeted advertising. Based on the insights from previous sections, recent business developments in Web, IPTV, mobile, and converged environments are pointed out, further giving an overview of existing and future potentials. Then, the framework of German privacy laws is outlined. Using the example of Web advertising, privacy concerns of targeting are analyzed closer. The section ends with an examination of legal issues in the context of stream manipulation required for targeted advertising in IPTV.

Eventually, section 7 summarizes the results of the uses case analyses and draws conclusions regarding targeted advertising activities in the ICT space ending up with recommendations Telco operators might want to keep in mind when developing future strategies in the context of targeted advertising.

1.2.2 Interview Proceeding

As a basis for guided interviews a questionnaire focusing on the general market situation in the context of targeted advertising, typical use cases, technical platforms, and privacy and standardization aspects was developed. The questionnaire was discussed and improved with experts at Detecon International GmbH. Guided interviews with technology experts are a tool for qualitative research and can be used to gather concrete information on specific technology topics but also incorporating respective business aspects. A quantitative analysis would have been too time-intensive while probably not yielding much more valuable results within the scope of this work. A typical characteristic of questionnaire-guided interviews is to confront the interviewee with open questions allowing her to freely respond and focus on aspects she thinks of as important within her respective context. The questionnaire hence serves as orientation and does not necessarily be answered in the original order of questions. As a consequence it is more challenging for the interviewer to stay focused and later extract and aggregate relevant aspects. The background for the sample composition in the case of qualitative analyses is different from the motivation in quantitative research. While statistical representativeness is not necessarily required, it is rather important to choose a sample that assures representativeness with regards to the content. This means that interview partners should be selected such that constructive results within the scope of this work emerge [130]. Hence, the spectrum of interview partners was chosen in order to cover technology vendors and Deutsche Telekom Group units focusing on targeted advertising and/or technology aspects in Web, IPTV, and mobile environments. Depending on the interview partners' background, the questionnaires have been slightly modified in order to also obtain more specific information in the context of the interviewees' area of focus. With the interviewee's consent the interviews have been recorded using a voice recorder. Based on these recordings and notes taken during the interview sessions, the main thoughts have been summarized in structured protocols that can be found in the appendix at the end of the book. An exact transcription is not required in this context.

The basic idea behind the guided interviews that were performed was collecting initial input for the development of use cases and about recent market developments. However, with ongoing progress of the work, it became obvious that additional input on specific topics would be necessary in order to gain deeper insights e.g. about identity management or recommendation technologies. Therefore, several informal interviews have been performed in addition. Albeit these interviews are not attached in the annex, the interview partners and the respective interview contexts are also listed in the below overview.

Table 1:   Overview of interview partners

Questionnaire/Guided Interviews			
Company	**Expert/Position**	**Context**	**Conducted**
Nokia Siemens Networks GmbH & Co. KG	Dietmar Maierhöfer/ Advertising Solution Consultant	Vendor, Multi-channel Advertising, Mobile TV & Video	2009-08-07, 2009-11-26
SeaChange International, Inc.	Joseph "Yossi" Weihs/ Director Product Management	Vendor, IPTV, Targeting	2009-08-27
Sun Microsystems, Inc.	Taras Bugir/ Strategic Sales Manager Global IPTV	Vendor, IPTV, Targeting	2009-08-28
Deutsche Telekom AG, T-Home	Torsten Topaloglu/ Expert Targeting & Permission Marketing	Web Portals, Targeting	2009-08-13, 2009-10-09
Deutsche Telekom AG, Products & Innovation	Sebastian Thiele/ Product Manager IPTV	IPTV, Advertising	2009-08-28

Informal Interviews			
Detecon International GmbH	Holger Diekmann, Managing Consultant Information Technology	IPTV, Network Architectures	2009-08-13
Detecon International GmbH	Stephan Dieter, Managing Consultant Strategy & Marketing	Advertising, IPTV	2009-08-13, 2009-10-09
Detecon International GmbH	Martin Pieperhoff-Sauter, Senior Consultant Communication Technology	Mobile Architecture & Services	2009-08-13
Nokia Siemens Networks GmbH & Co. KG	Rainer Schmäling/ Service Delivery Framework (SDF) Solution Consultant	Identity Management	2009-12-07
Sun Microsystems, Inc.	Bernd Kaponig/ Principal Engineer	Identity Management	2009-11-23
InteractiveMedia CCSP GmbH	Peter Eiermann/ Head of Projects & Producing	Web Portals, Ad Marketing	2009-09-16
Deutsche Telekom AG, Deutsche Telekom Laboratories	Thomas Buchholz/ Senior Expert Project Management	IPTV Architecture	2009-09-23

Questionnaire/Guided Interviews			
Company	**Expert/Position**	**Context**	**Conducted**
YOOCHOOSE GmbH	Uwe Alkemper/ CEO, Founder	Recommendation Technologies, Targeting	2009-08-14
APRICO Solutions, part of Royal Philips Electronics N.V.	Joseph Proidl/ CTO, Founder	Personalized TV, Targeted Advertising	2009-10-09

Note: Company names and job titles represent the current status at the time the interviews were conducted. See Appendix for protocols of the guided interviews.

2 Definitions and Related Work

After having introduced to the topic and methodology of this book, this section will provide fundamental information about targeted advertising and theoretical basics that will be relevant in the context of the further analysis. First, targeted advertising and basic types of targeting will be defined, before an introduction to the business environment and typical advertising value chains is given. This is followed by a short subsection about the basics of use case modeling. In the next step, the basic technologies of IPTV and mobile networks will be described, which are necessary for understanding the technological use case analyses in section 1. After this technology part, standardization organizations that are relevant in the context of targeted advertising as well as their key activities are listed. The section is closed with an introduction to the most important advertising formats in the context of Web, IPTV, and mobile advertising.

2.1 Foundations of Targeted Advertising

Before starting to describe and analyze use cases, the actual meaning of targeted advertising must be defined. A closer look at the term itself discloses that targeted advertising, from a business perspective, is a marketing concept aimed at addressing a specific target group. Targeted advertising falls under the umbrella of personalization strategies in Electronic Customer Relationship Management (E-CRM) whose goal is a differentiated alignment of marketing instruments towards the individual customer. The basic idea of individual marketing is the recognition of individual preferences and based on that the offering of personalized, customer individual services. The terms "E-CRM" and "Web personalization" have first been discussed in 1999/2000. However first personalization attempts failed due to a lack in efficient technologies and in the intensity of Internet usage that is required to analyze user behavior [12, 143, 72].

To avoid misunderstandings and confusion that may arise in the terminology complex concerning personalization and targeted advertising, it is useful to take notice of the following correlation: Personalization comprises targeted advertising on the one hand, but also content targeting methods and product recommendations on the other. Albeit this book focuses on targeted advertising, many of the concepts and technologies analyzed below are also valid for personalization in general. Moreover, attention should be paid to the fact that in marketing language the term personalization is often used in a narrower sense to describe one-to-one-marketing constellations where the user is known by her name (see section 2.1.2). The next section will introduce the generic personalization process with a specific focus on targeted advertising.

2.1.1 Targeted Advertising as Part of the Personalization Process

From a process-oriented perspective the activities required to realize personalization strategies can be divided up into the steps: tracking (data acquisition), profiling (data analysis), matching (individualization). Tracking implies the integrated acquisition of data by logging relevant user activity, collecting data entered by the user, and inclusion of data provided by other systems or purchased from external suppliers. In the profiling phase, the collected data is processed and analyzed. This includes filtering tools that organize and structure the data according to their applicability. Then, the profiling engine analyzes the data for interest and behavioral patterns in order to generate segmented user profiles. This may mean that predefined categories (e.g. sports, lifestyle,...) are assigned to the user. In the subsequent matching process, a recommender system compares the user interests to given target group specifications and recommends which groups fit best to the user profile. This recommendation is then applied to assign matching advertisements, content, or products. In advance, the advertisements, content, or products have to be categorized themselves to define which target groups will receive which advertisements, content or product recommendation [73].

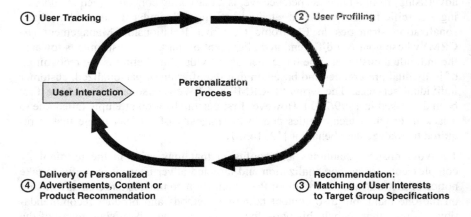

Figure 1: Generic personalization process (source: own illustration based on [143])

The concrete implementation of the matching process varies depending on the involved systems and on the personalization discipline (targeted advertising, content personalization, or product recommendations). In the case of targeted advertising the target group recommendations are sent to a campaign management that eventually initiates the delivery of the ads by an ad server according to the campaign policies booked by the advertiser. These may include time and content targeting as well as individual user targeting based on the target group recommendation of the recommender system. This means that the advertiser or ad agency determines which users shall be targeted by an ad campaign and according to these guidelines ads are matched to the user. In the case of content and product recommendations it may make more sense to not predefine the target group categories that are assigned to the content or product. They should rather undergo a similar profiling process like the user data that assigns attributes and thus categorizes the content or product.

2.1.2 Definition and Types of Targeting

In this subsection the term "targeting" will be defined and first implications for the use case development will be examined. This is followed by an overview of the most prevalent targeting methods.

Definition
Targeting can generally be defined as the automated and specific alignment of any advertising media according to different parameters. It enables the optimized delivery of digital advertising at defined audiences i.e. target groups minimizing losses due to waste coverage. Targeting increases the efficiency of advertising campaigns, while at the same time delivering more relevant ads to the customers [54, 155].

Targeting vs. Personalization
From a marketing perspective targeting must not be confused with one-to-one marketing respectively personalization in a narrower sense. While the ladder comprises the individual delivery of personalized ad messages to one defined customer (e.g. Mrs. Schmitt, Hamburg), targeting addresses users anonymously via a target group they belong to (e.g. women, age 20-49) [155]. Ad agencies will not ask an ad marketer to target Mrs. Schmitt personally. It rather works the way that a specific target group profile for a product will be defined in order to find similar customers. This has important consequences for the technical realization of targeted advertising as it implies that the ad recommendation and selection process is usually split up between one system that targets the user and one system that manages the ad campaigns and assigns matching ads. The recommendation that is made by the targeting system usually does not include a direct associa-

tion to an ad but to a target group that is then used to select matching ads from possible campaigns (see section 5.1 for a detailed description on the targeting process). However, it has to be pointed out that the above conclusions are not correlated with the possible targeting granularity that can be technically achieved in a distinct scenario. The target groups used in the recommendation process to represent special types of users must not be confused with the technical ability to create (anonymized) individual profiles.

Types of Targeted Advertising
The use cases that will be discussed in the next sections describe scenarios in different ICT channels thus covering a broad range of medium-specific technological subtleties. The determination of a target depends largely on the capabilities, processes and systems prevalent in the respective environments. However, in the following a general non medium-specific overview of possible targeting methods shall be given [39].

First of all, it has to be emphasized that the term targeting is more comprehensive than one might think at first sight. Actually each ad campaign is to some extent optimized in order to reach the right audience for a product. Targeting thus starts already with placing a sports-related billboard advertisement aside a soccer stadium or displaying an airline banner ad on a travel portal in the Web. Certainly, this book focuses on targeting opportunities and methods opened up when applying cutting-edge ICT technologies.

Content and Contextual Targeting
The basic and most simple targeting method is content targeting. One example for this method is the already above mentioned scenario of displaying banner ads in a website according to the category of the content the page is about. It is very common that marketers of a Web presence offer to book a distinct advertising space within a site of a special content category. The concept of this targeting method can also be applied to other advertising media beyond the Web. For example, an article about buying homes serves up an insurance ad, or a documentary film on animals provides a good place to inject a public service ad for animal protection [39].

Many sources call this targeting method contextual targeting as it matches the ad to characteristics of the content actually being consumed [222, 143, 39]. This is obviously a very narrow interpretation and the meaning of the term context goes far beyond this aspect. Instead of the content it can also be the context of the user herself that shall be targeted. In this case a differentiation between static and dynamic context information can be made. While the static context includes user "properties" like gender, age group, ZIP code,... that can be permanently stored in a user profile, the dynamic user context comprises the current situation of a user that may change at any time like e.g. the speed someone travels in a car or her current location. Eventually, from a technical point of view there will not be one single targeting technique that helps figuring out the user context. It is rather an aggregation of the results of the targeting technologies described here. As these thoughts reveal, one should pay attention to a clear usage of the terminology in order to avoid ambiguities.

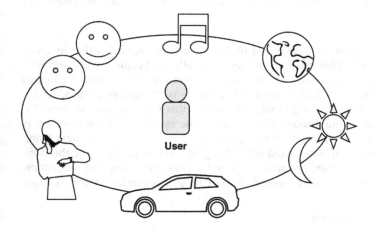

Figure 2: Aspects of dynamic changes in the user environment (source: own illustration)

Content/contextual targeting is closely related to what is known under the label language based targeting, which focuses on the occurrence of terms especially in the context of a Web page (compare Google AdSense). Language based targeting further comprises the two sub-categories keyword and semantic targeting. Keyword targeting uses terms a user enters in a search field on a website for selecting appropriate ads. Semantic advertising enhances the language based concept by analyzing the whole text of a website. This allows deriving the true meaning of ambiguous words (e.g. "Golf" can be a car or a sport) further improving the targeting results [155].

Technical Targeting
Technical targeting means that the user receives advertising that is tailored to her software and hardware environment [155]. This includes for example targeting according to the available bandwidth, which may be relevant in mobile and regular Web scenarios for users whose Internet connection is limited. Then, the ad delivery system can be instructed to avoid heavy ads that would lead to long

loading times. In addition, other technical characteristics like the device type (e.g. Set-Top-Box (STB) type, mobile phone type) or the browser type can be incorporated into the targeting process in order to only deliver ads that can be displayed correctly (ads must fit to the screen size and resolution). Finally, technical targeting can also be applied to target users with ads that fit to the technology they use (e.g. iPod ads for Safari users). Technical targeting requires the implementation of methods that allow detecting technical details about the user's hardware and software equipment.

Time Targeting

Time targeting enables the delivery of digital advertisements according to given time windows [155]. This method focuses especially on people's work and life-style schedules, such as serving ads to commuters between 7 to 10 am. It can also be used to perform so-called "roadblock" campaigns for upcoming product releases or events. Roadblocking in this case means that e.g. one and the same TV commercial is played out through all channels at the same time. Time targeting is mostly combined with other targeting approaches to refine the consumers being targeted (e.g. outdoor sports-related advertising on a sports portal while the Bundesliga plays i.e. on Saturdays between 3 and 6 pm). Time targeting also comprises a broader time-context beyond daypart related scenarios as for example seasonal targeting [39].

Sociodemographic Targeting

Sociodemographic targeting is based on user characteristics that stem from the field of social research, such as age, gender, income, nationality, ethnicity,... [143, 39]. An example for sociodemographic targeting would be to deliver specific ads to female users at an age of 20-29. Usually, these data are explicitly declared by the user herself when she registers for a newsletter or a community. Additional sociodemographic data input can be provided by predictive behavioral targeting methods [155]. Sociodemographic targeting may overlap with geographical targeting if the data includes e.g. the ZIP code of a user.

Geographical and Location-Based Targeting

Geographical or regional targeting includes the delivery of advertising based on geographical target areas. In classic Web or in IPTV scenarios the location of a user can be mined from the IP address [39, 155]. Location data may also be derived from existing user profiles that have been explicitly declared by the user (e.g. in communities) or provided through the integration of Customer Relationship Management (CRM) data into the profiling process. These sources usually deliver static location data as for example residence information in form of ZIP codes. The granularity of the geographical information (national, regional, single user location) may be limited due to technological constraints (e.g. the position of an ad insertion point in the IPTV network). Static location information may be stored in one user profile like behavior originated interest data thus allowing to consider this additional target group information in the same recommendation process.

Increasingly, so-called Location-Based Services (LBS) on mobile devices gain importance. The targeting concept is the same as described above. But the fact that mobile devices travel with their users leads to dynamic changes in the location information. Technically this data can be tracked using location area and cell information from mobile operators or based on Global Positioning System (GPS) receivers implemented in the handset [196]. However the integration of such dynamic changes in the context of a user (compare contextual targeting above) poses a challenge for the recommendation process, as the data cannot be stored in static profiles (see section 5.3.5 for more details on context-aware recommendation).

In either case the approach to incorporate geographical information into the targeting process offers powerful new advertising opportunities for regional and local businesses. Geographical and location-based targeting are thus especially valuable for promotional and impulse buys (e.g. induced through Short Message (SMS) couponing). In addition, it helps to reduce waste coverage (e.g. no advertising for an event in Munich if the user lives or currently stays in Berlin) [39, 155].

Behavioral Targeting
Behavioral targeting works by tracking the actions (e.g. Web browsing behavior, channel switching in IPTV) of users. Data mining methods help to detect patterns in the past user behavior that are aggregated to user interest profiles which become the basis of targeting. For example, if a user frequently browses websites with car-related content the targeting system may conclude that he is into automobile topics and thus recommends car related ads even after the consumer continues on to a non-auto related site. Behavioral targeting often includes tracking of interaction and transaction data meaning that the system tracks the purchase history of users to establish trends. People who bought one brand's shoes might for example be interested in more of the same, or those from another brand. It can also comprise retargeting methods that aim at locating users who already were on the way to buy an article but dropped off during the purchasing process [143, 39, 155].

The major benefit of behavioral targeting is that it allows to book advertising for specific interest target groups independent of the respective environment or content. At the same time the user is presented with advertising he is most likely interested in due to his past consumption behavior [155]. Behavioral targeting is one of the hottest topics in targeted advertising as the concept is leveraged by the tracking opportunities of modern bidirectional IP-based communication.

Predictive Behavioral Targeting
Predictive behavioral targeting enables the delivery of advertising to user groups whose profiles have been enriched using statistical predictions. These may be based on past behavior, questionnaires, and external data and may include attributes like sociodemographic and psychographic data or product and buying interests. Predictive behavioral targeting allows filling existing gaps in user profiles. Moreover, it increases the reach of campaigns as it allows to identify e.g. a potential interest in cars even if the user has not visited a car-related webpage before [155].

2.1.3 The Business Environment of Targeted Advertising

In the previous subsections targeted advertising has been identified to be part of the personalization process that aims at better addressing customers in order to increase advertising efficiency. A basic definition of targeted advertising and possible targeting methods has been given. On the way to develop the most promising targeted advertising scenarios in the ICT space, it is necessary to analyze the business environment in which advertising shall take place. Therefore, in this subsection the business model of targeted advertising will be classified in the context of recent developments in the ICT space in order to give an overview of the "big picture". Finally, the advertising value chains in TV and mobile will be introduced giving an impression of potential stakeholders.

2.1.3.1   *Classification of the Targeted Advertising Business Model*

Generically, targeted advertising can be considered as part of the two-sided business model concept recently emerging in the telecom industry. So far, operators mainly focused on delivering network infrastructure and related services to their customers. Expansion efforts were basically directed to replicate this business model in adjacent markets. For example fixed network operators moved into mobile markets or mobile players started offering fixed broadband services. Some launched content delivery services like IPTV and mobile TV. However, with more and more businesses making money with Internet-based services carriers run the risk of being degraded to pure "bit pipes" [129]. The idea of the two-sided telecom market, sometimes called "Telco 2.0", is to provide platforms through which two sides can interact or transact, meaning to build capabilities that support 3rd parties in interacting with the Telco user base. This includes the transformation towards an integrated services, content and data pipe provider that connects upstream (e.g. developers, retailers, media content providers, advertisers) and downstream customers (consumers and business customers in various segments) via advanced platform services. With the data operators hold on customers, and the ability to reach them through many different channels (e.g. email, SMS, IPTV, Web portals) operators own the necessary core assets. Targeted advertising is one example of these new business opportunities for operators. Other possible services include content delivery scenarios (music, TV, video, games), identity, authentication, and security management services, marketing and advertising, or billing and payments services [197].

The concept of two-sided markets originally stems from economics where the term describes market constellations in which one or several platforms enable interactions between end users, and try to get the two or multiple sides "on board" by appropriately charging each side. The theory of two-sided markets is closely related to the theory of network externalities. Classic examples of two-sided markets include TV networks and newspapers competing for advertisers as well as "eyeballs", or videogame platforms that need to attract gamers on the one hand and game developers on the other. Further reading on the theory of two-sided markets is e.g. provided by [169].

2.1.3.2 The TV Advertising Environment

Several stakeholders are involved in the delivery of TV advertising. The below depicted value chain shows the relation of these interest groups and how they act together in order to deliver an ad to the customer. The TV advertising value chain strongly depends on the structure of the TV industry in each country. The below overview is aggregated from a recent study of the IPTV advertising environment [111] and insights from the conducted expert interviews.

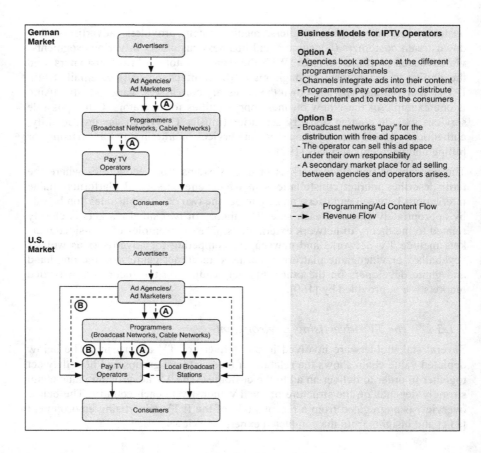

Figure 3: The TV advertising value chain (source: own illustration based on [111])

Advertisers

Advertisers finance the whole value chain. This comprises the costs of conceptualizing, creation, distribution and finally measuring the success of a TV commercial. Important for programmers and pay TV providers, they subsidize the cost of TV programming. Without the advertising money other revenue sources would need to be opened up or developed leading to an increasingly subscription or license fee based financing.

Ad Agencies

Ad agencies are hired by advertisers to develop the brand for the consumer product. They develop the creative guidelines and scripts for commercial production that is subcontracted to professional producers. Ad agencies organize the purchase of slots within a TV network's schedule to insert the commercials.

Ad Marketers/Media Buyers

The buying process of ad opportunities is usually performed or optimized by ad marketers that act as brokers selling the ad slots for the TV networks. Ads are usually sold on a Cost Per Mille (CPM) basis. Thus, the rate for a commercial is based on the number of viewers that the show can deliver. The price for ad slots depends on the format (e.g. 30-second commercials) and the advertising time.

Programmers

Programmers have different interests and a different focus of operation across different regions in the world. In the United States of America (U.S.) they typically fall into the two categories of broadcast networks and cable networks both offering single channels or a group of channels. Some premium subscription channels may be ad free. In Western Europe the industry structure is different. Here a differentiation must rather be made between commercial TV stations and public channels offering limited advertising opportunities depending on the daytime.

Broadcast Stations

Here again the industry is varying in different countries. In the U.S. broadcast networks are distributed nationally using a network of local broadcast stations that may be affiliated to retransmit the networks' shows. Local stations are provided with "avails" for regionally inserted advertising (see especially section 4.2.4.1). In Germany like most other European countries, this business of selling inventory for ad insertion is yet undeveloped because there are usually no networks selling their content to local broadcast stations. In addition, legal constraints may forbid touching the stream of the TV channels (see section 6.2.4). However, ad insertion is an opportunity for IPTV operators to become part of the TV advertising value chain.

Pay TV Operators

In the U.S. pay TV is more developed and accepted than in Europe. In addition to pay TV assets that are provided ad-free U.S. pay TV operators partly receive content from cable networks including avails for regional ad insertion. In Western Europe some pay TV operators are slowly starting to incorporate this component of the advertising business into their carriage deals. IPTV operators can be considered as a special kind of pay TV operators presenting a potential point of entry into the TV advertising market.

2.1.3.3   The Mobile Advertising Environment

Like above in IPTV environment several players are involved with the mobile advertising value chain. Many of the stakeholders are the same as in the Web environment. Their respective roles concerning the way mobile advertising is delivered to the customer is discussed below. The input for this overview is again derived from expert interviews and also taken from a recent study of the mobile advertising environment [112].

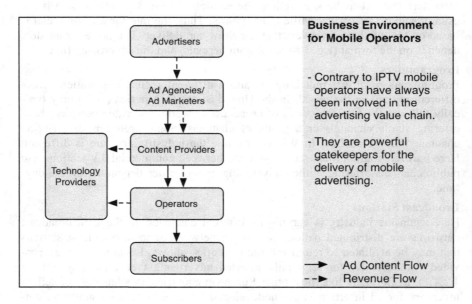

Figure 4:   The mobile advertising value chain (source: own illustration based on [112] and [149])

Advertisers

Major brands are starting to recognize some of the opportunities of mobile services. Their initial interest is often to use mobile as a complement of multimedia campaigns integrating the mobile platform with TV or print campaigns. This may include messaging with interaction capabilities ("call-to-action") and for promotion purposes (e.g. through mobile coupons).

Ad Agencies

Large ad agencies that already operate in the Web business start to look at mobile advertising but are waiting to see clear evidence of revenues. Meanwhile some small agencies are specialized on serving the mobile ad space, thus some acquisition activity is likely in the close future is likely.

Ad Marketers/Ad Networks/Ad Aggregators

Like in the online world ad networks work with mobile content owners/publishers in order to sell inventory. In the mobile Web the inventory typically consists of banner ads and rich media adapted to mobile requirements. Often the deal enables ad marketers to sell the whole inventory of a publisher's mobile website. Advertising is typically sold on a CPM basis, but Cost Per Action (CPA) and Cost Per Click (CPC) models are also used. The network/marketer then shares the ad revenue with the publisher.

In the case of message advertising the value chain is a little simpler as there are no actual publishers. Here ad marketing is usually realized through aggregators that have relationships with multiple carriers and can deliver the message across their mobile networks. SMS are sold on a per-message basis.

The actual ad delivery process is realized through campaign management technology and ad serving equipment. The campaign management is usually a software suite that enables the publisher or carrier to track ad inventory and manage the sales process. Ad servers store and serve advertising including the targeted delivery of advertising. Campaign management and ad serving build an interface function between content publishers, ad networks, and carriers. They may be operated by an ad marketer or by the carrier himself as technology vendors increasingly offer such solutions for integration directly into the carriers' networks.

Content Providers/Publishers

With growing 3G penetration and improved multimedia capabilities of mobile phones, content is more and more made available to mobile devices. This includes optimization of content and advertising for mobile viewing enabled through guidelines and standards e.g. developed by the Mobile Marketing Association (MMA, see below section 2.5). The iPhone and other cutting-edge smartphones are major drivers in this context as on the one hand they make regular Hypertext Markup Language (HTML) content available and on the other hand offer extended marketing opportunities through the emerging app concept (app = mobile application, e.g. made available through the Apple App Store or the Google Android App Market).

Operators/Carriers
The mobile carrier operates the mobile network thus enabling data and messaging services including advertising on it. One of the most important opportunities for operators to take part in the mobile advertising value chain are mobile portals through which users get access to the mobile Web. As the operator has access to subscriber data these central starting points to the Web offer excellent targeting possibilities. Another opportunity for operators to participate in the advertising value chain are advertising solutions that require network-based ad insertion (e.g. in message advertising or mobile TV advertising).

Technology Vendors/Mobile Content Optimizers
Technology vendors have a significant presence on a carrier's network through the already deployed network infrastructure. Content and ad management capabilities can thus be offered as extensions for existing solutions. Most carriers will first contact their existing business partners for such integrated solutions. Some technology vendors specialize in the delivery of rich media/video content over the mobile network. Their solutions often include tracking and targeting engines that allow carriers to develop consumer profiles in order to enable targeted ad delivery thus taking over campaign management and ad serving tasks.

2.2 Use Case Basics

As described in the methodology section, this work is based on a use-case driven approach. This means that in the next chapters typical targeted advertising scenarios in the ICT space will be identified. These scenarios will be basically described from a user perspective. Subsequently each use case will be analyzed in detail from a technical perspective delivering comprehensive results for a potential implementation. Hence, this subsection will give a short overview on use case modeling, in order to provide the reader with a basic understanding of the subject.

Use cases are important tools for the requirements analysis in software and systems engineering. They describe a system's behavior when interacting with the outside world [47].

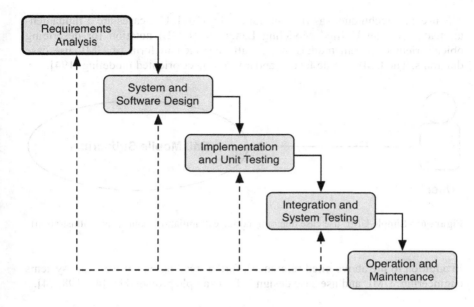

Figure 5:   "Waterfall" model of software engineering (source: own illustration based on [172, 194])

In most cases the requirement engineering process begins with a feasibility study that serves as a basis for decision-making if the software or system should be developed or not. In case of a positive feasibility report the actual requirements analysis can begin. The first step in the requirements analysis is a requirements elicitation aimed at identifying the needs and features of the system. This can be accomplished by modeling typical use cases that cover the desired system functions in form of exemplary process flows [21].

Based on a requirements specification or textual descriptions the functions of a system are described using concrete usage scenarios. Related scenarios can be aggregated to form use cases that describe the system's behavior under various conditions as the system responds to requests from stakeholders of the system. Use cases may fundamentally be written in text form but they can be depicted using flow charts or sequence charts. The results of the requirements analysis are the basis for system design and implementation, which are the next steps in systems engineering [21, 116].

The use case technique was first introduced by [104]. Use cases are a fundamental feature of the Unified Modeling Language (UML) notation for describing object-oriented system models and usually depicted in form of UML use case diagrams. The UML is a de facto standard for object-oriented modeling [194].

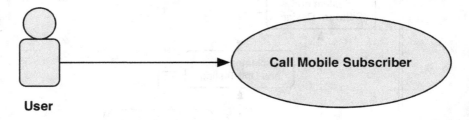

Figure 6:   Simple UML use case diagram mobile call initiation (source: own illustration)

In addition to the above-cited references, further reading on software and systems engineering, UML and use case design is for example provided by [48, 198, 74].

2.3   Basic Technology

As this book focuses especially on targeted advertising in ICT scenarios beyond the classic Web a short introduction to the underlying technologies shall be given. This comprises especially the basic IPTV and mobile communication architecture and respective data transmission modalities.

2.3.1 IPTV Basics

Internet Protocol Television (IPTV) is the transmission of digital video and audio signals through data networks, usually through the Internet in contrast to traditional radio frequency broadcast, satellite signal, and Cable Television (CATV) formats [84]. Historically, the usage of the term IPTV has often been heterogeneous. However, IPTV in the sense of this book must be distinguished from general Internet-based or Web-based multimedia services (Web TV, TV over Web/TVoW). IPTV is characterized by deployment scenarios that include the delivery over subscriber-based managed telecommunications networks and require end-user premises like Set-Top-Boxes (STB) for termination. According to the International Telecommunication Union focus group on IPTV (ITU-T FG IPTV) IPTV is defined as "multimedia services such as television/

video/audio/text/graphics/data delivered over IP based networks managed to provide the required level of quality of service and experience, security, interactivity and reliability" [101].

The basic IPTV services include linear/live television, Video/Content on Demand (VoD/CoD), and the Electronic Program Guide (EPG). Linear TV is a television service in which a continuous stream flows in real-time from the service provider to the terminal device and where the user cannot control the temporal order in which contents are viewed. In VoD the subscriber can view video content whenever desired. The content is stored on the provider's VoD server. The subscriber accesses the movie from a library directory, which may include a search engine that accesses movie description and rating. Subscribers typically have the ability to pause, play, rewind, fast forward the content, or even stop viewing it and return to it at a later time when using this service. The third basic service EPG comprises a structured set of data, intended to provide information on available content that may be accessed by end users [101].

These services are usually provided to the user through a STB that adapts the transmitted contents to a format that is accessible by the user [84]. Increasingly, IPTV includes additional interactive services and/or Web applications requiring the STB to possess hybrid functionality (compare section 4.2.5).

IPTV Network Architecture
The IPTV network architecture can be subdivided into the network components Super Headend, Core Network, Aggregation Network, Access Network, and Home Network. In order to give a basic understanding on how an IPTV network works, the tasks and functions of these components will be outlined in the following. For a more detailed description it can be referred to [216] and [85]. A basic introduction to IPTV is provided by [83].

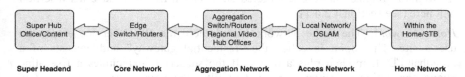

Figure 7: IPTV network architecture (source: own illustration based on [216, 167])

Super Headend: The part of a television network where the broadcast programming and on demand content is captured or ingested into the system. Here, video signals are selected and processed for further delivery through a distribution network. A variety of equipment is used at the headend, including satellite dishes to receive signals, decoding and encoding units, the VoD server management, the digital rights management, the middleware server, the EPG server, further application servers, and also ad insertion systems for ad replacement on national/operator level [84, 216].

Core Network: The central network component that provides interconnection and transfer between edge networks and transports all of the system's content. The core network is the "backbone" for the IPTV broadcast system [84, 216]. Actually, to save bandwidth the programs in IPTV are not broadcasted to the users like in terrestrial, satellite or cable TV. Broadcasting means that all programs are simultaneously transmitted to each user no matter which show she is effectively watching. In IPTV, channels are exclusively transmitted directly to specific viewers (unicast) or they are simultaneously sent to multiple users that are watching the same channel (multicast). Unicast transmission is used for delivering on demand services. Linear TV is usually transmitted via multicast, which helps to save bandwidth compared to the unicast method [83].

Aggregation Network: The aggregation network carries the broadcast content from the regional video headends to the access network that distributes it to the subscribers. Regional video hub offices can be equipped with VoD servers, broadcast servers for regional live TV content and ad insertion technology for regionally targeted advertising (see section 4.2.4.1).

Access Network: The "last mile" that connects individual subscribers or devices to the IPTV network. It provides a network translation from switched network technology used in the aggregation and core network to Digital Subscriber Line (DSL) technology. Digital Subscriber Line Access Multiplexers (DSLAMs) transfer the signals from optical fiber to copper wire for DSL delivery [216]. The DSLAM is usually the multicast-endpoint in the IPTV transmission. If an operator wants to realize one-to-one targeted ad insertion he must place his insertion unit here (see section 4.2.4.1).

Home Network: The home network starts where the IPTV service enters the user's site. This point is called the "residential gateway" and consists of a broadband/DSL modem plus a router. If the subscription includes a fixed-line phone connection a splitter is needed to filter the voice data out of the data stream. The DSL modem translates the modulation protocol of the access network into a standard home networking technology (e.g. Ethernet or powerline). Finally, the IPTV data will be delivered to the television via an STB, potential Internet data to computers within the home [84, 216].

The graph below depicts an exemplary IPTV network including typical components at the super headend, the regional headend, and the customer's site.

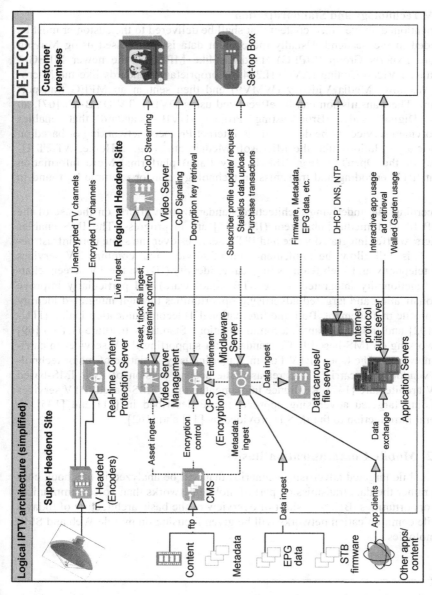

Figure 8: Simplified IPTV architecture (source: Detecon)

IPTV Technology and Standardization
As mentioned above video content that shall be delivered to the customer must be encoded in the headend. Usually the content data is compressed using Moving Picture Experts Group (MPEG) standards like MPEG-2, the newer MPEG-4 Advanced Video Coding (AVC)/H.264, or proprietary standards like the Microsoft Windows Media Video 9 (WMV9) and then sent in an MPEG transport stream. The transmission can be effectuated using DVB-IPTV/DVB-IPI [67], an open Digital Video Broadcasting Project (DVB) standard that enables audio/video services to be delivered via Internet Protocol networking or based on proprietary solutions like the Microsoft Mediaroom[2] (e.g. T-Home, AT&T U-verse) or the OpenTV[3] (e.g. BSkyB, Sky Italia) platforms. More information about IPTV encoding and transmission technology can for example be found in [27].

Concerning the underlying architecture standardization efforts on the use of the 3GPP IP Multimedia Subsystem (IMS) [5] are in progress. The IMS enables carriers to offer integrated voice and IPTV services over the same core infrastructure. This will allow the implementation of services that combine TV services with telephony and Web features (e.g. caller identity (ID) on the TV screen, chatting functionality integrated in the STB middleware) and particularly improve personalization and targeted advertising opportunities through integrated identity and profile management. Both the International Telecommunication Union (ITU-T) [102] and the European Telecommunications Standards Institute (ETSI) [69] are working on IMS-based IPTV standards for supporting IPTV services in carriers' networks. The Open IPTV Forum, a pan-industry initiative of major technology vendors and carriers, has released the second version of their IMS-based IPTV architecture [147]. Reference implementations of IMS-based IPTV services including targeted advertising approaches are described in [11] and [135]. A general introduction to the IMS is provided by [44] and [162].

2.3.2 Mobile Communication Basics

The mobile targeted advertising scenarios that will be analyzed in this book concern rather the data transmission part of mobile networks than voice communication opportunities. Below, a short of overview of the basic architecture of today's mobile communication networks will be given focusing on mobile Web and SMS technologies.

---

[2] http://www.microsoft.com/mediaroom/
[3] http://www.opentv.com/. Since 2010 OpenTV is part of the NAGRA Kudelski Group.

GSM Network Architecture

The Global System for Mobile communication (GSM) is a globally accepted standard for digital cellular communication. The GSM standardization group (at that time called Groupe Spécial Mobile) was established in 1982 by the European Conference of Postal and Telecommunications Administrations (CEPT) to create a common European mobile telephone standard. The GSM responsibility was later transferred to the ETSI and phase 1 of the GSM specifications were published in 1990 [93, 94, 68].

A GSM network is divided into three major systems: the Network and Switching Subsystem (NSS), with the Operation and Support System (OSS), and the Radio Subsystem (RSS). The basic architecture of a conventional GSM network can be depicted as follows.

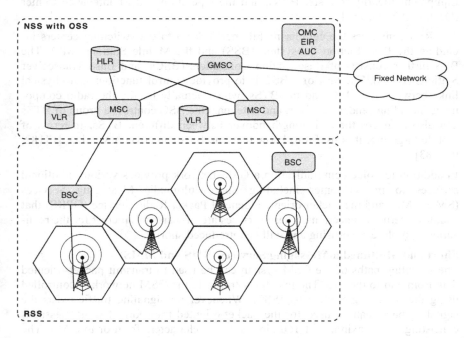

Figure 9: Architecture of the GSM system (source: own illustration based on [183])

The NSS performs call processing and subscriber-related functions consisting of several core components that will be of importance in the context of mobile targeting. One of these is the Home Location Register (HLR), which is a database used for management and permanent storage of subscription data. This comprises a subscriber's service profile, location information, and activity status. In contrast, the Visitor Location Register (VLR) contains only temporary information about visiting subscribers. Telephony switching and controlling calls to and from other telephone and data systems are handled by the Mobile Services Switching Center (MSC). The VLR and the MSC are always integrated. When a user roams into its MSC area the VLR requests the respective subscriber data from the HLR. Finally, the Gateway Mobile Services Switching Center (GMSC) connects the GSM network to the Public Switched Telephone Network (PSTN) being often implemented in an MSC. Operation support and management of the GSM subsystems is realized by the OSS consisting of the Authentication Center (AUC), the Equipment Identity Register (EIR), and the Operation and Maintenance Center (OMC) [182, 93, 183].

The RSS comprises the cellular mobile network up to the switching centers including the Base Station Subsystem (BSS) and the Mobile Stations (MS). The BSS further consists of Base Station Controllers (BSCs) and Base Transceiver Stations (BTSs). The task of a BSC is to provide control functions and physical links between the MSC and the BTSs, which actually handle the radio components including sender, receiver, and antenna. One BSC controls a group of BTSs and also manages the switching/handover between different BTSs. In terms of mobile targeting, it is useful to know that one BTS can cover several cells [182, 93, 183].

In addition to voice communication a GSM network provides various additional services to the customer including Short/Multimedia Messaging Services (SMS/MMS) and the packet-oriented General Packet Radio Service (GPRS) that enables Internet connections. These services are of a special interest for the realization of mobile advertising and will be introduced shortly.

Short and Multimedia Messaging Services (SMS and MMS)
The signaling paths of the GSM system can be used to transmit packet-oriented data from and to the MS. The telephony traffic in the GSM network is controlled using the Signaling System #7 (SS7). Whenever no signaling traffic exists the signaling paths can be used for the packet-oriented transport of short messages consisting of a maximum of 160 alphanumeric characters from or to a MS. The basic SMS network infrastructure can be depicted as follows.

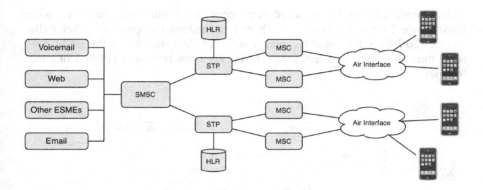

Figure 10: Basic SMS network architecture (source: own illustration based on [95])

The network infrastructure and basic components used in the SMS delivery process are the same as already described above. SMS are transmitted by a Short Message Service Center (SMSC) operating in a store-and-forward-mode that relays messages when the MS is powered off and try again when the device is on again. The signaling interconnection is enabled by Signal Transfer Points (STPs) that act as a router for SS7 messages and link the network elements [95, 210].

SMS comprises two basic point-to-point services. Mobile-Originated (MO) short messages are transported from the MO–capable handset to the SMSC and can be destined to other mobile subscribers or external short messaging entities including Internet hubs or e-mail receivers. Mobile-Terminated (MT) short messages are transported from the SMSC to the handset. The source can be other mobile subscribers via Mobile-Originated Short Messages (MO–SM) or External Short Messaging Entities (ESME) as depicted in the illustration [95, 210].

The Multimedia Messaging Service (MMS) is part of the GSM phase 2+ and as such uses the GPRS network for data transmission. MMS is not based on SMS technology thus enabling larger messages with multimedia content. However, the MMS delivery is also managed by a store-and-forward unit called Multimedia Messaging Service Center (MMSC) that is connected to the GPRS network. More information on MMS can be found in [210] and [182].

Packet-Switched Mobile Communication
When GSM phase 1 was completed the standard included circuit-switched data transmission up to 9.6 kbit/s. In 1995 phase 2 incorporated a large variety of supplemental services that are comparable to Integrated Services Digital Network

(ISDN) standards but no enhanced data speed. Such improvements came with GSM phase 2+ standardized in 1998 that introduced the general packet radio service (GPRS). GPRS enables packet-switched data transfer in the GSM network thus allowing for direct access to Packet Data Networks (PDNs) like the Internet.

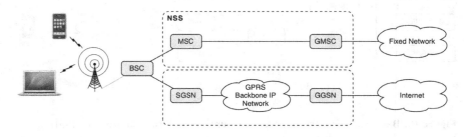

Figure 11: Circuit- (NSS) and packet-switched (GPRS Core) GSM subsystems (source: own illustration based on [36])

In order to provide these packet-switched services the operator must build a new GPRS core network including the so-called GPRS support nodes (GSN). The Serving GPRS Support Node (SGSN) resides at the same hierarchical level as a visited MSC/VLR and therefore performs comparable functions such as routing and mobility management. It is basically a switching center for routing data packets to a defined exit node. The Gateway GPRS Support Node (GGSN) provides gateway functionality comparable to a GMSC. It coordinates the data traffic between external PDNs (e.g. the Internet) and the GPRS core network [94, 210].

From the MS to the BTS data packets and voice traffic are transmitted basically using the same network infrastructure. The connection from the SGSN to the RSS is implemented through a Packet Control Unit (PCU) that is attached to the BSC [210].

Increasingly mobile Internet access is realized based on the Universal Mobile Telecommunication System (UMTS) that can be considered as the 3G GSM successor standard and is downward compatible with GSM, using the GSM Phase 2+ enhanced core network. However, UMTS requires a new Radio Access Network (RAN) called UMTS Terrestrial Radio Access Network (UTRAN) that is used instead of the GSM RSS. Existing network elements in the NSS and the GPRS core network, such as MSC, SGSN, and HLR can be extended to adopt the UMTS requirements [94]. In modern GPRS networks that integrate Enhanced Data Rates for Global/GSM Evolution (EDGE) technology a transmission speed of up to 384 kbit/s is possible. Using High-Speed Downlink Packet Access (HSDPA) UMTS allows a download rate of up to 7.2 Mbit/s [183]. For more information on the core architecture and components of GSM, GPRS, and UMTS networks it can be referred to [182] or [210].

Mobile TV Technology

UMTS provides unprecedented opportunities for mobile data transmission especially in the context of mobile Web usage. Likewise, the mobile network can be used to deliver mobile TV and video services. This usually requires a point-to-point connection between a content server and the user. As a consequence, the content server must establish and maintain a distinct connection for each recipient. This works well for on demand services, as subscriber requests are asynchronous and the load is thus rather distributed over time. However, in the case of live TV simultaneous usage is inherent and with increasing numbers of subscribers scaling problems emerge. Real-time service requires content servers to deliver content to several users at a time generating a tremendous amount of outbound traffic. In addition, the radio access network can easily become a bottleneck, if multiple recipients stay in the same mobile cell. Then, simultaneous streaming of multiple video streams rapidly congests the (limited) bandwidth of a cell making continuous TV reception impossible. This lack of scalability reduces the quality in true real-time scenarios (e.g. transmission of a live event like soccer) making it uncomfortable to use for subscribers. Hence, point-to-point based mobile live TV is technically possible, but extremely limited and economically almost unfeasible. As a result, mobile TV services using this technology (e.g. Deutsche Telekom MobileTV[4] and Vodafone MobileTV[5]) still cannot really succeed. Therefore, mobile live TV consumption on a mass basis requires point-to-multipoint radio bearers capable of transmitting data packets simultaneously from a single source to multiple destinations in a broadcast manner [20]. This can basically be realized based on two different technology approaches.

One option is to extend the existing mobile network infrastructure by implementing the Multimedia Broadcast and Multicast Service (MBMS) first specified in 3GPP Release 6 in 2004 [3]. MBMS is an IP datacast type of service that can be offered via existing GSM and UMTS networks. The infrastructure provides the possibility to use an uplink channel for interactions between the service and the user, which is an advantage compared to broadcast networks. MBMS has basically two modes of operation: the broadcast mode and the multicast mode. While broadcast refers to the ability to deliver content to all users (e.g. terrestrial or satellite TV services) in a push type service, multicast services are delivered to

---

[4] http://www.t-mobile.de/mobiletv/
[5] http://www.vodafonelive.de/cp/portal/tv-video/mobiletv/

users who have joined a particular multicast group (e.g. IPTV, see section 2.3.1). The broadcast mode hence allows a point-to-multipoint transmission of multimedia data (e.g. text, audio, picture, video) from a single source to all subscribers. In contrast, the multicast mode provides a point-to-multipoint service in which data is transmitted from a single source to a specific multicast group. This means that only users who are subscribed to the specific multicast service and have joined the multicast group associated with the service can receive the multicast transmission. The implementation of MBMS in mobile networks affects nodes in the mobile core and access networks, but it does not interfere with already existing GSM and UMTS services. This means that mobile devices not supporting MBMS will still work in networks that offer MBMS services [202, 77]. In addition, MBMS requires a new network component, the Broadcast Multicast Service Center (BM-SC), which is responsible for providing and delivering mobile broadcast services. It serves as an entry point for content-delivery services that want to use MBMS. It sets up and controls MBMS transport bearers to the mobile core network and can be used to schedule and deliver MBMS transmissions. MBMS features defining broadcast and multicast services for specific geographical areas at a granularity down to the size of individual radio cells enabling for example special transmissions to accompany local live events (e.g. soccer games, music festivals). The geographical broadcast or multicast service area is defined through an MBMS service area. Each node in the core network holds a list of downstream nodes to determine to which nodes service data has to be forwarded. Multicast services are managed by a dynamic distribution tree keeping track of users currently registered to the service, respectively tuned in to a channel. Compared to conventional point-to-point type streaming in GSM or UMTS networks MBMS can yield performance gains. Using MBMS, the content server providing the TV signal delivers just on stream per channel to BM-SC. Further on, the data flow for each channel in the core and the radio access network is solely replicated when necessary [20]. The figure below illustrates the performance advantages of MBMS over common point-to-point transmission.

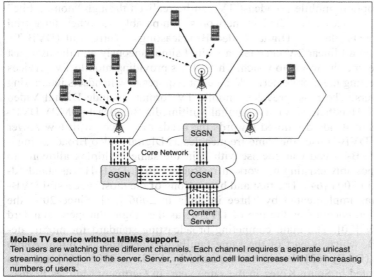

Mobile TV service without MBMS support.
Ten users are watching three different channels. Each channel requires a separate unicast
streaming connection to the server. Server, network and cell load increase with the increasing
numbers of users.

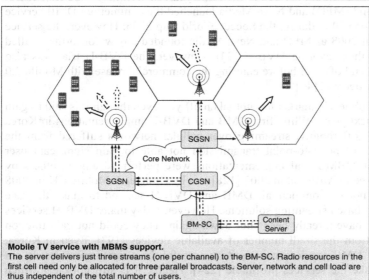

Mobile TV service with MBMS support.
The server delivers just three streams (one per channel) to the BM-SC. Radio resources in the
first cell need only be allocated for three parallel broadcasts. Server, network and cell load are
thus independent of the total number of users.

Figure 12: GSM/UMTS based mobile TV service with vs. without MBMS
(own illustration based on [20])

As a second option, mobile broadcast TV can be realized through "non-mobile" broadcasting services over distinct networks comparable to other terrestrial broadcast formats like e.g. Digital Video Broadcasting – Terrestrial (DVB-T). This means that all linear TV channels are aired simultaneously and the user just tunes in to the one she wants to watch. This allows providing mobile TV services without congesting the mobile network, albeit it requires new handsets integrating special receivers. The most prevalent mobile TV formats include Digital Video Broadcasting – Handheld (DVB-H), Digital Multimedia Broadcast (DMB). DVB-H is a DVB sub-standard tailored towards the needs of devices with low power consumption. DVB-H uses the same frequencies as Digital Video Broadcasting – Terrestrial (DVB-T) and can coexist with it in the same multiplex allowing to benefit from possibly existing network infrastructure [63]. DVB-H was standard-ized by ETSI in 2004 [64]. The first and by now one of the most successful DVB-H services was implemented by Three in Italia in 2006 [58]. Since 2007 the European Union encourages the use of DVB-H as the single European standard for mobile TV [70]. The main competing broadcasting standard for mobile de-vices is DMB, which is part of the same family of standards as Digital Audio Broadcasting (DAB) [62]. It was standardized by ETSI in 2005[6] [65] and was first implemented in South Korea in the same year. In Germany Mobiles Fernse-hen Deutschland (MFD) and Neva Media launched the commercial DMB service "Watcha" in June 2006 during the Soccer World Cup 2006. However, the service was stopped in 2008 as MFD and Neva Media founded a new consortium called "Mobile 3.0" then favoring DVB-H [34]. However, the DVB-H trial was also stopped at the end of 2008 before entering the commercial phase with Mobile 3.0 returning their licenses [49].

To date, the mobile TV market has not taken off yet, even though it is said to gain steam in the next years. While first DMB and DVB-H implementations in Korea and Italy took off rapidly, streaming over cellular networks suffered from the inherent limits of point-to-point transmission not able to gain significant user numbers. First MBMS trial implementations were performed among others by Hutchison Three in Australia in 2007 [128] and by Orange/ T-Mobile UK in 2008 [35], but did not go commercial. DMB and DVB-H seemed to make the race against UMTS based streaming solutions. However, today many DVB-H services across Europe have already been shut down again. They could not gain traction and suffered from the small number of available devices [193]. Even in Korea, where several DMB services were quite successful for a time, operators do not manage to make the services profitable [224]. Hence, it is still not clear which mobile phone TV standard will dominate the industry in future. DMB and DVB-

---

[6] Latest version dates from 2009 [66].

H still hold a time to market advantage over MBMS technologies, though MBMS is continuously being enhanced by the 3GPP [92]. It is also part of the next generation mobile network standard Long Term Evolution (LTE), which due to its increased bandwidth might MBMS based mobile TV and other MBMS data casting (e.g. news, traffic info) services help to break through [134].

2.3.3 Implications for the Use Case Development

The above-depicted IPTV network structure reveals that targeted ads can be integrated with the IPTV content stream either at some network node from the headend to the access network or within the STB. In case of network-based targeted advertising technologies like the already mentioned local ad replacement the granularity of targeting will depend on the location of ad insertion technology inside the IPTV network. Concerning the use case development for STB-based methods the capabilities and restrictions of these devices must be considered. As mentioned the different tasks of an STB make it a complex hybrid device offering various services (linear TV, VoD, EPG,...) that can be starting points for targeted advertising scenarios. On the other hand the computing power of STBs is very limited compared to network-based solutions.

As can be concluded from the above explanations on mobile network technologies mobile targeted advertising mainly affects the areas of messaging and mobile Web related services. In the case of message advertising use case development will have to consider how the GSM infrastructure can be used to realize targeted advertising and to what extent additional system units must be integrated. Special attention must be paid to the fact that with the HLR, information about the user's location is inherently available and can be exploited for location-based services. Aside from messaging the spread of packet-switched mobile network infrastructure especially of 3G technologies and the enhanced capabilities of modern smartphones drive the development of targeted advertising use cases in the mobile Web. Due to the increasing user numbers mobile Web scenarios provide increasingly excellent targeting opportunities. Despite these new possibilities enabled by cutting-edge mobile technology, the use case development must take into account the inherent limitations of mobile devices for example in terms of form factors and screen sizes. Further limitations are caused by the diversity of mobile operating systems and platforms and with regard to mobile TV and video also due to possible bottlenecks concerning the network infrastructure.

2.4 Standardization Efforts in the Environment of Targeted Advertising

According to NSN [129] the development of targeted advertising related technologies in the ICT space is not driven by standards bodies. There are no consortia focusing exclusively on targeted advertising in this area. However some standards bodies' efforts concern specific technologies that are also relevant within the scope of targeted advertising in the ICT space. This concerns for example the standards developments in the U.S. cable industry that can be partly adopted for the IPTV world (e.g. ad insertion technologies). Another driver are the advertising related standards and technologies originating from the Web and recently mobile world that can be consulted to derive implications for the ICT space. The following list provides an overview of relevant standards organizations.

Table 2: Standards organizations in the context of targeted advertising

Network-Related Standards

Standards Body/ Consortium	Description
DVB Digital Video Broadcasting	The Digital Video Broadcasting Project (DVB) is an industry-led consortium of over 250 broadcasters, manufacturers, network operators, software developers, regulatory bodies and others in over 35 countries committed to designing open technical standards for the global delivery of digital television and data services. Currently, more than 500 million DVB receivers are deployed worldwide. http://www.dvb.org/ *Targeted advertising related standardization activities:* Multimedia Home Platform (MHP): The MHP defines a generic interface between Java based interactive digital applications and hardware on which those applications execute.

Standards Body/ Consortium	Description
A GLOBAL INITIATIVE	The original scope of 3rd Generation Partnership Project (3GPP) was to produce Technical Specifications and Technical Reports for a 3G Mobile System based on evolved GSM core networks and the radio access technologies that they support. The scope was subsequently amended to include the maintenance and development of GSM Technical Specifications and Technical Reports including evolved radio access technologies (e.g. GPRS, EDGE) and the IMS, therefore heavily relating to future converged services. http://www.3gpp.org/
Open Mobile Alliance	Being the successor of the WAP Forum, the Open Mobile Alliance (OMA) is a consortium of wireless industry players. The mission of the OMA is to facilitate global user adoption of mobile data services by specifying market driven mobile service enablers that ensure service interoperability across devices, geographies, service providers, operators, and networks while also keep focusing on business aspects. http://www.openmobilealliance.org/ *Targeted advertising related standardization activities:* OMA Mobile Advertising V1.0: The MobAd Enabler specifies an enabling architecture allowing to implement mobile targeted advertising services.

Cable Industry Standards

Standards Body/ Consortium	Description
Society of Cable Telecommunications Engineers	The Society of Cable Telecommunications Engineers (SCTE) is a non-profit professional association providing technical leadership for the telecommunications industry and serves its members through professional development, standards, certification and information.

Standards Body/ Consortium	Description
	http://www.scte.org/ *Targeted advertising related standardization activities:* · SCTE 30: Digital Program Insertion Splicing API · SCTE 35: Digital Program Insertion Cueing Messages · SCTE 130: Digital Program Insertion Interface
C A N O E	Canoe Ventures is a venture of leading U.S. cable operators aimed at aggregating the collective capabilities of their digital infrastructure and collaborating with industry leaders in technology, research, programming and more to re-energize TV. http://www.canoe-ventures.com/ *Targeted advertising related standardization activities:* Canoe Ventures' main focus is the development of advanced advertising products and services for the cable environment.
CableLabs	Founded in 1988 by cable operating companies, Cable Television Laboratories, Inc. (CableLabs) is a non-profit research and development consortium that is dedicated to pursuing new cable telecommunications technologies and to helping its cable operator members integrate those technical advancements into their business objectives. http://www.cablelabs.com/ http://www.advancedadvertising.tv/ *Targeted advertising related standardization activities:* · Participation in SCTE 130 and Enhanced TV (ETV) standards development · OpenCable Application Platform (OCAP): Java based interactive TV standard, which is based on the DVB MHP · Enhanced TV Binary Interchange Format (EBIF): Non-Java based interactive TV standard developed for legacy STBs

Advertising Format Standards

Standards Body/ Consortium	Description
	The Interactive Advertising Bureau (IAB) is comprised of more than 375 leading media and technology companies who are responsible for selling 86% of online advertising (U.S.). The IAB focuses on strengthening the growth of the interactive advertising marketplace. The IAB educates marketers, agencies, media companies and the wider business community about the value of interactive advertising. http://www.iab.net/ *Targeted advertising related standardization activities:* Development of ad format standards for the Web (e.g. UAP)
	The Bundesverband Digitale Wirtschaft (BVDW, = German Association for the Digital Economy) e.V. is a German organization representing the interests of companies in the field of interactive marketing, digital content and interactive added value. http://www.bvdw.org/
	The Online-Vermarkterkreis (OVK, = Circle of Online Marketers) is the central body of online marketers in Germany. Twenty-one of the largest German online marketers have come together under the umbrella of the BVDW to raise the profile of online advertising. The circle's primary aims are to increase market transparency and planning reliability as well as standardization and quality assurance measures for the industry. http://www.ovk.de/ *Targeted advertising related standardization activities:* · Definition of ad format standards · Special working group focusing on targeting topics

Standards Body/ Consortium	Description
	The Mobile Marketing Association (MMA) focuses especially on the growth of mobile marketing and its associated technology. MMA members include agencies, advertisers, hand held device manufacturers, carriers and operators, retailers, software providers and service providers. http://www.mmaglobal.com/ *Targeted advertising related standardization activities:* Definition of mobile ad format standards

2.5 Definition of Ad Formats

In the previous subsections basic definitions of targeting and related terms have been given. Basic technologies in IPTV and the mobile environment have been defined. Before in the next section the actual use case development can begin, it is necessary to provide an overview of common ad formats in the relevant ICT channels. As already mentioned targeting technologies from the Web increasingly drive developments in the entire ICT space due to the spread of all-IP networks. Therefore the overview of ad formats starts with the Web environment before subsequently the typical ad formats in TV and the mobile space will be analyzed. This will lead to a comprehensive understanding in terms of which ad formats are most appropriate for each channel. Certainly some ad formats will better apply to one or the other. This will lead to a better understanding of possible advertising scenarios and give a first impression of targeting potentials.

2.5.1 Web Advertising Formats

Targeting and the delivery of personalized ads are today widely established on the Web. Since the relevant media channels for targeted advertising are more and more converging based on IP technology, most of the Web ad formats can likewise be deployed in use case scenarios in the IPTV or mobile space. It thus makes sense to first research on standard display advertising formats in the Web, in order to give and overview of existing standards in this area. Newsletter marketing and other non-display ad formats shall not be subject of this work.

Advertising in the Web is characterized by a diversity of different ad formats in terms of appearance and the underlying technologies. The variety ranges from simple text and banner ads to rich media formats. A basic distinction can be made between in-site/in-page (banner, skyscraper, rectangle) and on-site/on-page (pop-ups, Flash layer) display ad formats. Technologies that are used to enable these advertising forms include GIF/JPG, HTML, DHTML, Flash, and video/audio/ streaming.

2.5.1.1 Interactive Advertising Bureau

In 2002 the American Interactive Advertising Bureau (IAB) began a process to reduce the number of ad sizes for the purposes of reducing the costs and inefficiencies associated with the planning, buying and creating of online media [91]. The IAB is an advertising business organization in the U.S. that develops industry standards, conducts research, and provides legal support for the online advertising industry. The result was the Universal Ad Package (UAP), a set of four ad sizes that all compliant member publishers have agreed to support.

Table 3:   UAP specifications[7] (source: [91], images 20% of original size)

Format	Size	Dummy Image	Weight
Medium Rectangle	300x250px	iab.	40k
Rectangle	180x150px	iab.	40k
Wide Sky-scraper	160x600px	iab.	40k
Leaderboard	728x90px	iab.	40k

In addition to these basic ad formats, the IAB offers as series of Ad Unit Guidelines with further recommendations on rectangles and pop-ups, banners and buttons, as well as skyscrapers. Moreover, the IAB gives a detailed technical and methodological description of more complex ad formats like Pop-Ups/Pop-Unders, Rich Media Advertisements, and Video Ads [91]:

Pop-Ups/Pop-Unders: Any advertising that utilizes a Web browser initiated additional window to deliver an ad impression either directly above or below the existing browser experience. Each user should be exposed to no more than one Pop-Up ad for each visit to an online site.

---

[7] The UAP ad formats are part of the OVK standard forms of online advertising. A textual definition will therefore be given in the next section.

Rich Media Advertisements: Ads with which users can interact (as opposed to solely animation and excluding click-through functionality) in a Web page format. These ads can be used either singularly or in combination with various technologies, including sound, video, or Flash, and with programming languages such as Java, JavaScript, and DHTML. Rich Media Ads can be static (e.g. HTML) and dynamic (e.g. Active Server Pages, ASP) Web pages, and may appear in standard ad formats such as banners and buttons.

Video Ads: The Digital Video Ad Format guidelines contain definitions and recommendations for the most common current in-stream ad formats, including Linear Video Ads, Non-Linear Video Ads and will be discussed in the section about IPTV ad formats below.

The European counterpart of the IAB is the IAB Europe[8], which represents the interests of companies from the areas of digital and interactive marketing at European level in form of a business association. The IAB Europe is a consortium of 23 country members and maintains own working groups that make recommendations for best practice and voluntary guidelines, which are then ratified by the national members and trade association partners.

2.5.1.2   Online-Vermarkterkreis (Circle of Online Marketers)

In Germany, the IAB is represented by the Online-Vermarkterkreis (OVK)[9] as the body of online marketers in Germany. The OVK consists of 21 of the largest German online marketers and works under the umbrella of the Bundesverband Digitale Wirtschaft e.V. (BVDW, = German Association for the Digital Economy). In addition to the already mentioned targeting working group, the OVK has an Ad Technology Standards working group, which develops online advertisement standards that are constantly extended and adapted to market developments. The OVK's standard forms of online advertising are defined as follows [157]:

---

[8] http://www.iabeurope.eu/
[9] http://www.ovk.de/

Table 4:   OVK standard forms of advertising[10] (source: [157])

Format	Pixel	Weight	Possible formats
Full Banner	468x60	40K	GIF/JPG/Flash
Leaderboard	728x90	40K	GIF/JPG/Flash
Expandable Leaderboard	728x300 (90)	40K	GIF/JPG/Flash
Rectangle	180x150	40K	GIF/JPG/Flash
Medium Rectangle	300x250	40K	GIF/JPG/Flash
Standard Skyscraper	120x600	40K	GIF/JPG/Flash
Wide Skyscraper	160x600	40K	GIF/JPG/Flash
Expandable Skyscraper	420(160)x600	40K	GIF/JPG/Flash
Universal Flash Layer	400x400	40K	Flash
Flash Layer	individual	40K	Flash

Full Banner: The Full Banner (also called a Fullsize Banner) is a classic among the forms of advertising. It is increasingly superseded by the Leaderboard. The Full Banner is generally placed at the top of a page.

Leaderboard: The Leaderboard offers more space than a standard Full Banner. Like the Full Banner, it is placed prominently at the top edge of the site.

Expandable Leaderboard: The Expandable Leaderboard has initially the same format as the Leaderboard. As soon as the user moves the mouse cursor over the banner, it expands to full size. As soon as the mouse cursor moves off the banner, it returns to its original format.

Rectangle/Medium Rectangle: A Rectangle is integrated in the editorial setting of a website and is surrounded on at least three sides by the editorial content.

Standard Skyscraper/Wide Skyscraper: The Skyscraper is a tall ad normally used to the right of the content.

Expandable Skyscraper: As soon as the user moves the mouse cursor over the Expandable Skyscraper, it expands to full size. As soon as the mouse cursor moves off the banner, it returns to its original format.

Flash Layer/Universal Flash Layer: The Flash Layer does not have a fixed format. It is placed directly over the content when an Internet page is opened. The advertisement must be programmed entirely in Flash to this end. Unlike the "standard" Flash Layer, the Universal Flash Layer has a visible area with a standardized size.

---

[10] The four formats Leaderboard, Rectangle, Medium Rectangle and Wide Skyscraper are analog to the respective formats of the UAP.

2.5.1.3   Vendor Specific Advertising Formats

The standard online advertising formats of the IAB U.S. and the OVK that have been introduced in the two previous sections are kind of a least common denominator in the Web advertising business. As the Internet is a fast developing place that lives from creative ideas, ad marketers and agencies do not restrictively use these standard formats. In addition, they also offer special formats with individual specifications (e.g. Banderole Ad, Tandem Ad, Fireplace,...) [97, 188]. In the context of this book, it is not necessary to give an exhaustive description of all possible ad opportunities. It is sufficient to provide a good overview in order to enable defining of relevant ad formats in terms of technological differences when it comes to targeted ad delivery.

2.5.2 IPTV Advertising Formats

The choice of formats for IPTV advertising is an aggregation of adapted Web advertising formats, established linear TV ad formats, formats that are used in Web TV scenarios, and interactive formats that have originally been introduced in cable TV. In the following these ad formats will be introduced shortly except for the Web advertising formats that have already been described above. Finally, the relevant formats for IPTV will be summarized.

2.5.2.1   Classic TV Ad Formats

In the TV world open standards for ad formats like in the Web are not available but over years some industry standards have developed. TV ad marketers typically provide an inventory of possible ad types that can be booked by advertisers or ad agencies. The available ad formats differ for each ad marketer and TV programmer, however most of them basically differentiate between "classic spots" and "special ads".

Table 5:   Ad formats in linear TV (sources: [99, 188])

	Classic Spot	Special Ads
Definition	Full-screen ad during commercial break (at least two successive ads) that is legislated by airtime regulation.	Special Ads use an exclusive positioning (outside a commercial break) and/or ad format (often not full-screen) that intends higher ad awareness and response.
Variants	· 15"/20"/30" (standard) · Tandem · Direct Response TV (DRTV)[11]	· Exclusive positioning · Special creations · Sponsoring
Example	Program [part 1] | Ad 1 | Ad 2 | Ad 3 | Ad 4 | Program [part 2]	Sponsoring | Program [part 1] | Special Creation | Program [part 2] | Exclusive Positioning

Special ads can be further classified into Exclusive Positioning, Special Creations, and Sponsoring. A short overview of these formats is provided in the following table. For further information please visit [99, 188].

---

[11] DRTV describes ad spots that allow the viewer to actively contact the product vendor via service hotlines, telefax, or email.

Table 6: Overview of special ad formats in linear TV (sources: [99, 188])

Exclusive Positioning	Special Creations	Sponsoring
  (source: Kabel1)	 (source: ProSieben)	 (source: ProSieben)
Advertisements with an exclusive positioning outside of a commercial break.	Advertisements that are created especially for the surrounding editorial format.	Advertiser serves as content sponsor. Sometimes also called presentership.
Examples: · Single Split · Program Split · Credential Split · Trailer Split · Pre Split · Single Spot · News Countdown · Diary	**Examples:** · PromoStory/Infomercial · Raffle/Quiz · Spot Premiere · Move Split · Cut In · Crawl	**Examples:** · Program Sponsoring · Trailer Sponsoring · Title Sponsoring · Rubric Sponsoring · Block Sponsoring

2.5.2.2 Web TV/IAB In-Stream Video Advertising Formats

Advertising in the context of video services is already very common in the Web, be it explicit video/Web TV sites (e.g. YouTube, Hulu[12]) or other websites offering videos as an added value (e.g. on news sites like Spiegel Online). As mentioned in section 2.3.1, IPTV is basically different from Web TV as it is delivered over a distinct managed network. However, in terms of advertising formats the concepts realized in the Web TV environment may also be applied to IPTV espe-

---

[12] http://www.hulu.com/

cially in on demand scenarios. The most common in-stream video ad formats are summarized in the IAB Digital Video In-Stream Ad Format Guidelines & Best Practices and will be introduced below. In-stream video is generally played or viewed from a video player and must be distinguished from in-banner video that is displayed in standard display ad units (see above section 2.5.1).

The IAB Video Ad Guidelines basically distinguish between linear and non-linear video ads in the context of in-stream advertising [90]:

Linear Video Ad: The ad is presented before, in the middle of, or after the video content that is consumed by the user in very much the same way a TV commercial can play before, during or after the chosen program. These three variants are called Pre-, Mid-, and Post-Roll respectively Interstitial Advertising. One of the key characteristics of a Linear Video Ad is that the user watches the ad in addition to the content as the ad takes over the full view of the video. Linear Video Ads may allow the user to interact with an ad message within the video window.

Non-Linear Video Ad: The ad runs concurrently with the video content, so the users see the ad while viewing the content. Non-Linear Video Ads can be delivered as text, graphical ads, or as video overlays shown directly over the content video itself. An Overlay Ad can also be delivered over a linear advertising experience as well in order to animate the user to interact with the ad. Rather than overlaying the content, Non-Linear Ads can also reside outside the live video frame but within the video window. This format is called Invitation Ad and is used when publishers do not wish to overlay the content.

Figure 13: Non-Linear Overlay Ad (bottom), Non-Linear Non-Overlay Invitation Ad
(top) (source: YouTube[13], 2009/10/31)

Both Linear and Non-Linear Video Ad formats have the option of being paired
with so-called Companion Ads that are defined by the IAB as follows [90]:

Companion Ads: Commonly text, display ads, rich media, or skins that wrap
around the video experience. These ads come in a number of sizes and shapes and
typically run alongside or surrounding the video player. Companion Ads may
offer click-through interactivity and rich media experiences, such as expansion of
the ad, for further engagement opportunities.

---

[13] http://www.youtube.com/

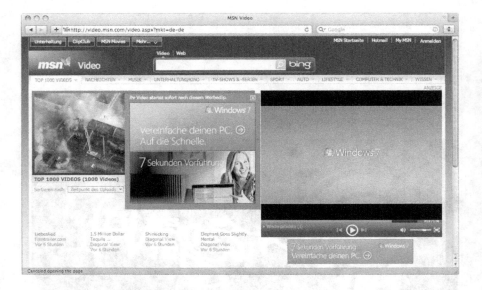

Figure 14: Linear Pre-Roll Video Ad with Companion Ads (left and below) (source: MSN Video[14], 2009/10/31)

2.5.2.3   Interactive Advertising Formats

The first successful interactive advertising realizations have been implemented in the UK by the BBC and Sky Media in 1999/2000. As will be discussed in later sections there exist some open standards concerning the technology of interactive television systems, but not in terms of ad formats. However some commonly accepted ad formats have evolved that are described in the following. The definitions are aggregated from [153, 26, 190] and information provided through Deutsche Telekom [203]:

Red Button/"Request-For-Information" (RFI): The Red Button is the best-known interactive advertising format. The name is derived from the way a user initiates the interaction with the television system. In case of interaction opportunities an overlay is displayed in a distinct area of the screen (e.g. upper right corner) telling

---

[14] http://video.msn.com/

the user that more information on the current show or ad spot is available when she presses the red button on her Remote Control (RC).

Figure 15: Red Button advertising examples (source [153])

Impulse Response: Basically an enhancement of RFI that enables the advertiser to ask simple questions, such as name, email, phone number, etc. It can also be used to perform surveys and polls. Impulse Response takes the form of overlaying pop-ups that appear in the bottom third of the TV picture. An example might be a cooking show that allows requesting a recipe by first pressing the red button on the RC and then entering the email address. Finally, the recipe will be mailed to the user.

Dedicated Advertiser Location (DAL): An interactive advertisement taking viewers from their programming to an interactive environment they could explore, play games and learn more about the products. DAL's have a customized feeling and can use a variety of rich media including videos, additional audio content, animation, games and others. The DAL may include Impulse Response functionality to report user data back to the advertiser. DAL applications are usually handcoded and have a high degree of design flexibility.

Figure 16: DAL advertising example (source: [153])

Mini DAL: A variation of the DAL that does not tear away the user from the programming, as the advertising environment covers only about 3/4 of the screen. The Mini DAL can also include Impulse Response functionality through an additional overlay displayed on the screen.

Microsite: Scaled down low bandwidth DALs, authored using a library of preformatted templates to save time and cost. Microsites can be built by advertising agencies using approved content creation tools. They are suitable for direct call-to-action, combining the speed of Impulse Response overlays with a "poster" page of additional information and data capture options.

2.5.2.4 Summary of IPTV Relevant Ad Formats

The potential advertising formats for IPTV have been described in the previous subsections. As this book has a clear technological focus it does not make sense to distinguish between all kinds of formats that have been mentioned above. Rather the formats with similar technical characteristics should be aggregated to groups in order to facilitate the use case development. The following groups can be identified:

Display Ad Formats: From a technological point of view it does not make a difference if a banner, a rectangle, a pop-up or an overlay is displayed on the TV screen (overlay in this case only describes the semi-transparent nature of this display ad and not a technology). Even the more complex splitscreen and wallpaper formats that are used in the Web but also in traditional linear TV can be considered as some kind of display ads. All ad formats that are displayed over or besides the content will therefore be referred to as display ads.

Ad Spots/Commercials: The classic 30-second ad spot as part of an ad block interrupting the content stream.

Interstitials: Advertisements displayed before, after, or as an interruption of streaming content, thus also called pre-, mid-, and post-roll ads.

Interactive Ads: Red Button, DAL, Mini DAL, and Microsite formats as described above.

2.5.3 Mobile Advertising Formats

The Mobile Marketing Association (MMA) regularly releases the Mobile Advertising Guidelines [138] providing recommendations for ad units in mobile advertising and has standardized the Universal Mobile Ad Package (UMAP) [140] defining the most frequently used mobile ad units corresponding to the IAB UAP standard known from the classic Web. The MMA basically differentiates the following mobile media channels: Mobile Web, Messaging, Applications, and Mobile Video and TV. The guidelines recommend ad unit usage best practices, creative technical specifications, as well as guidance on ad insertion and delivery necessary to implement mobile advertising initiatives. In the following, a short introduction containing the most important facts about mobile ad formats shall be given.

2.5.3.1 Mobile Web

The MMA Advertising Guidelines provide recommendations for the most prevalent advertising units on the mobile Web. This includes banner advertising and text links. From these pre-defined formats appropriate ads can be selected that fit best a particular mobile phone's display. The mobile Web features text and graphics optimized to match specific screen solutions and browser capabilities of each user's mobile phone. The recommended ad formats are as follows [138]:

Mobile Banner Ad: A universal color graphics ad unit displayed on a mobile website. It is defined as a still image intended for use in mass-market campaigns aimed at audiences across all mobile phone models, network technologies and data bandwidths.

WAP 1.0 Banner Ad: A supplemental black-and-white graphic for use in campaigns that target older phones.

Text Tagline Ad: A supplemental ad unit displaying only text that may be used in older mobile phones.

The MMA guidelines for mobile banner ads contain a series of specification components, i.e. aspect ratios, media formats, dimensions, and files sizes. The recommended ad formats are given in 4:1 and in 6:1 aspect ratios and in the sizes Small Image Banner, Medium Image Banner, Large Image Banner, and X-Large Image Banner. Publishers should always deliver the whole set of ad units in order to reach as many devices as possible.

Figure 17: Mobile Web Banner Ad units in 6:1 and 4:1 aspect ratio (source: [42])

2.5.3.2   Text Messaging (SMS)

SMS advertising has the same restrictions as regular messaging between mobile phones. SMS is a text-only medium that does not support rich media and the length is restricted to 160 characters. The MMA Mobile Advertising Guidelines distinguish between two kinds of recommended ad units [138]:

Initial SMS Ad (Appended): is a universal text ad unit of variable length appended to the primary non-advertising content of the message. It uses the remaining space after the actual content and can be made available for advertiser usage by the publisher. The content must not be compromised by the ad unit.

Complete SMS Ad (Full Message): is a universal text ad unit with up to 160 characters completely available for advertiser usage. There is no primary, non-advertising content in the message and this ad unit is typically delivered as a reply to an initial SMS ad or "Text (keyword) to (short code)" call-to-action. In addition, these ads may be delivered as part of an ongoing opt-in mobile advertising campaign.

In case of appended SMS advertising a clear separation between the text message content and the ad should be made. This is usually realized through an indicator, e.g. "**", "Ad:" or comparable. SMS advertising can also include interactive features like "call-to-action" or links to mobile websites.

2.5.3.3 Multimedia Messaging (MMS)

Multimedia Messaging Service (MMS) is a rich media messaging service allowing mobile users to send and receive messages that can include graphics, photos, audio, video and text. As such, it provides marketers with significantly enhanced ad opportunities compared to SMS.

Possible ad units for MMS are: MMS Short Text Ad, MMS Long Text Ad, MMS Banner Ad, MMS Rectangle Ad, MMS Audio Ad, MMS Video Ad, MMS Full Ad. As a consequence of the various form factors and screen sizes of mobile phones, the MMA recommends a series of specification components that are basically aligned to the definitions for the mobile Web [138].

Figure 18: MMS Pre-Roll Ad example (source: [138])

2.5.3.4   Mobile Video and TV

The mobile video advertising units defined by the MMA are very similar to the IAB in-stream video advertising formats [138]:

Linear Ad Breaks: take over the full mobile display screen and replace the streamed or downloaded video content for a given period of time. Ad unit formats include Billboard Ads (static image or brand logo), Bumper Ads (short video advertisement or sponsorship), Pre-, Mid-, Post-Roll Ads, Book Ending Ads (Pre-Roll Ad with corresponding Bumper Ad).

Non-Linear Ad Breaks: share the mobile display with the streamed or downloaded video content for a given period of time. Ad unit formats include Overlay Ads and Companion Ads.

Interactive Mobile Video and TV Ads: are advertisements that allow for user interaction including clicking, browsing, zooming. Guidelines for these types of mobile TV and video advertisements are still being researched by the MMA but may include click-to-web, click-to-call, click-to-SMS, click-to-video, click-to-download, click-to-locate, click-to-ad, etc.

2.5.3.5   Mobile Applications

The mobile application advertising guidelines address applications installed on the mobile phone that host ads inside the application design and logic. A problem in this context is the wide range of application types comprising managed platforms, virtual machines, native applications and widgets. However the recommended ad units for mobile applications are as follows [138]:

In-App Display Advertising Units: can be further differentiated into Mobile Application Banner Ads and Mobile Application Interstitial Ads. In both cases the above described specifications for Mobile Banner and Mobile Interstitial Ads apply.

Integrated Ad: is an advertisement that is integrated with the application or game experience (also known as product placement) and is formatted to be compatible with the main content type used in the application context.

Branded Mobile Application: many downloadable application advertising campaigns are custom designed to support the needs and expectations of the target audience.

Sponsored Mobile Application: publisher's downloadable application, which features a sponsoring arrangement at various places across the application.

Figure 19: Branded Mobile Application/Game example (source: [138])

3 Use Case Identification and Description

In the previous section the foundations of targeted advertising have been described and an overview of use case methodology and basic technologies in the ICT space has been given. As a first step towards the definition of concrete use cases typical ad formats from the Web, TV, and mobile world have been introduced in order to give a feeling of possible advertising scenarios.

This section focuses on the identification of relevant targeted advertising use cases and gives a description from a user perspective. The choice of scenarios includes cases stemming from the Web, IPTV, and mobile environments and finally two converged cases. In each subsection the respective selection of use cases will be explained before in the following the single cases are described and motivated individually. A detailed technical analysis follows in section 1.

3.1 Targeted Web Advertising

As mentioned in the definitions section targeting approaches first appeared in the Web space in the late 1990ies, at that time summarized under the umbrella of Web personalization. Even though these first attempts of exploiting user data and behavior for the purpose of individualization failed due to small Internet user numbers, hardware constraints, and low bandwidth, today targeted advertising is well established in the Web. NSN [129] says targeted advertising actually causes a paradigm change in terms of Internet business models away from single paid services towards ad financing. Many large Internet portals use targeting technology to identify customers, track their usage behavior and finally provide them with personalized Web offerings. The personalization does not only comprise ad targeting, but also content and product targeting, which means the delivery of target group specific content and product offerings based on user interest profile data. With the whole ICT space transforming to an all-IP world and the Internet being a strong driver in this process, it is only consistent to start the use case analysis with a classic Web example. However, as the focus of this book lies on the ICT space and thus more on IPTV and mobile scenarios, the examination of targeted Web advertising will concentrate on one exemplary use case.

The typical targeted advertising scenario comprises display advertising using classic ad formats as described in section 2.5.1. From a technological point of view, there is no difference whether e.g. banner ads or wallpapers are delivered as all these formats are served in form of a simple image file (e.g. .PNG, .GIF) respectively integrated in HTML code. The screenshot below is taken from the T-Online Web portal representing a standard ad supported Web page.

Figure 20: Targeted online advertising on T-Online Web portal (source: T-Online[15], 2009/10/04)

Short Description
The user browses a website offering of a company. The website includes online advertisements according to the standards of the IAB/OVK. While the user is browsing the site, a targeting system tracks the online behavior of the user and builds an interest profile from the topics of the visited pages. According to these

---

[15] http://www.t-online.de/

profiles the targeting system recommends targeted ad delivery that is realized by an ad server.

Motivation
The analysis of a targeted Web advertising scenario can deliver useful insights for two reasons: First, business model and technology are already well developed and established and therefore allow to derive principle characteristics of a targeted advertising architecture also valid in other ICT channels. Second, in a convergent ICT environment, most services are based on IP technology. This means that major elements of the technology used in the Web can be applied for use in other channels like IPTV and mobile.

3.2 Targeted Advertising in the IPTV Environment

Targeted advertising in the IPTV environment is by far not as established as in the Web. According to NSN [129] and Sun [40] the market situation in IPTV in terms of subscriber numbers is comparable to early Web targeting times. The definition of target groups requires a critical mass of users that has to be reached before the tipping point for efficient realizations can be crossed. However, the technology is generally sophisticated enough to realize targeted advertising in IPTV, they say. As will be shown there are several promising use case scenarios for example based on adapted Web technology or standards from the cable industry that can potentially make targeted advertising in IPTV a future success story.

The identification of possible targeted advertising scenarios in the IPTV domain can be supported using an option space in the form of a morphological box ("Zwicky Box"). The morphological analysis is a creativity and problem-structuring technique for exploring the possible solutions to a multi-dimensional, non-quantified problem complex. The approach begins by identifying the characteristics of the problem complex and assigning each of these a range of relevant values. By choosing a value from each row of the resulting matrix, possible use cases can be derived as paths through the matrix. The point is to examine all of the configurations in the field, in order to establish which of them make sense, are interesting and viable, and which are not [228, 168]. For the purpose of identifying potential use cases in the IPTV domain, the appropriate morphological option space can be depicted as follows.

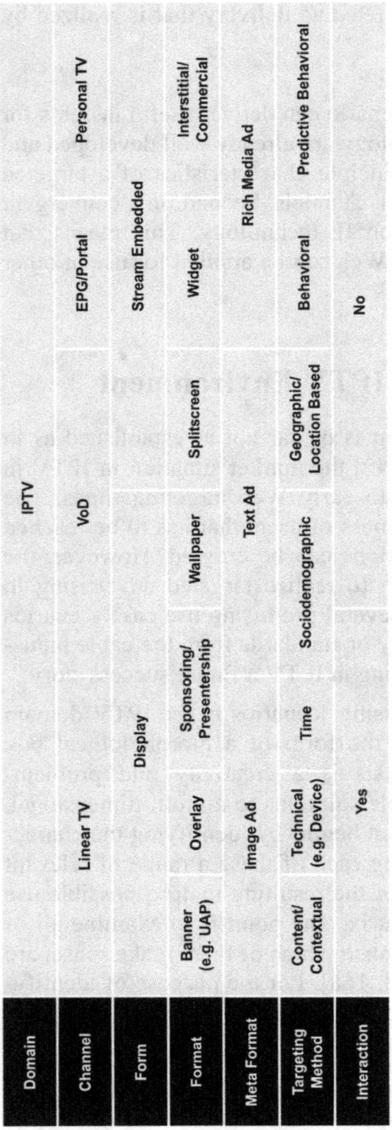

Domain	IPTV			
Channel	Linear TV	VoD	EPG/Portal	Personal TV
Form	Display		Stream Embedded	
Format	Banner (e.g. UAP)	Overlay	Sponsoring/Presentership	Wallpaper	Splitscreen	Widget	Interstitial/Commercial
Meta Format	Image Ad		Text Ad		Rich Media Ad	
Targeting Method	Content/Contextual	Technical (e.g. Device)	Time	Sociodemographic	Geographic/Location Based	Behavioral	Predictive Behavioral
Interaction	Yes			No

Figure 21: Option space: IPTV targeted advertising opportunities (source: own illustration)

In the IPTV domain there are basically four different channels that can be used for targeted advertising. This includes the three basic services linear TV, VoD, and EPG as described in section 2.3.1 and in addition personal TV services based on personal video recording (PVR) functionality. Ad formats for IPTV advertising can be chosen according to the ad format definitions in section 2.5.2 and may comprise different meta formats in terms of text, image, or rich media styles. However, from a technological point of view the form in which ads are presented within the channels is more important. A basic distinction can be made between display and stream embedded ads. The former comprises all formats that are delivered in form of e.g. HTML pages that are in one or the other way displayed over the content. As will be shown, this process can take place in the network or in the STB. Stream embedding comprises ads that interrupt the TV stream in the manner of classic commercials, which requires specific ad insertion technology usually based in the network. An important feature of IPTV is the opportunity of offering interactive services including targeted advertising. Finally, each targeted advertising scenario is characterized through the applied targeting technologies whose realization largely depends on available kinds of user data respectively data sources (e.g. interest profiles, CRM, location info). Certainly, several targeting methods can be combined in one use case thus aggregating several paths in the above option space.

According to SeaChange [218] and NSN [129] some of the most interesting use case scenarios can be found in the context of banner/overlay advertising as well as in the EPG environment where existing Web standards and technologies can be adapted. The same is true for targeted advertising in on demand scenarios that are very similar to interstitial advertising on video Web pages. Deutsche Telekom [203] identifies interactive ads as a very promising targeted advertising opportunity as these formats are already pretty established in the cable sector and can easily be adapted for the IPTV environment. Sun [40] and SeaChange [218] further see a great potential for inline advertising based on ad insertion/replacement although mainly interesting for the U.S. market where these technologies have already been used in the cable sector for years. Another very interesting concept is to offer personalized TV channels based on PVR and EPG technologies that integrate targeted advertising as part of the individual programming.

In order to achieve a systematic depiction, the interesting uses cases can be grouped into the categories display advertising, ad insertion, EPG advertising, and personal TV channel advertising. As will become obvious, in most of the scenarios this breakdown fits with the underlying technologies in terms of system architectures. In the following sections the most promising use cases will be described with a user-centric focus in order to provide a basis for a more detailed technical analysis in the next chapter. In addition, each scenario will be motivated

individually. The following diagram introduces the selected scenarios largely
using UML use case diagram notation. Attention should be paid to the fact that
this selection is certainly not exhaustive.

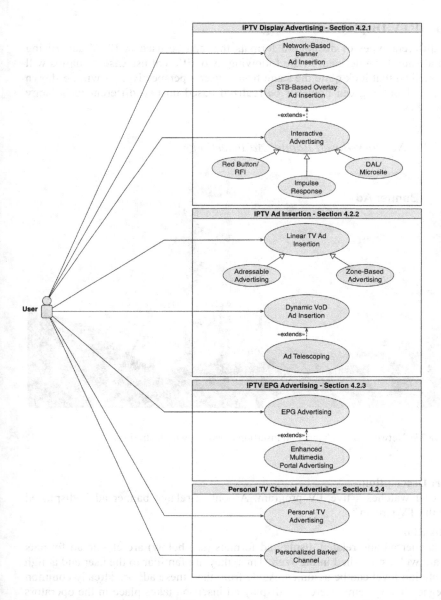

Figure 22: Use case diagram: IPTV targeted advertising (source: own illustration)

3.2.1 IPTV Display Advertising

The different types of display ad formats that can be used in IPTV advertising have already been defined. In the following, two different use case scenarios will be described that look quite the same from a user's perspective. As will be shown display advertising can however be realized based on two different technology approaches.

3.2.1.1 Network-Based Banner Ad Insertion

Figure 23: Network-based banner ad insertion (source: own illustration)

Short Description
The user watches a live TV program. A content-related banner ad is displayed over the TV stream.

Motivation
The banner ad and related display ad formats (see below) are classic ad formats that are well established in the Web. Thus, they are familiar to the user and a high acceptation level can be assumed. Aside from that, these ads are already common on legacy TV systems. Here, the display ad insertion takes place in the operators network. One of the questions being discussed in the technical use case analysis below is which targeting opportunities the operator has in this case.

Alternative Realization Formats
Overlay, wallpaper, splitscreen, sponsoring/presentership

3.2.1.2   Set-Top-Box-Based Overlay Ad Insertion

Figure 24: Local/STB-based overlay ad insertion (source: own illustration)

Short Description
The user watches a live TV program. A personalized overlay ad is displayed over the content.

Motivation
Display ad insertion can also take place at the user's site. In principle, the same display ad formats as mentioned in the previous case are imaginable. Though, as the STB's computing power is limited, the most interesting scenario in this case will be a transparent overlay ad locally displayed over the content stream. The fact that the ad insertion takes place in the STB has consequences for the targeting process that will be examined in the technical use case analysis.

Alternative Realization Formats
Banner

3.2.1.3 Interactive Advertising

Figure 25: Interactive IPTV advertising (source: own illustration)

Short Description

During a live TV transmission (either regular programming or classic advertisement spots), an overlay is displayed offering the user to press the red button (or some other key) on the RC to receive more information on the current programming or ad. In a next step, the user is asked for personal information and a confirmation that she wants to be contacted. Finally, more detailed product information is sent to the user by email or even regular mail. This process is known under the term Request-For-Information (RFI).

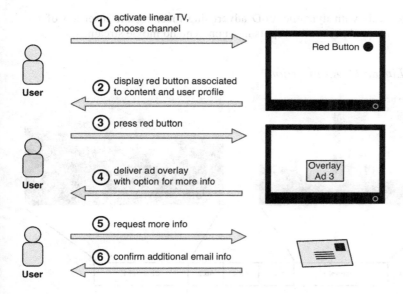

Figure 26: Interactive IPTV advertising flow, user perspective (source: own illustration)

Motivation
Red button and DAL scenarios have already been realized in cable networks providing first experiences in terms of customer acceptance and realization issues. This know-how can be exploited to achieve a successful implementation in IPTV networks. Compared to cable or satellite TV, IPTV has the major advantage that IP communication is inherently bidirectional, offering best conditions for interactive applications. In addition, a tight integration with Internet services is possible. Interactive advertising is therefore one of the most promising advertising use cases in the IPTV environment.

Alternative Scenarios
Impulse response, DAL, mini DAL, microsite

3.2.2 IPTV Ad Insertion

The following two use cases describe the possibilities of ad spot or interstitial advertising in IPTV scenarios. In the first case, default ad spots inserted by the broadcaster, are replaced by the operator according to the targeted audience. The

second case deals with dynamic VoD advertising meaning the insertion of targeted pre-, mid-, and post-roll ad spots in an on demand movie stream.

3.2.2.1   Linear TV Ad Insertion

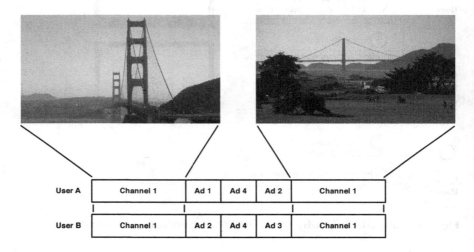

Figure 27: Linear TV ad insertion (source: own illustration)

Short Description
Users watch a live TV program interrupted by classic TV ad spots. Although
watching the same channel, they do not necessarily consume the same ad spots in
the ad break. Targeted commercial spots replace default spots originally inserted
into the broadcast stream.

Motivation
Local ad insertion can open up new revenue streams for operators by attracting
new advertising customers. This offers targeting opportunities on personal or
regional level especially for local advertisers, who could otherwise not afford
advertisements in national broadcast TV. Local ad insertion technology is originated in the U.S. cable network environment. First digital systems became available in the early 1990ies leading to the development of a sophisticated know-how
and a developed vendor network. As most cable vendors offer comparable solutions for IPTV networks, operators can benefit from a wealth of experience, when
implementing this cable-originated ad insertion technology [187].

Possible Scenarios
Addressable advertising, zone-based advertising

3.2.2.2 Dynamic VoD Ad Insertion

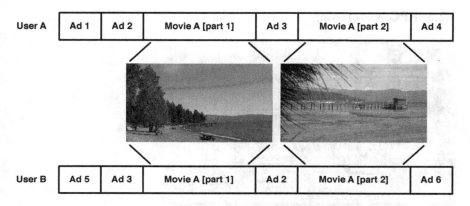

Figure 28: Dynamic VoD ad insertion (source: own illustration)

Description
User A (female) and User B (male) watch separately the same on demand movie. In each case, the movie is framed by two pre-roll ads and one post-roll ad, and interrupted by a mid-roll ad. While User A mainly receives specific ads targeted to a female auditorium, User B consumes male-specific ad spots.

Motivation
VoD advertising stands out as a compelling advertising scenario because it allows the advertiser to engage audiences with highly relevant messages. Viewers who select particular programs from VoD platforms see advertisements uniquely associated with that particular viewing session resulting in really one-to-one personalized ad sessions [186].

Another reason why IPTV operators should consider the implementation of VoD advertising is that interstitial (pre-/mid-/post-roll) advertising is already common in Web TV scenarios and turns out to be an accepted ad format at least among the Web users. According to the ARD/ZDF-Onlinestudie 2009 [15] 62% of German Internet users watched video content in the Web. Revenues generated by Web video ads grew in 2008 by 402% [114]. Hence, a deeper analysis of a realization of these ad formats in an IPTV environment seems appropriate.

Alternative Scenario
Ad telescoping

3.2.3 EPG Advertising

Figure 29: Targeted EPG banner advertising (source: APRICO[16], 2010/01/29)

Description
User browses EPG to obtain information on current TV programming. A classic banner ad is being displayed alongside the EPG content. The banner can be targeted to the current context and according to the user's profile.

Motivation
The EPG is a highly attractive customer interface potentially guiding the customers. Targeted advertisements thus reach the customer in an open mood for consuming ad information offerings. As EPG systems are mostly based on Web technology, existing targeted Web advertising concepts can be applied to this scenario.

---

[16] http://www.aprico.tv/. In 2012 APRICO was acquired by Axel Springer Digital TV Guide [18]. APRICO was formerly part of Royal Philips Electronics N.V.

Alternative Scenarios
Enhanced multimedia portal advertising, TV widgets

3.2.4 Personal TV Channel Advertising

Personal TV channels follow the concept of offering the customer an individually customized TV programming. The approach is hence inherently based on analyzing user tastes and computing appropriate recommendations thus allowing to exploit the program personalization technology for targeted advertising purposes. The first of the below described scenarios allows to create channels based on special content characteristics a user likes and uses PVR technology to record matching TV shows. The second use case is an adaptation of the "barker channel" approach normally used for promoting purposes.

3.2.4.1 Personal TV Channels

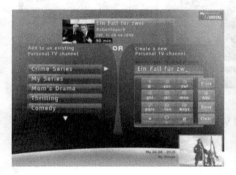 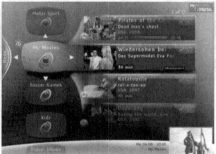

Figure 30: APRICO personal TV channel, (1) "My Crime Series" channel creation, (2) "My Movies" channel list including targeted ad spot (source: APRICO[17], 2010/01/29)

Short Description
A user enters a movie or TV program characteristic (e.g. title or actor name) or chooses a show from the EPG to create a new dedicated personal TV channel upon this information. She is then offered a channel list filled with content that is

---

[17] http://www.aprico.tv/

tailored to her preferences. Relevant ads that suit the viewer's channel's profile are inserted into the channel list and can be watched like the other content.

Motivation

The personal TV channel concept, introduced by APRICO Solutions[18], promises to better reach potential customers than this is possible with traditional advertising spots. Due to the fact that the viewer watches her own personalized TV channel, she is more open-minded for the offered program and it is more likely that she consumes the targeted advertising spots in full length without zapping away. From a technical point of view, personal TV channels are interesting because the channel profile targeting is different from the previous solutions based on user interest profiles.

3.2.4.2 Personalized Barker Channel

Figure 31: Personalized barker channel on ITV Digital (UK) (source: YouTube[19], 2012/04/30)

Description

A barker channel is a TV channel used to list or promote programs on other channels [103]. Its name was derived from a barking dog that wants to attract attention. The screenshots depicted above are taken from the ITV Digital Barker Channel, which is a collection of short clips of the user's favorite TV shows that is continuously repeated. It is imaginable to enhance this scenario by including VoD programs and ad spots that fit the user's personal interest profile.

---

[18] http://www.aprico.tv/
[19] http://www.youtube.com/

Motivation
The principle of the barker channel is already established in the digital cable TV and satellite TV environment, where it is used to promote mostly paid programs on other channels of a TV network. Following a similar approach like the personal TV channel described in the previous section, a personalized barker channel has basically the same advantages. In some sense, a personalized barker channel comes like a personal TV channel with a zapping-like appearance potentially promising to address a special clientele of more passive lean back users.

3.3 Targeted Advertising in the Mobile Environment

In the mobile domain targeted advertising is not yet as widespread as in the Web. However the initial position for targeted advertising deployment is somewhat different than in the IPTV environment. With more than 100 million mobile connections in Germany [29] the basis for personalized services is very broad also due to the inherent individuality character of mobile devices. Contrary to IPTV, the low spread of targeted advertising has to date been an issue of technological possibilities accompanied by user skepticism. However, according to NSN [129] the emergence of high-performing Web enabled smartphones like the iPhone and the increasing availability of broadband wireless technologies like UMTS emerge as a driver of mobile targeted advertising. Most interviewed experts agree that the mobile space will be a future key playground of targeting efforts [40, 129, 206, 218]. As many mobile subscribers plan to purchase next generation mobile devices [30] the conditions for targeted advertising are excellent, promising to cross the chasm in near future. Especially the delivery of location-based advertising is often considered as the "holy grail" of mobile advertising enabled through improved location-awareness of cutting-edge mobile services [87].

Like in the IPTV section above, the potential mobile targeted advertising use cases can again be derived from the below depicted option space readable as morphological box.

Domain	Mobile						
Channel	On-Portal Browsing	Off-Portal Browsing	Messaging	On-Device Applications/ Downloadables	Mobile Linear TV	Mobile VoD	
Form	Display	Stream Embedded	Message				
Format	Banner	Text Ad	Sponsoring/ Presentership	Wallpaper	Splitscreen	Widget	Interstitial
Meta Format	Image Ad	Text Ad	Rich Media Ad				
Targeting Method	Content/ Context	Technical (e.g. Device)	Time	Sociodemographic	Behavioral	Geographic/ Location Based	Predictive Behavioral
Mode	Push	Pull					
Interaction	Yes	No					

Figure 32: Option space: mobile targeted advertising opportunities (source: own illustration)

The mobile domain provides advertising opportunities in the mobile Web, in the context of messaging scenarios, within on-device applications, and in mobile video scenarios whereas the mobile Web and the mobile video channel can be further differentiated into on- and off portal browsing respectively mobile linear TV and mobile on demand services. In terms of ad presentation towards the customer again display and stream embedded ads can be distinguished though the messaging channel requires the introduction of a third advertising form here just called message. Display ads occur mainly in on-/off-portal Web scenarios and within on-device applications but can also be used in the context of mobile video, which is apart from that dominated by stream embedded advertising. As described in the IPTV section the advertising form allows conclusions to be drawn about underlying technologies. The choice of ad formats in mobile use cases follows the MMA guidelines described in section 2.5.3. The meta format of mobile ads has traditionally been restricted to plain text due to device and bandwidth limitations, but increasingly more complex image and even rich media ads gain traction depending on the used advertising channel (e.g. SMS is by standard restricted to text). As mentioned the mobile medium is characterized by its individuality and location-awareness inherently providing targeting systems with basic customer data available in the HLR offering good conditions for sociodemographic and geo-targeting. Besides that, special attention must be paid to device targeting as mobile devices are typically characterized through a diversity of form factors. The realization of other targeting methods depends on available data. As for example tracking of user actions is not yet widespread in mobile use cases the possibilities of behavioral targeting methods are limited. Finally, mobile advertising is often categorized by the ad delivery mode as push or pull advertising, especially in the context of messaging. Push message advertising often includes interaction possibilities through "call-to-action" dialogues or linking to mobile websites.

According to Sun [40] and NSN [129] typical mobile targeted advertising scenarios include banner advertising on mobile websites especially operator portals, such as the T-Online Web'n'Walk portal, providing some kind of homepage for mobile subscribers of a certain operator. Sun [40] further sees good opportunities for targeted pre-/mid-/post-roll ads in mobile video scenarios. The maybe highest potential for targeted advertising on mobile phones though lies in messaging. NSN [129] emphasizes that especially direct message marketing, where users opt-in to receive targeted ads compensated by free talking time or SMS, and subsidized messaging, either in form of sponsored news services or person-to-person messaging, have already proven to be successful. Another category of mobile advertising use cases comprises on-device applications and downloadables. This channel is currently dominated by iPhone or Android apps that can be downloaded from a central app store, often for free but sponsored by in-app advertising.

In the following subsections, a description of the most interesting use cases in mobile advertising will be given though without claiming to be exhaustive. Again each use case is motivated individually in order to explain why this special case was selected. The use case diagram below depicts the selected cases grouped in the categories mobile Web advertising, message advertising, on-device advertising, and mobile TV advertising, effectively representing different underlying technologies.

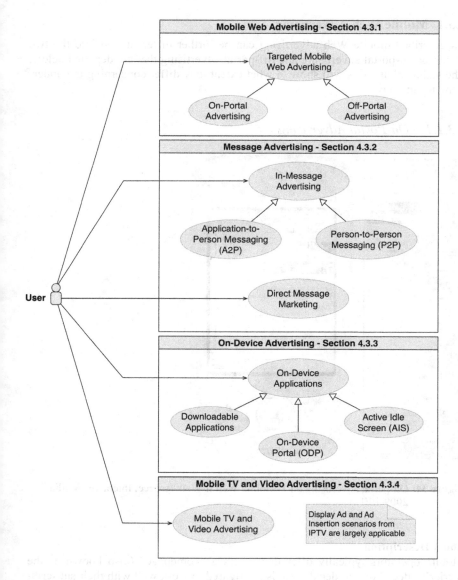

Figure 33: Use case diagram: mobile targeted advertising (source: own illustration)

3.3.1 Mobile Web Advertising

As described mobile Web advertising can be further differentiated into the two scenarios on-portal advertising and off-portal advertising that are depicted below. The technical analysis will show to what extent they differ concerning the underlying technology.

3.3.1.1 On-Portal Advertising

Figure 34: On-portal advertising on T-Mobile Web'n'Walk (source: InteractiveMedia[20], 2009/10/11)

Short Description

Mobile operators typically offer their users a "homepage" (also known as the carrier's "deck" or "on-deck") that is configured to work well with their subscrib-

---

[20] http://www.interactivemedia.net/

ers' browsers and devices. The operator portal provides a variety of links to branded, mobile-specific external sites in order to make it easier for subscribers to navigate. It also includes online advertisements according to the standards of the MMA and targeted to user-specific personalization data [137, 138].

Motivation
As operator portals are based on Web technology, targeted on-portal advertising is basically similar to targeted Web advertising described in section 3.1. From a technical point of view, special attention should be paid to the questions how user identification and profiling can be realized in a mobile scenario compared to the Web case, and to what extent the targeting potential of the mobile phone as a highly individual device can be leveraged in this context.

3.3.1.2 Off-Portal Advertising

Figure 35: Off-portal advertising at FUSSBALL.DE (source: InteractiveMedia[21], 2009/10/11)

Short Description
Simply put, targeted off-portal advertising is the mobile counterpart to targeted advertising on classic Web pages, typically realized through user-specific banner or text ads according to the MMA guidelines. In contrast to on-portal Web serv-

---

[21] http://www.interactivemedia.net/

ices, the terminology "off-portal" (or "off-deck") is used by the MMA for mobile Web pages with a "direct-to-consumer" characteristic. This means that their success does not depend on carriers preloading the services through their branded portal [136].

Motivation

As mobile users browse increasingly outside their operator portal, off-portal sites are becoming important destinations for mobile Web browsing, with sites such as Yahoo!, Facebook, BBC and Sky offering tailored mobile experiences [137]. Even though the scenarios off-portal and on-portal barely differ concerning the underlying technology, a key difference to the on-portal case lies in the user identification opportunities necessary for tracking and profiling. This is due to the fact that a common Web content provider will not be able to access the same resources like the mobile network operator.

3.3.2 Message Advertising

All mobile phones shipped today or in the past few years support SMS or its rich-media equivalent MMS. Accordingly, the installed base of messaging enabled phones creates a large addressable market for messaging-based mobile marketing campaigns. From a technical perspective, message advertising can be divided up into the two types in-message advertising and direct message marketing, whereas in-message advertising occurs in the two forms Application-to-Person (A2P) and Person-to-Person (P2P).

3.3.2.1 In-Message Advertising

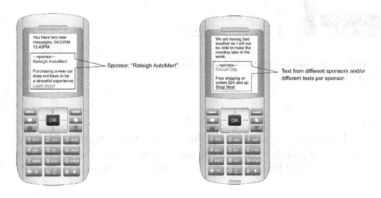

Figure 36: In-message advertising, (1) A2P, voicemail sponsoring, (2) P2P (source: [201])

Short Description
In-message advertising can be basically differentiated into A2P and P2P scenarios. In a typical A2P service, media publishers and businesses provide content (e.g. news, sports, gossip) and services (e.g. operator services like voicemail, overdraw alert from a bank) using an automatic application that sends the messages to a customer's mobile phone. If there is enough space left within the messages they provide inventory into which ads can be inserted. Users can for example subscribe to theses services on a daily or weekly basis (push), or request them ad-hoc (pull). Usually, the content is provided for free in exchange for viewing these ads [137].

The range of possible A2P services further includes interactive scenarios where users can participate in votings and contests often combined with other media activity such as TV shows. Finally, in-message advertising can be applied to A2P pull services where media publishers or search providers use SMS or MMS to answer user search requests or inquiries subsidized by inserted ad messages. This can be directory inquiries for phone numbers or any kind of mobile-enabled Web searches.

P2P messaging refers to scenarios where users communicate among each other via personal messages. Like in the case of A2P these messages allow the insertion of ads into the available space up to the size limit. In return, operators reward subscribers with free messaging or free talking time [137].

Motivation
As SMS is the most widely used mobile phone service after voice [137], the potential especially of advertising in P2P messaging is enormous. However, mobile messaging involves completely different actors i.e. systems than the previously described mobile Web scenarios. Therefore, the technical analysis must examine which components are necessary for ad insertion into SMS or MMS and where they are situated in the network infrastructure. Like all mobile advertising scenarios ad supported messaging can exploit the specific benefit of individuality a mobile phone provides. Again the question is how an individual user can be identified in the messaging scenario in order to target her personally. Moreover, the inherently delivered context of the message opens up enhanced targeting opportunities beyond pure subscriber data.

Possible Scenarios
Sponsored A2P messaging (ad sponsored push services, ad sponsored interactive scenarios, search and inquiry pull services), subsidized P2P messaging

3.3.2.2   Direct Message Marketing

Figure 37: Blyk ad funded mobile communication, MMS with Web link (source: Blyk[22], 2009/10/11)

Short Description

Beyond the above-described in-message advertising scenarios messaging also enables direct mobile marketing campaigns containing advertising or promotional content. Here, the subscriber opts in to occasionally receive pushed advertising messages and is in return compensated by free talking time or SMS. This business model can be further extended towards ad funded mobile communication as e.g. offered by Blyk or E-plus (Gettings[23]).

A special opportunity of direct message marketing lies in the location-awareness of mobile services. Local businesses like coffee shops or restaurants may launch promotion campaigns including the pushing of advertising messages whenever an opted-in user comes close to their location. Such messages can maybe include coupons for free drinks in combination with a paid breakfast.

Finally, direct message marketing can be used to enable subsidized messaging. Contrary to the scenario described in the previous section, in this case the ad is not inserted into the actual message. Rather an additional targeted direct market-

---

[22] http://www.blyk.com/
[23] http://www.gettings.de/

ing message is pushed to the sender (or receiver) in return for each transmitted message.

Motivation
From a technological point of view direct message marketing is at first sight quite easy to realize, as there is no need for a network-based ad insertion unit. As long a user has opted in for the service it can be realized in the manner of an arbitrary SMS application. However, the realization of targeted advertising requires at least a targeting system capable of analyzing subscriber information stored in a CRM system or the HLR. In this context it has to be discussed how the targeting system can attain and apply location information about a mobile device in order to realize the above mentioned couponing scenario.

Possible Scenarios
Ad funded mobile communication, location-based couponing, subsidized P2P messaging

3.3.3 On-Device Advertising

Figure 38: AdMob iPhone in-app advertising (source: AdMob[24], 2010/01/29)

---

[24] http://www.admob.com/

Short Description
On-device advertising comprises the three scenarios mobile applications/downloadables, Active Idle Screen (AIS), and On-Device Portals (ODP). Due to the emerging application stores, most smartphone vendors integrate with their mobile phone operating systems (e.g. Apple App Store, Google Android App Market/Google Play, Nokia Ovi Store[25]), mobile applications are a rapidly developing segment of the mobile market. They consist of software running on a mobile device and which performs certain tasks and provides utility for a mobile phone user [137]. Typical ad formats in this context are banner ads, text ads, and also display or even rich media ads presented in a pre-/post-roll manner before the application has started or after it was closed.

ODPs and AISs are specific kinds of on-device applications. The infrastructure can be pre-installed on the mobile phone or be downloaded to the handset, using a technology such as Java or Flash. ODPs were originally deployed to simplify the download of free mobile content like ringtones and games much like today's app stores. They provide the user with similar services like mobile Web portals as described in section 3.3.1.1 with the difference that some data is cached on-device, so no connection is required for the user to browse the basic content set [139]. AIS advertising aims at leveraging the fact that the idle screen is the starting and finishing point for all tasks associated with a mobile phone thus promising high Click-Through Rates (CTRs) [212].

Motivation
Mobile applications have evolved to provide the user with rich services that are however not necessarily permanently connected to the Internet. In this respect, mobile applications are distinctly different from browsing the mobile Web, which makes them interesting as a use case. Some mobile applications (e.g. games) run completely disconnected, while others connect occasionally (e.g. ODPs and AIS solutions may connect occasionally in order to update the local cache), and still others are constantly connected (e.g. browser-based apps, multi-player games) [137]. The question is how targeting and ad delivery can be managed in this environment and to what extent technologies of other scenarios may be applied.

Possible Scenarios
Downloadable applications, On-Device Portals (ODP), Active Idle Screen (AIS)

---

[25] http://www.apple.com/de/iphone/apps-for-iphone/, https://play.google.com/store, http://store.ovi.com/

3.3.4 Mobile TV and Video Advertising

Figure 39: Deutsche Telekom Mobile TV on iPhone (source: T-Mobile[26], 2009/10/31)

Short Description
Mobile TV and video typically comprises scenarios where content is delivered over a mobile network and is played via a media player installed on the mobile phone. As depicted above Deutsche Telekom for example offers an iPhone application that can be downloaded from the App Store, respectively for other device types the player is available on the Web'n'Walk portal. Mobile TV can alternatively be broadcasted to the mobile handset using for example the Digital Video Broadcasting - Handheld (DVB-H) standard. Since the mobile environment also offers linear TV and on demand services, similar use case scenarios as in IPTV are imaginable. In addition, mobile TV comprises podcast-like scenarios where videos are completely downloaded to the mobile device before playing.

Motivation
Due to the similarity of mobile TV and video services to the IPTV world, these scenarios do not need to be remodeled completely. The analysis should rather focus on the differences in content transmission and the resulting issues that have to be considered when realizing targeted advertising. Therefore, the single IPTV advertising scenarios will be examined to what extent they can be transferred to

---

[26] http://www.t-mobile.de/. In 2010 the T-Home and T-Mobile German operations merged to form Telekom Deutschland GmbH, the T-Mobile brand was discontinued in Germany and replaced with the Telekom brand. See http://www.telekom.de/.

the mobile domain and which specific changes in the implementation must be made.

Possible Scenarios
Banner ad insertion, linear mobile TV and video ad insertion, Electronic Service Guide (ESG) portal advertising

3.4   Targeted Advertising in Converged Scenarios

The previous sections included various targeted advertising scenarios in the Web, IPTV and on mobile phones. While all of these cases affected exclusively one of these domains, this section will focus on so-called converged scenarios. Convergence in telecommunications means the integration of products and services across multiple ICT channels in order to offer a comprehensive user experience to the customer. Telco consolidation has led to a situation where most operators are not anymore focused on either fixed or mobile products. However, the integration of business lines and especially underlying platforms and technologies causes multiple challenges that have to be tackled. The next two use cases will give examples on how convergence can influence targeted advertising in the ICT space. Crucial points include especially the management and integration of user data needed for targeting and the consistent delivery of unified ads through multiple channels.

3.4.1 Targeted Advertising in a Triple-Play Environment

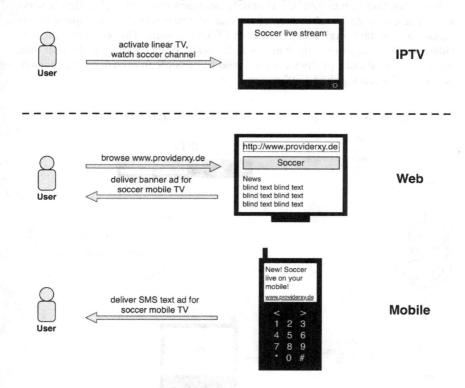

Figure 40: Targeted advertising in a triple-play environment (source: own illustration)

Short Description

The above scenario depicts a targeted advertising use case scenario integrating the three channels Web, IPTV, and mobile. Such constellations are often called triple-play services. Here, the starting point is a user switching on her TV to watch a special soccer channel she is subscribed to. As a reaction to her subscription and subsequent watching behavior, she is provided with targeted advertising not only in IPTV, but also on websites and her mobile, operated by the same provider whose IPTV service she is subscribed to. In this special scenario she receives a banner ad and a direct-marketing SMS containing information about the new soccer programming the operator offers in mobile TV.

Motivation
Telcos operating in multiple ICT channels can reach users through different serv-ices. If a customer is subscriber of several of these services, the operator has access to user data originating from each of the channels. This environment pro-vides excellent targeting opportunities as the operator can aggregate the user data and derive more exact profiles than it would be possible in each separate channel, potentially increasing the ad efficiency.

3.4.2 Dynamic Ad Replacement in Pre-Recorded Content

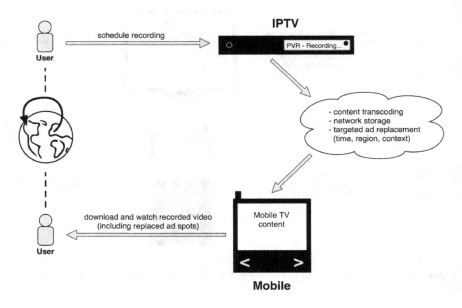

Figure 41: Dynamic ad replacement in pre-recorded content (source: own illustration)

Short Description
The above illustrated use case scenario comprises dynamic ad replacement in previously recorded content according to the user's current situation. The use case flow from a user's perspective can be described as follows. A user is about to go on a business trip for three weeks. She is fan of a monthly regional sports show that is unfortunately not available on the Web. As she wants to watch it anyway, she schedules her home Digital Video Recorder (DVR), which is connected to an

IPTV network, to record the next episode that will be broadcasted during her absence. Three days later, she comes back to her hotel in the evening and decides to watch the recorded TV show via her mobile phone. She activates the program manager that allows managing her IPTV account. Her favorite TV show has meanwhile been recorded and uploaded to a Web storage provided by the operator. In addition, the content has been transcoded to a mobile video format and is ready for viewing. The user downloads the recorded programming and then starts watching. As always the sports show is interrupted by an ad break after 30 minutes. But instead of the normal commercials, regionally targeted ad spots have been inserted. Thus she learns that the local gym five minutes from her hotel offers a promotion allowing her to work out for free in the next week. Two weeks later she gets homesick and decides to watch the same show again. As the promotion of the gym is over the ad is replaced by another sports related commercial.

Motivation

Due to its complexity, this scenario includes several key issues that have to be analyzed in the technical use case analysis. For example, the recorded content must automatically be uploaded to the Web storage and then be transcoded to a mobile compatible format. In order to replace the ads within the recording, the system must be able to somehow recognize when ads start and when they end. Eventually, the advertising platform does not only have to support network-based replacement of ads, but must also be capable of inserting ads within the mobile device in order to provide the user with updated commercials once the recording was already downloaded.

4 Technological Use Case Analysis

In the previous section an introduction to targeted advertising opportunities in different ICT channels has been given. The analysis of potential scenarios has led to the definition of several particularly interesting use cases in the Web, in IPTV, in mobile networks and also in converged environments. The selected use cases have been described from a user perspective aimed at providing the reader with a basic understanding of the respective matters.

The next step is now to analyze the underlying technology that is needed to realize the use cases. In order to provide a comprehensive and consistent overview the examination will follow a unified structure. First, the major players involved in targeted advertising will be defined for each of the three ICT channels and their roles will be basically defined. Then, the analysis steps one level down and examines the most important actors of the use cases. In IPTV and mobile they are commonly defined at the beginning of the respective subsection attempting to avoid redundancies in the single use case descriptions. The actual analysis of the use cases starts with an introduction to the subject matter of the scenario and an illustration of the concerned logical units. The tasks of these actors are further concretized and the use case flow is described according to the chronological order. Finally, the issues and challenges of each case are examined in a detailed textual analysis. In cases where concepts of other already described scenarios are picked up, the analysis focuses on supplemental issues without depicting the whole case again.

4.1 Targeted Web Advertising

As described in section 3.1 targeted advertising in the Web is not the main focus of this book. Therefore, one exemplary use case has been selected in order to representatively cover essential aspects. The purpose of this subsection is to describe the crucial points of targeting in the Web and to provide an overview of fundamental architectural structures that are also valid in the context of targeted advertising use cases in IPTV, in the mobile domain and in converged scenarios. At this point reference should be made to the detailed generic description of targeted advertising platforms in section 5.1 that has been developed based on this Web scenario.

4.1.1 Players in the Web Advertising Environment

The first step in the technological use case analysis is to define players or stakeholders involved in how advertising is finally delivered to the consumer. The most influencing stakeholders affecting the environment of a targeted advertising platform in the Web include the User, the Targeting Platform Operator, the Website Publisher and the Ad Marketer. A short description of their roles follows below.

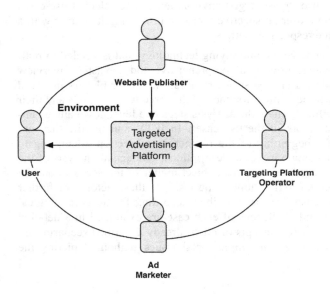

Figure 42: Players in the environment of a targeted Web advertising platform (source: own illustration)

User
The User browses a website/portal in the Internet. She can be new and unknown to the website or have a portal profile from previous visits that may even be enriched by other existing customer data, e.g. from CRM systems.

Website Publisher
The Website Publisher provides website offerings to customers, optionally using a Content Management System (CMS). The Web service is at least partly financed by targeted advertising.

Targeting Platform Operator

The Targeting Platform Operator hosts the different components that build up the targeting system. This includes tracking and analyzing user behavior for interest profile creation and the actual targeting and recommendation process.

Ad Marketer

The Ad Marketer sells advertising space on the respective website to advertising agencies/advertisers. He operates an ad delivery system that comprises campaign management and ad serving capabilities. Campaign management includes organizing the ad delivery according to campaign rules and scheduling information, and based on target group recommendations from the targeting platform.

4.1.2 Use Case Actors in the Targeted Web Advertising Platform

The basic roles of the stakeholders in targeted Web advertising have now been defined. The next step is to go one level down to examine the functional components in the responsibility of the respective players. This means that the actual actors of the technical use case descriptions in the following subsections will now be defined.

User Domain

PC: provides an environment that enables running a Web browser to interact with the Internet. Web pages are downloaded from a Web/Portal Server (definition below) using the standard HTTP protocol and may include different kinds of display ads.

Website Publisher

CMS: is used for creating and managing HTML content of the Web portal. Content that is requested by the user is delivered via the Web/Portal Server. The website layout must include fields that are reserved as advertising space.

Web/Portal Server: accepts, processes and answers website requests from the browser on the user's PC. The HTML code of delivered Web pages includes ad links referring to the ad delivery system. Once a page is being parsed and displayed by the browser the ad delivery process is initiated.

Targeting Platform Operator

Profiling Engine: tracks the user's browsing behavior and aggregates this information to user-specific interest profiles. Individual users are identified via user identification (ID) cookies stored on the PC. User profiles may be enriched by additional information from other profiling assets like customer data from CRM systems or even information about the user's Internet subscription if this data is available.

Targeting Intelligence: analyzes user profile data that it receives from the Profiling Engine in order to give recommendations, about which target group a user fits in. The Targeting Intelligence matches user profiles to target groups and determines the highest similarities. The best matches are written into a recommendation cookie on the user's PC in order to forward them to the Campaign Management (definition below) when ad delivery is requested.

Ad Marketer

Campaign Management: manages ad campaigns of advertising customers (ad agencies or advertisers). Depending on the portfolio of the Ad Marketer the campaigns can include different display ad formats and booking models. This may include ad delivery based on classic targeting methods like time, content and other context criteria as well as individual targeting based on the target group recommendations from the Targeting Intelligence. Information about delivered ads is stored in a campaign report that may be generated from data collected directly by the Campaign Management or that could be provided by a central statistical unit designed for feedback and reporting purposes.

Ad Server: delivers display ads that have been selected by the Campaign Management directly to the PC.

4.1.3 Targeted Advertising on an Operator Web Portal

As the T-Online Web portal is a classic example for a Web page implementing targeting technologies, it has been chosen for an exemplary analysis. The underlying system architecture can be depicted as follows.

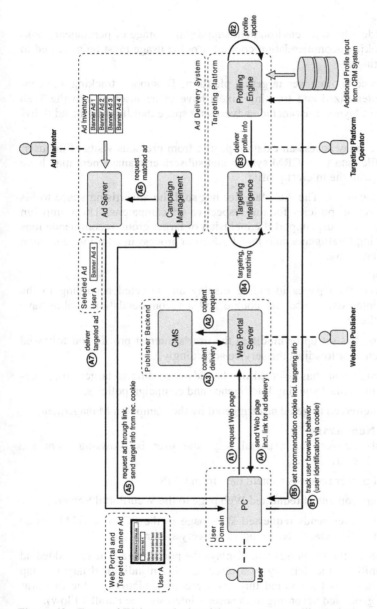

Figure 43: Targeted Web portal advertising (source: own illustration)

Pre-Conditions

PC: must provide a browser environment supporting storage of permanent cookies (user ID cookie, recommendation cookie). Cookie usage must be activated in the browser settings.

CMS: integrates code of chosen targeting platform. To support tracking, the content must be categorized and tracking pixels have to be inserted into the Web page. The content layout must include advertising space that links to the ad delivery system.

Profiling Engine: may access an existing profile from previous visits of the user. Additional profile data from CRM system and subscriber management may have been integrated with the interest profile.

Campaign Management: The Ad Marketer has sold the advertising space to his customers and set up policies for the respective ad campaigns. The Campaign Management system must support the inclusion of target group recommendations from the Targeting Intelligence into its ad selection process in addition to content and contextual targeting.

Post-Conditions

PC: has received Web pages including display ads targeted according to the user's current interests. A user ID cookie and a recommendation cookie have been stored on the PC.

Profiling Engine: has set up or modified the user's interest profile and followed her browsing behavior to adjust the service accordingly.

Campaign Management: has selected display ads according to target group recommendations from the Targeting Intelligence and campaign policies.

Ad Server: has delivered targeted ads triggered by the Campaign Management.

Main Flow (A Numbers)

A1. PC requests delivery of a portal page the user is browsing from the Web/Portal Server.

A2. Web/Portal Server requests content data from CMS.

A3. CMS delivers content of requested Web page to the Web/Portal Server.

A4. Web/Portal Server sends requested Web page to the PC. The HTML code includes an ad link that refers to the ad delivery system.

A5. The browser on the PC parses and displays the portal page. The embedded ad reference initiates the delivery of a targeted ad. An individual target group recommendation is transmitted through a recommendation cookie that was previously generated according to the user's interests (see Parallel Flow).

A6. Campaign Management selects appropriate ad according to campaign policies and target group recommendation transmitted via recommendation cookie and triggers delivery through Ad Server.

A7. Ad Server delivers selected ad for integration into current portal page.

Parallel Flow (B Numbers)

B1. Websites the user is browsing are tracked by the Profiling Engine. The tracking request is initiated by a tracking pixel integrated in the code of the Web page. User identification is realized using a permanent identification cookie that is stored on the PC.

B2. Profiling Engine generates or updates user profile if already existing. The profile contains information about the user's interests and her browsing behavior, e.g. the frequency of her visits on portal pages of a certain category. Additional profiling information from CRM and subscriber management systems is integrated if available.

B3. User profile information is delivered to Targeting Intelligence.

B4. Targeting Intelligence analyzes similarities of user profile and predefined targeting groups and determines the best matches.

B5. Target group recommendations are stored on user PC using a cookie. This recommendation cookie can be read out when requesting targeted ads.

Technical Use Case Analysis

Targeted advertising on websites is very popular since it promises to improve the efficiency of online campaigns by addressing users according to their special interests. Targeting technologies are used in the Web environment since more then ten years. Today's solutions are already very sophisticated. Therefore, an analysis of the underlying technology can give a good general understanding of systems and elements required for targeted advertising and introduces general concepts that recur in the other use cases in IPTV and mobile scenarios. Below the crucial points in Web targeting will be examined. For a comprehensive overview please see section 5.1 where a deeper analysis of the entire targeted advertising process in the Web is provided further attempting to derive a generic architecture for targeted advertising purposes.

User Identification and Tracking in Targeted Web Advertising

In order to address single users or user groups it is unavoidable to first identify them. As already described in the actor definition above, in the Web this is usually realized through cookies that are locally stored on the PCs of the users. When a user browses the website for the first time, the targeting system sets a user ID cookie containing identification information. While the user is browsing through different pages of the Web portal, tracking requests are sent back to the Profiling

Engine. These are initiated by tracking pixels integrated in the single pages and include the user ID taken from the cookie and the category of the currently visited site [225].

Due to legal constraints the targeting system must assure that the collected usage data cannot be associated to an individual user. This is can be realized using an "anonymizer" that separates the user ID stored in the cookie from the IP address of the customer. Such a system must also guarantee that the anonymized user ID afterwards cannot be resolved to the IP address anymore [208]. However the targeting platform operator is not required to request permission for cookie storage on the local system from the user ("Opt-In") [115]. A more detailed overview of the anonymization process and about the regulatory framework concerning user data collection is given in section 6.2.

The cookie method however has one weakness that can be a problem for targeting. If several different users (e.g. different members of a family) use one PC to browse the Web, there is no chance to distinguish between them. It is always the same cookie based on which the user identification in the Profiling Engine takes place. Hence, the profile of this "user" will be completely distorted and ad efficiency will probably not be improved. This problem can only be avoided through login functionality on the Web portal. However, this means that content access is either restricted to registered users only, or the operator must find a way to convince the user to login voluntarily (e.g. via incentives).

Profile Enrichment Possibilities
From the browsing behavior the Profiling Engine creates user interest profiles. Depending on the content categories browsed websites belong to and the frequency a user visits particular websites, the profiles are updated in order to represent the user preferences. The profile quality can be further improved through the integration of additional user information from other sources. Portals that provide community functionality and require a login can for example access enhanced profile information from explicitly or implicitly created user profiles. In the special case of an operator Web portal even CRM information can be used to enhance the profile quality. If the customer is connected to the Web via an Internet connection of the operator, the user can already be identified based on network authentication information (compare section 5.2.3.1) opening up the opportunity to provide the targeting system with enhanced customer data from other operator systems like the subscriber database. To further comply with the above mentioned privacy regulations the user ID must be pseudonymized (see section 6.2).

Recommendation and Ad Selection
In the above-depicted scenario target group recommendation and actual ad selection are not directly consecutive. One might guess that these steps are always realized in one logical unit that analyzes a user profile, selects appropriate ads and then initiates the ad delivery through an ad server. Here, the tasks of identifying the user's preferences and select best matching ads are allocated in two distinct systems and not conducted in direct temporal sequence. The Targeting Intelligence is provided with profile information about a user that is compared to predefined target groups. This means that in the actual recommendation process the individual user is associated with target groups and not directly with advertisements. The resulting target group recommendation is not directly forwarded to the Campaign Management. As already mentioned it is rather stored on the user's device in order to be read out and forwarded in case of ad delivery requests [225].

The delivery of ads is initiated as soon as the user browses a website containing a field destined for a display ad. The request works like a common image link to a media server though in addition, the target group recommendation from the recommendation cookie is being transmitted within the same procedure. The Campaign Management receives the target group recommendations and selects an ad from ad campaigns appropriate for the target group the user belongs to. Additional targeting rules specified by the campaign policies (time, content,…) and business as well as legal specifications are considered [225].

As will become obvious from the use case descriptions in the next sections, the implementation of the targeting process may vary in other scenarios depending on the respective situation. However, the crucial points in the targeting process, like the issue of user identification, remain mostly the same.

Personalization Opportunities beyond Targeted Advertising
Although the focus of this book lies on targeted advertising, it should be noticed that similar targeting technology could be applied for other personalization disciplines. As was mentioned in section 2.1.1 personalization also comprises content and product targeting. The target group recommendations computed by the Targeting Intelligence may be used to customize the actual content a Web user is presented with. This can be achieved by enabling the CMS to read out the recommendation cookie and adjust the content accordingly. In addition, the operator can use the customer information delivered by the Targeting Intelligence for cross- and up-selling or for customer retention activities.

4.2   Targeted Advertising in the IPTV Environment

The analysis of targeted advertising scenarios in the IPTV environment is one of the core points of this book. As figured out in section 3.2 the most interesting use cases in IPTV include network- and STB-based display advertising, interactive advertising, ad insertion in linear TV and VoD scenarios, advertising in the EPG, and advertising in the context of personal TV channels. Following the proceeding applied in the Web advertising case, first of all the relevant players in targeted IPTV advertising will be identified.

4.2.1 Players in the IPTV Advertising Environment

As the introduction to the TV advertising value chain in section 2.1.3.2 has shown, several players or stakeholders are involved in how advertising in the TV environment is finally delivered to the consumer. The following most influencing stakeholders affecting the environment of a targeted advertising platform in the IPTV domain can be identified: User, IPTV Operator, Broadcaster, Ad Marketer. The roles of these players are described below.

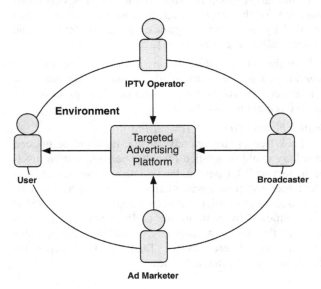

Figure 44: Players in the environment of a targeted advertising platform in IPTV (source: own illustration)

User
The customer of an IPTV service offered by the IPTV operator. She watches linear TV, VoD or consumes other IPTV services using an STB.

Broadcaster
The Broadcaster provides the IPTV operator with a TV broadcast transmission of linear TV content including default advertising spots.

IPTV Operator
The IPTV Operator receives live TV content from the Broadcaster that is processed in the headend for distribution using an IPTV middleware. The headend is also the home of VoD delivery equipment. In addition, the IPTV Operator hosts the different components that build up the targeting platform. To realize ad replacement in the IPTV stream, he offers ad insertion capabilities in the headend or in the access network.

Ad Marketer
The Ad Marketer sells IPTV ad opportunities to advertisers or ad agencies. He operates an ad delivery system organizing the ad delivery according to campaign rules and scheduling information, and based on target group recommendations delivered by the targeting platform.

4.2.2 Use Case Actors in the IPTV Targeted Advertising Process

The basic roles of the stakeholders in the delivery of targeted IPTV advertising have now been defined. Again, the next step is to examine the level of functional components in the responsibility of the involved players. As several IPTV advertising use cases with varying architectures will be analyzed in the following sections, recurring actors are first defined more generally. A more detailed and specific description of actors' roles will be given at the beginning of each use case analysis. This approach gives a good introduction to the advertising use cases in the IPTV environment and helps to avoid redundancy in the individual use case descriptions.

User Domain
TV/STB: receives the data packets transmitted through the IPTV network. This can be a linear TV stream, VoD, EPG data, advertisements, or other data. The STB is necessarily compatible with the operator's IPTV middleware and acts as client counterpart of the IPTV distribution server (D-server).

Broadcaster
Broadcasting Station: provides the IPTV operator with a TV broadcast transmission of linear TV content. The content is delivered in real-time to the headend of the operator using a common video codec.

IPTV Operator – Network Infrastructure

Processing/Distribution: processes linear TV stream received from the broadcasting station for further usage, this includes e.g. transcoding. Delivers content via core, aggregation and access network to the user's STB enabled by the IPTV middleware. Since the use case descriptions focus on the ad and not on content delivery, this combined actor has been introduced to represent several actually separated systems. This is of course a strong simplification.

Ad Insertion/Splicing Units: provide ad insertion capabilities to the Ad Marketer. This can include display ad insertion as well as the insertion of ad spots triggered by cue-tones.

VoD Server: stores on demand movies that it receives from an ingest server being part of the CMS. Ad spots for VoD ad insertion are also stored and delivered by the VoD server.

VoD Management: operates the VoD movie and ad spot play-out by the VoD Server.

IPTV Operator – Targeting Platform

Profiling Engine: tracks user behavior and aggregates this information to user-specific interest profiles. In case of channel changes and other relevant user actions, it receives updates from the Presence Engine (defined below). Further input may be provided through a link to the Campaign Management's (defined below) reporting system or a distinct statistic unit that could merge feedback information of different sources. In addition, other profiling assets like the user's VoD watching history or subscription data can be integrated via an interface to Business Support Systems (BSS), Operations Support Systems (OSS), or CRM systems.

Presence Engine: triggers profile updates. The implementation could include delivering status changes in addition to bare channel information to the Profiling Engine in order to create an extended behavioral profile. Optionally, a Presence Engine already being used for other presence services in the network could be attached to the platform instead of a new implementation.

Targeting Intelligence: analyzes user profile data that it receives from the Profiling Engine. It then sends matched target group recommendations to the Campaign Management (defined below).

Ad Marketer

Campaign Management: manages ad campaigns of Ad Marketer's customers who are offered to book different advertising opportunities. This may include ad delivery based on classic targeting methods like time and content, enhanced context targeting, e.g. on regional basis, and also personalized targeting on household or user level. Information about delivered ads is stored in a campaign report.

Ad Server: delivers different ad types (banner ads, overlay ads, ad spots) to an ad insertion point in the IPTV operator's network or to the user's STB.

These basic definitions are applicable to all IPTV use cases described in the subsequent sections. Depending on the respective use case scenario variations of the roles may occur and not all of the actors have to appear in each of the cases. Additional actor information will be added.

4.2.3 IPTV Display Advertising

Display ad insertion IPTV comprises all kinds of display ad formats that can be inserted into an IPTV stream. This can be simple text or banner ads or more advanced graphical formats like a wallpaper. A basic distinction from a technical point of view has to be made concerning the location where the insertion takes place. In principle, it is possible to differentiate between the STB and some place in the network. The following two sections will illustrate and analyze display ad insertion using the examples of network-based banner ad insertion and STB-based overlay ad insertion.

4.2.3.1 Network-Based Banner Ad Insertion

The following technical use case analysis describes a network-based banner ad insertion scenario. Depending on the capabilities of the ad insertion unit, other display ad formats like wallpaper, overlay, or even a splitscreen are imaginable. However, this does not have any consequences for the targeting process.

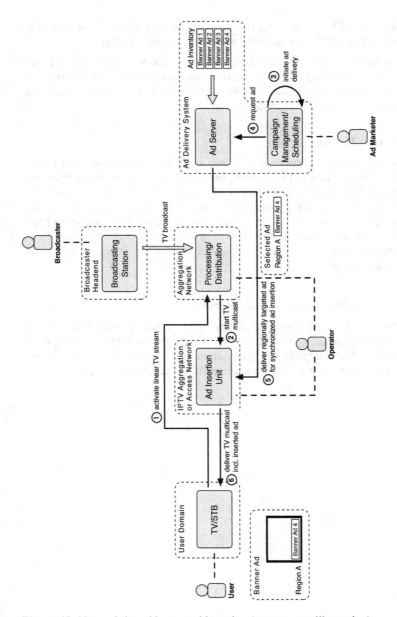

Figure 45: Network-based banner ad insertion (source: own illustration)

Actors

TV/STB: The user has selected to watch a linear TV channel. The TV Stream received by the STB includes banner advertising. As there is no profile based targeting, every STB receives by default the same ads in the same content stream unless the operator does targeting on regional level. Then, the user's STB can be considered to be part of an addressable regional user group.

Broadcasting Station: see basic actor definition

Processing/Distribution: see basic actor definition

Ad Insertion Unit: In this case the Operator does no user tracking. He only provides an ad insertion point for ad delivery of the Ad Server, located in the headend or at other points in the network.

Campaign Management: initiates ad delivery according to a time schedule based on TV guide data that defines ad opportunities. Alternatively (not depicted here), the broadcast stream may include a trigger initiating the ad delivery process. The Campaign Management selects appropriate ads based on content info and location data.

Ad Server: delivers banner ads to the Ad Insertion Unit.

Pre-Conditions

Ad Insertion Unit: To enable regional targeting, ad insertion infrastructure must be installed on a regional level in the IPTV network. Depending on the desired granularity, this can be in the access or in the aggregation network.

Campaign Management: Ad Marketer has set up policies for the ad campaigns of his customers that are translated into rules applied by the Campaign Management.

Post-Conditions

TV/STB: has received a linear IPTV stream that included banners displayed over the content. STB belongs to a special regional user group that all have received the same advertisements.

Campaign Management: has selected ads based on content and contextual targeting.

Ad Server: has delivered ads according to the campaign scheduling optionally including regional targeting.

Flow

1. User has activated linear IPTV stream on her STB. The STB requests delivery of chosen linear TV channel.

2. TV broadcast ingest is continuously being processed in IPTV operator's headend. As the user's STB demands streaming of a TV channel, her STB is

included into the IP multicast group of the respective channel to deliver the linear TV stream.

3. Campaign Management schedules the delivery of a banner ad according to the campaign policies. This includes contextual targeting based on content meta-data, time and regional info.

4. Campaign Management submits ad choice to Ad Server and triggers ad delivery.

5. Ad Server delivers selected banner ad that is synchronously being inserted into the content stream by the Ad Insertion Unit.

6. Delivery of multicast stream including inserted banner ad.

Technical Use Case Analysis
The use case depicted above describes a possible scenario for banner ad insertion within the operator's network. Before digging deeper into the issues of the actual insertion technology, it is important to understand what network-based ad insertion means in terms of targeting granularity.

Targeting Granularity of Network-Based Ad Insertion
Graphic ads are already well known in traditional linear TV. One example would be a pop-up ad that informs the viewer about other TV shows on a channel. However, in traditional linear TV every viewer receives the same display ads meaning that these ads can only be targeted according to the current content and basic contextual features like the time. In order to address single users or regional user groups, the targeting system must be able to identify them. One way to address single households is to deliver ads directly to the user's STB. Then, every user receives the same content stream and ads are locally inserted by the STB of the user. In this case the identification of single households via STB ID is easy. On the other hand, the advertising possibilities are restricted by the computing power and divergence of the used STBs. This scenario will be discussed in the next section.

If display ad insertion shall be realized on network-level, the provision of computing power is no problem. Network-based video processing can enable the insertion of very rich, complex graphic overlays because the rendering capability is now dependent upon powerful, network-based overlay processing engines, rather than upon the lowest common denominator of set-top processing capabilities. However, linear IPTV is transmitted to the customer using multicast streaming. Targeting on household level would thus require to have installed the video processing equipment at the multicast endpoint. This again would make the targeting efforts very expensive, so that the advantage of being able to insert high-quality display ads vanishes facing the high expenses. As a consequence, network-based display ad insertion will be most promising when realized at aggregation network locations (compare figure above). Then, the expenditures for the insertion technology are likely to be outweighed by the advantage of being able to insert a wide range of top-quality display ads and the expected leverage effect on advertising efficiency. Ad insertion on a regional level is also called zone-based advertising, even though this term is more commonly used in the context of ad splicing in linear TV (see section 4.2.4.1).

Once an operator has decided to go for network-based display ad insertion, he faces the problem of how to insert the advertisements into the IPTV stream. TV broadcasters widely use graphic overlays to insert display ads into their TV programs relying on baseband video technology. If the operator decides to place the insertion infrastructure into the headend, he can potentially use the same baseband technology as broadcasters. While processing the content received from the programmer, there will be a point where he can access the uncompressed and not yet encrypted content. But as described above, he will not be able to target much more than the content and the time. This will probably not be the preferred option of the operator. So what opportunities does he have to insert display ads e.g. in the aggregation network?

Pixel versus Compressed Domain and the Factor of Encryption
One way that operators can insert the digital display ads into video programming is by using baseband technology as described above. When realizing this approach on regional level, operators must first decode each MPEG program to the pixel domain, insert the ad there, and then re-encode the program. Due to the complexity of this process, current pixel domain solutions can typically insert display ads into just a few programs per rack unit of equipment space. A problem is that the decoding and encoding process can erode the video quality [205]. Considering the fact that the IPTV stream usually is encrypted for reasons of Digital Rights Management (DRM), it is almost impossible to follow the baseband approach. In either case the method is very low performing and very expensive.

Another opportunity is to insert the digital display ads directly into a compressed MPEG video stream. The cable industry has developed more advanced all-digital network-based video processing solutions capable of manipulating compressed MPEG programs that are also available for the IPTV space. Following this approach, operators can place graphic ads right into the native digital video format without needing to convert it. Therefore, there is no need to decode and re-encode each program, minimizing the risk of picture degradation [207]. Though, the encryption of the content still restricts the opportunities of the operator. But as ad spots being part of the IPTV stream can be left unencrypted, the operator can at least use display ads to customize these spots by inserting specified display ads (see section 4.2.4.1). The display ad insertion then takes place while ad spots are played. In this context, encryption does not cause a problem. However, the newest development is that technology vendors like BigBand Networks[27] start offering platforms that are also able to insert ads into encrypted content [213].

Concluding, display ad insertion in the compressed domain offers several key advantages. First of all, it can be far cheaper than insertion in the pixel domain because the digital hardware and software needed to carry out the MPEG operation is much less expensive than the baseband equipment for the pixel domain. Second, digital display ads can be inserted into more video programs and much quicker under the MPEG compression method [205]. Third, new cutting-edge solutions allow inserting ads even in encrypted content offering far more opportunities.

Further Aspects of Network-Based Display Ad Insertion
Network-based display ad insertion has some further advantages compared to STB-based ad insertion. The central location of video processing capabilities simplifies the maintenance of the infrastructure. Updates only have to be deployed to the network devices and not towards the whole entity of STBs. There is no need to manage the installation of new software to the multiple models of STBs that might be attached to the IPTV network. Since the display ads are included in the stream itself, the operator must only provide one piece of overlay content for an ad campaign element, instead of one for each STB device or model. Additionally, some technology vendors provide integrated solutions that include network-based display ad insertion as well as ad splicing technology. Hence, the operator could easily integrate both advertising technologies with his network infrastructure (see section 4.2.4.1) [205].

Nevertheless, the major drawback of network-based display ad insertion is that really personalized one-to-one targeting is only possible if the infrastructure is installed very close to the user's site meaning in the access network. In most cases, this scenario will probably be too expensive.

4.2.3.2   Set-Top Box Based Overlay Ad Insertion

This use case describes the scenario of local overlay ad insertion realized by an ad insertion enabler inside the STB. Other display ad formats like non-transparent banners or simple text ads could also be realized in similar scenarios as long as they do not require too much local computing power. Anyway, this does not make a difference concerning the targeting possibilities in this use case. As will be shown, user identification and user presence are the two major issues.

---

[27] http://www.bigbandnet.com/

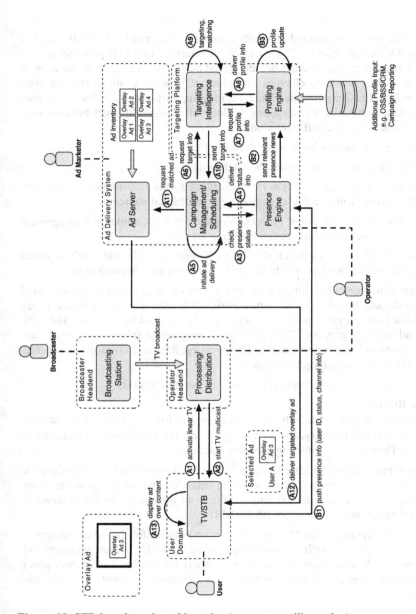

Figure 46: STB-based overlay ad insertion (source: own illustration)

Actors

TV/STB: The user has selected to watch a linear TV channel. The STB receives the linear TV stream from the IPTV distribution server. The STB provides a local ad insertion enabler that displays ads delivered by the Ad Server over the content stream. It pushes presence changes and channel switch events to the Presence Engine and the Profiling Engine. The STB may support user login for single user identification. Otherwise the targeting is done on household level because user and household cannot be differentiated.

Broadcasting Station: see basic actor definition

Processing/Distribution: see basic actor definition

Profiling Engine: tracks user behavior according to the information sent by the STB and received from the Presence Engine or additional sources.

Presence Engine: answers user presence requests of the Campaign Management and forwards presence updates to the Profiling Engine.

Targeting Intelligence: analyzes the user's interest profile and derives target group recommendations that are delivered to the Campaign Management.

Campaign Management: initiates ad delivery according to a time schedule based on TV guide data that defines ad opportunities. Alternatively (not depicted here), the broadcast stream may include a trigger that is detected by the STB and initiates the ad delivery process. The Campaign Management selects appropriate ads based on content and contextual info like location data and on target group recommendations from the targeting system.

Ad Server: delivers personalized ads directly to the user's STB.

Pre-Conditions

TV/STB: must be able to locally insert overlay ads for display over the stream. For user-specific ad delivery, the STB, respectively the middleware, must support user login. Then the user must login before watching.

Profiling Engine: must be able to identify the STB/household or single user to enable the targeting system to track viewing behavior and set up an interest profile. It may have access to an existing profile from previous viewing sessions or provided from other sources (OSS/BSS/CRM).

Campaign Management: Ad Marketer has set up policies for the ad campaigns of his customers that are translated into rules applied by the Campaign Management. The Campaign Management system must support the inclusion of target group recommendations in its ad selection process in addition to content and contextual targeting.

Post-Conditions

TV/STB: has received a linear IPTV stream that included overlay ads locally displayed over the content. The household or the single user was targeted because of the past viewing behavior and the therefore created interest profile.

Profiling Engine: has identified the user's STB or the user herself. It has set up or modified an interest profile and tracked the TV consumption to adjust the interest profile.

Targeting Intelligence: has derived target group recommendations and delivered them to the Campaign Management.

Campaign Management: has selected ads based on content targeting, contextual targeting and on target group information from the Targeting Intelligence.

Ad Server: has delivered ads according to the campaign scheduling and personalized target group recommendations of the Targeting Intelligence.

Main Flow (A Numbers)

A1. User has activated linear IPTV stream on her STB. The STB requests delivery of chosen linear TV channel.

A2. TV broadcast ingest is continuously being processed in IPTV operator's headend. As the user's STB demands streaming of TV channel, her STB is included into the IP multicast group of the respective channel to deliver the linear TV stream. Presence and channel info updates are sent to the Presence and the Profiling Engine (see parallel flow).

A3. Campaign Management checks user presence status to find out if user is active.

A4. Presence Engine confirms to Campaign Management that the user is active.

A5. Campaign Management schedules targeted ad delivery if user is active.

A6. Campaign Management requests target info from Targeting Intelligence in order to include it into ad selection process.

A7. Targeting Intelligence requests user profile from Profiling Engine.

A8. Profiling Engine delivers current user profile to Targeting Intelligence.

A9. Targeting Intelligence analyzes user profile and matches appropriate target group attributes.

A10. Targeting Intelligence sends target group recommendation to Campaign Management.

A11. Campaign Management matches content, context and target group rec-
      ommendation to campaign policies and submits ad choice to Ad Server and
      triggers ad delivery.

A12. Ad Server delivers targeted overlay ad to STB.

A13. STB displays delivered ad over the content.

Parallel Flow (B Numbers)

B1. STB continuously pushes user presence updates (user ID, user status, channel
     info) to Presence Engine to keep it up-to-date.

B2. Presence Engine analyzes presence information from STB according to pre-
     defined rules. In case of relevant changes it informs the Profiling Engine
     about the user's status.

B3. Profiling Engine updates the user profile according to the user's viewing
     preferences. The Profiling Engine can derive information about the user's in-
     terests from her viewing behavior. The user profile is enriched by data from
     other sources like subscriber information provided by the OSS/BSS/CRM
     systems including demographic data.

Technical Use Case Analysis

From a user perspective, network-based banner ad insertion as described in the
previous section and local overlay ad insertion may resemble each other a lot. At
first sight, both cases use display ad formats to communicate the ad message. And
to the user it does not really matter, whether the ad message is being presented as
a banner ad or as an overlay ad in form of a rectangle. In fact, both use cases
might even be realized using similar display ad formats that look exactly the
same, so that there is eventually no difference that could be recognized by the
viewer.

What makes the difference happens on the technology level. First, it has to be
mentioned that the choice of the ad format strongly depends on the capabilities of
the ad insertion technology. While banner ad insertion in the previous case is
realized in the network, the overlay process here is performed by the STB. It has
to be pointed out that STBs actually are very simple personal computers with
adapted standard operating systems [71, 27]. They are optimized for a cheap
realization of their main task, which is to decode the IPTV stream. The decoding
is usually realized on a hardware basis. But besides that the hardware equipment
is very basic, most often following a "system-on-a-chip" architecture. Thus, the
available processing power for advanced graphical operations is very limited
compared to powerful network processing units, specially geared towards ad
insertion.

But, more important than the impact on the ad format choice, ad insertion at the user's site offers more specific targeting possibilities compared to the network based solution. The Ad Server sends advertisements directly to a distinct STB. Thus ad campaigns can address single households instead of regional groups like in the banner case. It is therefore possible not only to target according to contextual data, e.g. special time frames and content types. The Campaign Management knows which ads work best at which time and in combination with which channel or program. In addition, it now receives a user-specific target group recommendation from the Targeting Intelligence that may include demographic and exact location data but especially information about the user's interests and behavior. This recommendation is the result of an analysis of the profile information collected by the Profiling Engine optionally including OSS/BBS/CRM data, e.g. provided from the operator's subscriber management. The involved actors and their roles can be compared to their counterparts in the Web scenario. So far, it can be stated that STB-Based Display Ad Insertion is a trade-off between lower graphic processing power and a higher personalization level. However, the initiation of the profiling process and the identification of the user raise some questions that require a closer look.

User Identification in IPTV Set-Top-Boxes
User identification for targeting purposes in the Web is realized using an identification cookie (see sections 4.1.3 and 5.1.1). The IPTV client software solutions installed on contemporary STBs do not provide a cookie support. This may be the case in an integrated portal environment with Web browsing capabilities, but cannot be considered to be given. Though, the IPTV middleware comprises a subscriber management using distinct device IDs that can be provided to the local ad insertion enabler via an interface.

The STB device ID enables targeting down to household level. This yet does not necessarily mean that a distinct user can be addressed because no one knows who is sitting in front of the TV unless the user has somehow logged in. In the Web world this problem is not as serious because most users have their own computers or at least own user profiles. The implication of this issue in the IPTV scenario is obvious. Let's say the User A is a family dad. What happens if the rest of the family (Users B, C, D) uses the same STB to watch TV? If there is no login opportunity, the user will probably never be targeted on a really personal level. The solution of this problem can be an identity management solution implemented in the IPTV middleware allowing to differentiate individual users that need to login on the STB. The Profiling Engine being part of the targeting system would then be linked to the middleware subscriber management system in order to track viewing preferences of each distinct user of the household. For the sake of customer satisfaction, the STB would probably best be launched with a default "family" profile to enable viewing without the need to have an own profile. Despite the fact that the need for users to login might feel a little uncomfortable, in future the problem can be solved through automatic user recognition. This could be done via an analysis of the users' zapping behavior [98] or using a facial recognition system. The users can also be encouraged to login by providing an enhanced STB user interface more like a user portal page that welcomes the user with integrated personal information and services like e.g. email, chatting and other interactive services. A completely different approach of targeting single users is the personal TV channel concept. Here, the personalization is based on channel profiles rather than on single user profiles. This approach will be discussed in detail in section 4.2.6.

Importance of Presence Information for User Profiling

As mentioned in the introduction to this chapter, it occurs that users turn on their STBs to watch a TV show but forget to turn it off, when they are not actively watching anymore. It does not really matter if they are just leaving the room for few hours, go to bed, or go on holiday while the STB is still working [218]. In each case, the user absence affects the targeted advertising process in two ways. First, the personal user profile can be extremely distorted. The Profiling Engine tracks the viewing behavior according to the channel info pushed by the STB. It just knows that the user turned on the STB and started watching a TV program on a certain channel. If the user leaves without turning off the device, the Profiling Engine will believe that she is still watching the same channel and modify the profile according to this information. Second, the advertisements will still be delivered to the STB unnecessarily charging the network capacity. In contrast to network-based display ad insertion, the display ads are not transmitted as part of the multicast stream. Each overlay has to be delivered separately to the STB. This process requires a lot more resources in terms of bandwidth and ad serving capabilities that are partly wasted in case of unnecessarily delivered ads. In addition, it makes the campaign reporting eventually meaningless. The advertiser will not only receive false information about how often his ads have been displayed. Depending on the billing model he will possibly be charged for advertising that in fact wasn't consumed by any customer.

A smart solution for this problem is the implementation of a Presence Engine triggered by the STB. Generally, presence information indicates the availability of a user for real-time communication activities. It also indicates the level of the user's activity for the device publishing the presence information [171]. For example, in converged scenarios a Presence Engine is needed to enable enhanced services like chatting. Here, it is used as an indicator for user activity answering the question if the user sits in front of the TV or not. Thus, rules must be defined that are applied in order to analyze if the user is still watching or not. This can for example include the definition that a user is considered to be not actively consuming anymore, if she has not changed the channel for two hours. In the case of interactive advertising (see next section), it is imaginable to include missing reactions to interaction offerings in the presence status analysis. In each case, the Presence Engine must always be kept up-to-date about the activity level of the user. This can either be realized in push or pull communication with the STB.

In order to tackle the issues mentioned above, the Presence Engine must provide interfaces towards the Profiling Engine and the Campaign Management. The Presence Engine analyzes the information of the STB and derives the current status (e.g. the user ID, the presence status, and channel information) according to the predefined rules (e.g. user is more than to hours away = inactive). Changes in the status are forwarded to the Profiling Engine. By including the time a user is actively watching a program, profile distortion caused by misinterpretation of channel switching information can be avoided. The problem of delivering ads to inactive users causing waste of bandwidth and wrong reporting can be solved as follows. Before initiating ad delivery, the Campaign Management requests the presence status of the user to find out if a scheduled ad delivery is reasonable. Otherwise the ad delivery will be cancelled.

4.2.3.3   Interactive Advertising

The interactive advertising use case described here can be understood as an extension of the overlay ad case analyzed in the preceding section. The red button overlay is displayed in the same manner as the standard overlay ad. The process depicted below continues the flow described in the previous section and therefore starts with step 14. It is reduced to the additional elements necessary to realize interactive features. While several forms of interactions are imaginable, the depicted flow illustrates the Request-For-Information (RFI) scenario. The other scenarios will be described in the textual analysis.

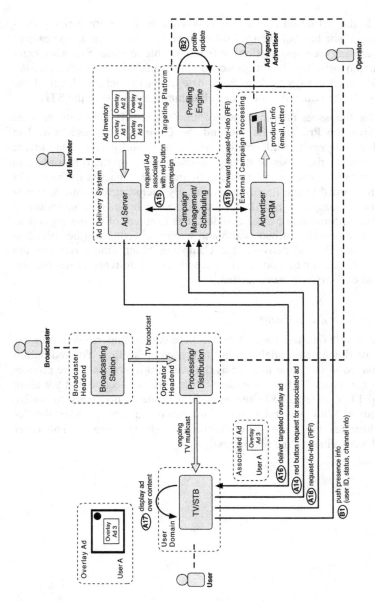

Figure 47: Interactive Red Button advertising, Request-For-Information (RFI) (source: own illustration)

Actors

TV/STB: see description in STB-based ad insertion use case. The user is provided with interactivity features, in this scenario represented by red button functionality. Information about the user's reaction facing the displayed red button overlay and her further behavior is sent to the Profiling Engine.

Broadcasting Station: see basic actor definition

Processing/Distribution: see basic actor definition

Profiling Engine: tracks user behavior according to the information sent by the STB. Particularly, this includes her reactions concerning the interactivity features. One opportunity would be to rate her interaction with the ad in terms of at which level of the interaction she possibly aborts the process.

Campaign Management: initiates delivery of second overlay ad with further interaction feature (RFI option) upon red button request. A possible RFI is processed and forwarded to the ad agency or advertiser. In case of more complex interactive scenarios, the Campaign Management must refer to the Dedicated Advertiser Location (DAL) or microsite when requested by the user.

Ad Server: delivers second overlay ad directly to the user's STB.

Ad Agency/Advertiser: receives RFI request from Ad Marketer's Campaign Management and initiates mailing of further information to the user.

Pre-Conditions

TV/STB: see post-conditions in STB-based ad insertion use case. In addition, the STB comes with an RC enabled for interactive features such as action buttons of different colors. The STB has displayed an ad message asking the user to press the red button of her RC in order to receive more information on the advertised topic.

Profiling Engine: see post-conditions in STB-based ad insertion use case. The Profiling Engine has identified the user herself or the household she lives in via the STB ID. It has set up a new profile or selected a possibly existing user profile.

Campaign Management: see post-conditions in STB-based ad insertion use case. According to a time schedule indicating ad opportunities in the current programming, the Campaign Management has initiated the delivery of an interactive ad set. The ad selection is based on content and context targeting as well as on the target group recommendation of the Targeting Intelligence. The Ad Marketer must of course support interactive campaigns including RFI functionality. The Campaign Management must have an interface to communicate RFIs to Ad Agencies/Advertisers that subsequently contact users by email or regular mail.

Ad Server: has delivered the red button overlay ad selected by the Campaign Management to the STB.

Post-Conditions

TV/STB: has received a linear TV stream from the IPTV distribution server. The STB has locally displayed overlay ads being part of a red button campaign over the content stream. Red button commands of the user have been transmitted to the Campaign Management.

Profiling Engine: has updated the user profile according to her reaction towards the red button campaign.

Campaign Management: has triggered the delivery of a second ad containing more information about the advertised product. A subsequent user request for more info has been forwarded to the respective Ad Agency/Advertiser.

Ad Server: Triggered by the user's red button activation, the Ad Server has delivered a second more detailed overlay ad offering an RFI opportunity.

Ad Agency/Advertiser: has received an RFI concerning the advertised product.

Main Flow (A Numbers)

A1 – A13. Same flow like in STB-based overlay ad use case but with red button overlay ad instead of standard advertisement.

A14. User has pressed red button on her RC. STB requests delivery of the more detailed second overlay ad belonging to red button campaign and forwards information about red button event to Profiling Engine (see parallel flow).

A15. Campaign Management requests Ad Server to deliver second overlay ad associated with red button campaign.

A16. Ad Server delivers second overlay ad to user's STB.

A17. STB displays delivered ad over the content. Ad offers option to request more info on advertised product.

A18. User chooses to receive more info. RFI is submitted to Campaign Management. Information about RFI event is forwarded to Profiling Engine (see parallel flow).

A19. Campaign Management forwards RFI to Ad Agency/Advertiser to initiate delivery of additional product info via email or regular mail.

Parallel Flow (B Numbers)

B1. STB submits user's reactions concerning red button campaign to Profiling Engine.

B2. Profiling Engine updates user profile according to her interaction behavior.

Technical Use Case Analysis

Interactive ad formats have first been invented in cable TV systems using back-channel functionality via the PSTN. Today the integrated return path of cable networks is used to send data back to the operator. Popular interactive TV providers include e.g. Sky [190] and BBC [26]. Due to the bidirectional architecture, IPTV provides an optimal environment for interactive TV applications.

Interactive TV, generally known as iTV, refers to any interactive content delivered to the TV [111]. As introduced in the ad format and use case descriptions in sections 2.5.2.3 and 3.2.1.3, examples include more simple red button campaigns with RFI capability, impulse response, DAL, mini DAL, and microsites that are simple websites featuring news and information. The more complex solutions can include interactive portals, games, or other interactive features. A subset of iTV is Enhanced TV (ETV) that is often defined as an umbrella for applications allowing consumers to interact with the video content on their TV screens [111]. It should though be noted that several definitions of ETV are circulating. Some sources speak of ETV when a particular program offers additional resources for viewers to better understand its content, most often via their computer, Web TV or mobile device [103]. CableLabs [43] defines ETV as a programming with an associated interactive software application. This application is delivered with the program, and its lifespan is tied to viewing of the program. Examples include voting contests of a game show or purchasing an item from an advertisement.

The figure depicted above describes a very simple red button scenario that enhances the STB-based overlay ad insertion scenario of the previous section. Thus, it includes the opportunity to address single households or users, if login functionality is provided, with personalized interactive ad campaigns. This means that a male and a female user could be provided with different advertisements matching the users' personal interests, but which are also related to the content and context. For example, a James Bond movie broadcasted via linear IPTV could be associated with a car ad for a man when Bond drives around, but with an interactive fashion advertisement as soon as the female co-star appears. To realize this scenario, the IPTV middleware must support active user feedback to the Campaign Management. It is assumed that the Campaign Management features enhanced ad campaigns consisting of a sequence of display ads (red button ad, advanced info ad). In addition, the Campaign Management must be enabled to forward the RFI via an interface to the Ad Agency the campaign originates from. This functionality could be included in a reporting process that already provides the Ad Agency with feedback concerning the ad campaign's success.

Critical Points for Successful Interactive Advertising

Generally, there are multiple approaches to realize interactive advertising. OpenTV [153] for example defines four "key pieces" of technology that are critical for the success of iTV advertising platforms:

1. An STB middleware that provides strong graphical capabilities being crucial to the visual impact of iTV advertising. It needs to support a store and forward capability to enable a response generation mechanism as well as measurements and profiling functionality for targeting purposes.

2. An advertising management platform that can coordinate all advertising campaigns and schedule them at the right time. Typically, this system resides in or near the headend facilities.

3. A response network that has the ability to process the transactions, collate them into reports and provide them back to the advertiser for fulfillment. After collection of all transactions, the server sends these orders, leads or RFIs to the appropriate advertiser or retailer.

4. The ability to measure the response for each advertisement and to produce helpful analytical data to be used in future campaigns. In order to enable targeting, the measurement platform tracks what consumers are doing, how they interact, how long they interact and what their preferences are for certain products and/or services. The privacy of viewers needs to be respected by enabling easy opt-out or opt-in mechanisms and by collecting only anonymous information for measurement and reporting.

General Interactive Advertising Delivery Process

iTV requires specialized client and server side software integrated with the middleware. Interactive content may be developed by the producer of a commercial or the ad agency responsible for the campaign. Then the content is inserted into the broadcast stream. According to the two display ad insertion cases described above, this can happen in the network or in the STB. The interaction is in either case enabled in conjunction with the client on the STB initiated when the right button is pressed on the RC. The red button overlay that announces the availability of an interactive service can be initiated according to a time schedule as described above in the pre-conditions, or it can be indicated by an in-stream trigger [96].

Concerning the delivery of interactive content to the STB, two levels of interactivity can be distinguished [27]. Traditionally, interactive content is carouseled continuously into the MPEG broadcast stream. A carousel provides a mechanism allowing data to be pushed from a broadcaster to multiple receivers by transmitting a data set repeatedly in a standard format. An STB receiver may tune to the data stream at any time and is able to reconstitute the data into a virtual file system [96]. Hence, the content is available when the consumer presses the button on the RC. In case of the more sophisticated interactive ad formats, the content for the DAL or microsite must be carouseled as well. The disadvantage of the carousel approach is that it provides a kind of offline interactivity, meaning that the user can only access the data that are broadcasted cyclically and only updated in defined time intervals. However, since the IPTV network is bidirectional, the content can be delivered in real-time over the network. Thus, only the trigger needs to be inserted into the broadcast stream, if it is used to indicate the availability of an interactive service. This method realizes true online interactivity, where the user is connected to the server, and additionally results in significant bandwidth savings compared to the one-way network carousel approach [111].

In order to support the deployment of iTV, several standards have been specified. Multimedia Home Platform (MHP) is the open middleware system designed by the European DVB Project. MHP defines a generic interface between interactive digital applications and the hardware on which those applications execute. Based on a Sun Java virtual machine, the MHP specification decouples the application from the specific hardware and software details of different compatible systems, enabling digital content providers to address all types of terminals ranging from low-end to high-end STBs, integrated digital television sets and multimedia personal computers [96]. OpenCable Application Platform (OCAP) was established as a standard by CableLabs in the United States as part of the OpenCable project. OCAP is based on the DVB MHP, consistent with the specification for Globally Executable MHP (GEM) [96]. According to the GEM specifications, in OCAP the various DVB technologies and specifications that are not used in the U.S. are removed and replaced by their functional equivalents. Today, the number of OCAP or MHP compatible STBs is still small. The reason is the Java architecture that requires powerful devices. Another open standard designed to offer interactive capabilities on legacy STBs with limited computing power is the Enhanced TV Binary Interchange Format (EBIF) also developed by CableLabs [111].

4.2.4 IPTV Ad Insertion

The subsequent two subsections will analyze the technology used for ad insertion in linear IPTV and in VoD. In linear TV, ad insertion is realized by inserting commercials ad some point in the network that has to be as close as possible to the user's site to achieve a finer targeting granularity. In the case of VoD ad insertion, one-to-one targeting is easy, because VoD is transmitted via unicast stream directly to the user.

4.2.4.1 Linear TV Ad Insertion

Ad insertion can be defined as the process of inserting an advertising message into a media stream such as a television program [84]. Basically, it follows the concept to replace commercials inserted by the broadcaster with more specified ad spots that are regionally or even one-to-one targeted. The following use case flow diagram describes the underlying technological process.

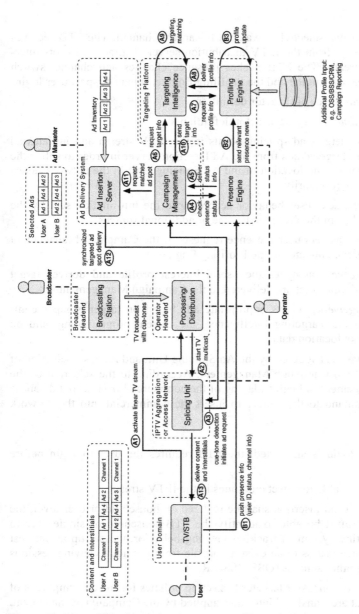

Figure 48: Linear TV ad insertion (source: own illustration)

Actors

TV/STB: The user has selected to watch a linear TV channel. The STB receives the linear TV stream from the IPTV distribution server. Targeted ad spots interrupt the IPTV stream. The STB pushes presence changes and channel switch events to the Presence Engine and the Profiling Engine. It may support user login.

Broadcasting Station: see basic actor definition

Processing/Distribution: see basic actor definition

Ad Splicing Unit: detects ad splicing points in the IPTV stream and initiates ad delivery. Receives targeted ads from the Ad Insertion Server in order to splice the spots into the stream. The location of the Ad Splicing Unit in the network determines the targeting granularity.

Profiling Engine: tracks user behavior according to the information sent by the STB and received from the Presence Engine or additional sources.

Presence Engine: answers user presence requests of the Campaign Management and forwards presence updates to the Profiling Engine.

Targeting Intelligence: analyzes the user's interest profile and derives target group recommendations that are delivered to the Campaign Management.

Campaign Management: selects appropriate ads based on target group recommendations from the Targeting Intelligence, the current programming, and on contextual info like location data.

Ad Insertion Server: is triggered by the Ad Splicing Unit and requests selection of appropriate ads from Campaign Management. According to the selection of the Campaign Management, it begins playing of the commercial from a spot database and sends a command to the splicer to insert the commercial into the network feed.

Pre-Conditions

TV/STB: if user login is supported, the STB requires the user to login before watching.

Ad Splicing Unit: is able to detect cue-tones in the IPTV stream.

Profiling Engine: if ad insertion shall be realized on household or user level, the Profiling Engine must be able to identify the STB/household or single user to enable the targeting system of tracking viewing behavior and set up an interest profile. It may have access to an existing profile from previous viewing sessions or provided from other sources (OSS/BSS/CRM).

Campaign Management: Ad Marketer has set up policies for the ad campaigns of his customers that are translated into rules applied by the Campaign Management.

The Campaign Management system must support the inclusion of target group recommendations in its ad selection process in addition to content and contextual targeting.

Ad Insertion Server: To allow targeting on user/household level, the Ad Insertion Unit must be located at the multicast endpoint in the network. A positioning deeper in the aggregation network allows regional/zone-based advertising. If the Ad Insertion Unit is located in the headend, all customers of the IPTV operator will receive the same ad spots.

Post-Conditions

TV/STB: has received a linear IPTV stream from time to time interrupted by targeted ad spots. The STB was either targeted directly or received the same IPTV stream like other STBs in a geographical zone.

Profiling Engine: If targeting is done on household or user level, the Profiling Engine has identified the user's STB or the user herself and set up or just updated her interest profile according to the TV consumption.

Targeting Intelligence: has derived target group recommendations and delivered them to the Campaign Management.

Campaign Management: has selected ads based on content targeting, contextual targeting and on target group information from Targeting Intelligence.

Ad Insertion Server: triggered by the Ad Splicing Unit, the Ad Insertion Server has delivered the ads selected by the Campaign Management.

Main Flow (A Numbers)

A1. User has activated linear IPTV stream on her STB. The STB requests delivery of chosen linear TV channel.

A2. TV broadcast ingest is continuously being processed in IPTV operator's headend. As the user's STB demands streaming of TV channel, her STB is included in IP multicast group of the respective channel to deliver the linear TV stream. Presence information is pushed to the Presence Engine (see parallel flow).

A3. Splicing Unit detects a SCTE 35 cue tone (see below) in the IPTV stream that indicates an ad insertion opportunity. The Splicing Unit requests a targeted commercial for insertion into the stream using a SCTE 30 message (see below). The request must include information about the channel the ad is destined for and the location of the Ad Insertion Unit.

A4. Campaign Management checks user presence status to find out if user is active.

A5. Presence Engine confirms to Campaign Management that the user is active.

A6. Campaign Management requests target info from Targeting Intelligence in order to include it into the ad selection process.

A7. Targeting Intelligence requests user profile from Profiling Engine.

A8. Profiling Engine delivers current user profile to Targeting Intelligence.

A9. Targeting Intelligence analyzes user profile and matches appropriate target group attributes.

A10. Targeting Intelligence sends target group recommendation to Campaign Management.

A11. Campaign Management matches content, context and target group recommendation to campaign policies and submits ad choice to Ad Insertion Server and triggers ad delivery.

A12. Ad Insertion Server begins play-out of ad spot that is being inserted into the content stream by the Ad Splicing Unit replacing another not targeted ad or filling a designated break. After having completed insertion it reports to the Campaign Management that logs information about the selected ads for campaign reporting purposes.

A13. IPTV stream containing targeted ad spots is delivered to the STB.

Parallel Flow (B Numbers)

B1. STB continuously pushes user presence updates (user ID, user status, channel info) to Presence Engine to keep it up-to-date.

B2. Presence Engine analyzes presence information from STB according to pre-defined rules. In case of relevant changes it informs the Profiling Engine about the user's status.

B3. Profiling Engine updates the user profile according to the user's viewing preferences. The Profiling Engine can derive information about the user's interests from her viewing behavior. The user profile is enriched by data from other sources like subscriber information provided by OSS/BSS/CRM systems including demographic data.

Technical Use Case Analysis

Given the fact that linear TV ad insertion has already been offered by U.S. cable operators for years, the development of ad insertion technology is driven by cable. Thus, the analysis of ad insertion systems necessarily focuses on technology originally developed for cable environments. There will be little architectural difference in contrast to IPTV networks, when it comes to concrete realization. However, most of the cable technology vendors meanwhile offer adapted solutions for IPTV [111].

The TV Ad Insertion Ecosystem

The process of splicing pieces of digital video into other pieces of digital video is called Digital Program Insertion (DPI). It is defined in the two American National Standards Institute (ANSI)/Society of Cable Telecommunications Engineers (SCTE) standards ANSI/SCTE 30 [184] and 35 [185] that have been developed by the Digital Video Subcommittee (DVS) of the SCTE in the U.S. SCTE 30 specifies the communication between an ad splicer and the ad delivery system. This includes notifying the ad delivery system to deliver the next advertisement for insertion into the specified channel. SCTE 35 standardizes the digital message embedded in a broadcast stream that notifies the splicer that an ad insertion opportunity is approaching [187]. Seamless splicing is the biggest challenge in ad insertion scenarios. In display ad insertion it may be fine if the ad appears a half second earlier or later. Hence, the insertion process can be triggered depending on a time schedule. But in the case of ad spot replacements, it is crucial to ensure seamless insertion best realized by an in-stream trigger like the SCTE 35 digital messages.

Linear ad insertion was already used in the analog world to replace the typical 30-second commercial spot. Cable systems received analog programming via satellite, and then inserted local advertising using analog switches and automated tape players that were triggered by Dual-Tone Multi Frequency (DTMF) cue tones inserted at the satellite uplink facility [111]. Now the DTMF cue tones are replaced by SCTE 35 digital messages, but the principle remains the same with completely digital equipment. According to the use case flow depicted above, the actual ad insertion process works as follows [111]:

- An ad marker inserts an SCTE 35 cue tone prior to the ad slot used for the operators avail. An avail is the advertising inventory "available" for purchase during a specific time period. Here, it refers to the breaks or default ad spots within network programming intended for insertion of local commercials [187]. The marking operation takes place at the point that the broadcast program stream is converted into an IP encapsulated MPEG-2 transport stream by a suitable encoder or transcoder. This would typically be the headend of the IPTV network [159].

- Local ads (= operator avails) are delivered physically or via data connection and uploaded to the ad insertion server that may be located at the headend or at regional offices.

- The Ad Splicing Unit detects the SCTE 35 cue tone and notifies the Campaign Management via an SCTE 30 message to manage the play-out of the appropriate ad. The splicer then matches the bit rate for the programming stream and splices the ad into the stream. Once the commercial insertion is complete, the successful play-out must be forwarded to the OSS/BBS system for verification and billing and to the Campaign Management for reporting purposes.

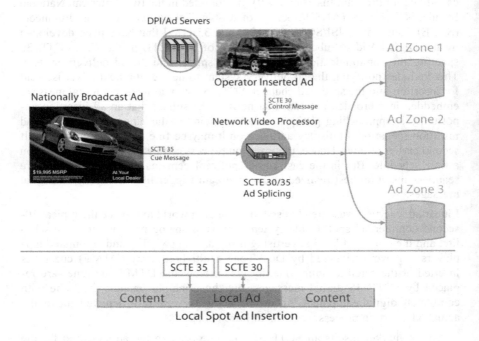

Figure 49: Zone-based linear TV ad insertion (source: RGB Networks [204])

The ad splicing operation takes place in the transport stream domain and requires intelligent video processing to support seamless frame accurate ad insertion at the splicer [52]. The MPEG-2 transport stream is a special transmission format intended for the transport of MPEG (MPEG-2 and MPEG-4 AVC/H.264) compressed TV programs in real-time over unreliable transport media like IP networks [27, 10]. Splicing in the transport stream domain enables ad insertion even when using DRM protected media as long as MPEG-2 layer headers and MPEG-4 AVC/H.264 Network Abstraction Layer (NAL) unit headers and slices are available unencrypted [159].

Zone-Based versus Addressable Advertising

Linear TV ad insertion most often appears in the form of zone-based advertising. The term is derived from the principle of targeting regional zones, e.g. neighborhoods of a city defined after the income level of typical inhabitants. Sometimes, U.S. operators offer a ZIP + 4 targeting based on the zip code of the area viewers live in. The ZIP + 4 code was invented by the U.S. Postal Service and uses the basic five-digit code plus four additional digits to identify a geographic segment within the five-digit delivery area, such as a city block. If the approach is broken down to STB level, local ad insertion is called addressable advertising. Addressable advertising would for example allow replacing all commercials for children's products with commercials for more appropriate items, in order to deliver only advertising relevant to the viewers [111]. In that case, however, another problem already described in the STB-based display ad insertion use case arises. The operator does never really know who sits in front of the TV, so that STB identification is only equivalent with user identification in single households. Hence, to achieve a really individual targeting, some kind of user login must be implemented. Concerning the possibilities of user identification and the importance of presence information in the context of targeted advertising, it can be referred to the explanation in the STB-based overlay ad insertion case in section 4.2.3.2.

Targeted Ad Insertion as a Business Optimization Problem

From the technical point of view, the realization of addressable advertising is no problem. The decision whether to realize zone-based or addressable advertising is rather a business optimization problem. For addressable advertising the Ad Splicing Unit must be located at the multicast endpoint in order to be able to deliver personalized ads in each unicast stream. The zone-based approach requires only having the equipment installed in regional offices being part of the aggregation network. Then targeting can only comprise the addressing of geographically different groups as described above. Thus, the operator must calculate if the expected revenue plus from user-specific advertising outweighs the investment and operating expenses for a local installation of the required equipment.

However, regardless of which of both approaches is followed, targeted advertising is expensive. It needs e.g. a lot of bandwidth to transfer ad spots from the Ad Insertion Server to the ad splicing point, or, if both are in one location, to keep local ad databases updated. As SeaChange says [218], it is really a question of "money per GHz", whether to implement targeted advertising or to use the network capacity to sell e.g. more broadband Internet. Sun [40] points out that it is not only the expenses of the technological realization that need to be considered when thinking of linear ad insertion. The idea of delivering maybe five different variants of an ad spot depending on the geographical location (e.g. depending on if someone lives at the sea or in the mountains) first requires that all these versions have to be produced. This makes targeted advertising campaigns more risky than traditional campaigns. A fact that, according to SeaChange [218], decelerates the acceptation of targeted advertising in linear TV in the conservative advertising business. It should be noted that these costs can be avoided by customizing the ad spots with much cheaper to produce display ad overlays inserted in the STB or in the network. An example would be to enhance the ad spot of a car manufacturer by an overlay ad containing promotion information of the local dealer. A new trend is to use both technologies, linear ad insertion and display ad insertion, in combination. RGB Networks offers a network video processing solution that is capable of inserting ad spots as well as overlay ads based on the SCTE 130 advanced advertising framework [204].

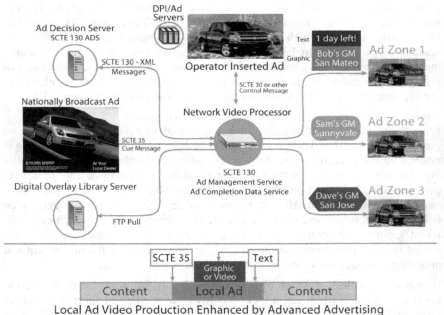

Figure 50: Linear TV ad insertion enhanced by overlay ads (source: RGB Networks [204])

Opportunities of the SCTE 130 Advertising Framework
The SCTE 130 standard (formerly DVS 629) defines a framework for advanced advertisement systems. Like SCTE 30 and 35, the SCTE 130 standard was developed for the cable industry. But considering the similarities in the video processing systems, Telco operators can leverage the work already done by the SCTE. SCTE 130 addresses content delivery platforms and covers aspects of ad management systems, ad servers, program splicing units, interactive/enhanced television (iTV/ETV), and digital video overlays. It provides a framework of messaging interfaces among a set of distributable advertising services. Some of the key messaging interfaces of the SCTE 130 framework include communication between the ad campaign management, content management, and content delivery systems [204]. Thus, the SCTE 130 framework can enable communication between various types of advertising systems and logical units in order to achieve an integrated advertising approach as in the car-advertising example described above.

Conditions for Ad Insertion in Europe
Linear TV ad insertion is an advertising model originating from the U.S. market, where the concept was already used in the analog world. In Europe, this approach is still very unusual. TV broadcasters do not offer avails for ad insertion to the TV operators, so that they cannot sell their own advertising inventory. In order to open up these advertising opportunities, IPTV operators must work with national programmers to find an effective compensation model for sharing revenues [111]. Besides the differences in the value chain, the fact that ad insertion could not prevail until now has further reasons. First, the regional differences in a country like the U.S. are much larger than for example in Germany. It is much more attractive to have different ad spots for people from Florida and from Alaska than it is for people from Hamburg compared to Munich. The ad spot of a car manufacturer intended for Florida can for example show a cabriolet in front of palm trees, while in Alaska it is maybe more appropriate to emphasize that the cars are winter proof. In Germany there would be no big difference between Hamburg and Munich in this example. Second, in the U.S. it is much easier to divide up a city in neighborhoods according to the income level or race of the inhabitants in order to specifically target them. In most European countries, these local differences inside one city are not that shaped out. Another Germany specific problem is that due to legal constraints, it is problematic to manipulate the TV stream of the public TV stations (see section 6.2.4). Albeit, the finer the granularities and the opportunities of targeting become, the more interesting is the approach of linear TV ad insertion also in Europe as long as there are no legal restrictions.

4.2.4.2   Dynamic VoD Ad Insertion

The realization of one-to-one targeting is easier in VoD scenarios than in the previous case of linear TV ad insertion, as the VoD movie reaches the viewer via unicast. From a user perspective VoD advertising looks very similar to interstitial advertising in the case of Web videos. The following illustration represents the technical realization of a VoD scenario that includes pre-/mid-/post-roll advertising. In the analysis, opportunities and challenges will be discussed and further applications of the underlying technology for ad telescoping purposes will be explained.

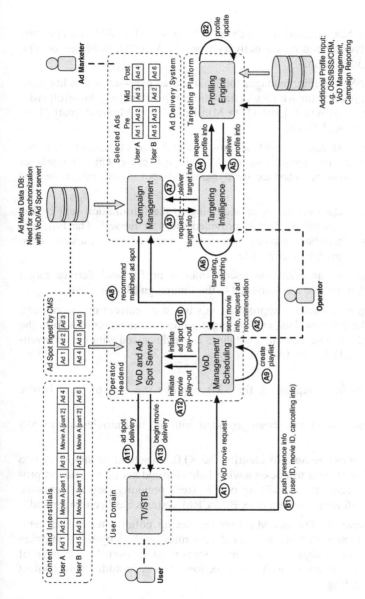

Figure 51: Dynamic VoD ad insertion (source: own illustration)

Actors

TV/STB: The user has selected to watch a VoD movie. The STB initiates the delivery and receives ad and movie delivery from the VoD/Ad Spot Server. The STB may support user login.

VoD Management/Scheduling: manages the VoD and ad play-out. The scheduling is realized using a playlist for which a systematic composition (e.g. Pre-Roll Ad 1 => Pre-Roll Ad 2 => Movie A [part 1] => Mid-Roll Ad => Movie A [part 2] => Post-Roll Ad) has to be defined.

VoD/Ad Spot Server: stores ads and VoD movies and delivers them directly to the STB. Content and ads are uploaded via the CMS ingest server. The Ad Marketer should be provided with an interface for dynamic ad spot ingest independent of movie content uploads.

Profiling Engine: tracks user behavior according to the information sent by the STB. It either identifies the STB or if provided the user herself. The Profiling Engine integrates subscriber data (e.g. previously watched VoD movies) from OSS/BSS/CRM systems into user profile.

Targeting Intelligence: analyzes the user's interest profile and derives target group recommendations that are delivered to the Campaign Management.

Campaign Management: selects appropriate ads based on current movie content, contextual info like location data, and on target group recommendations from the Targeting Intelligence. The campaign database is synchronized with the ad inventory stored on the VoD/Ad Spot Server.

Pre-Conditions

TV/STB: If user login is supported, the STB requires the user to login before watching.

VoD/Ad Spot Server: must have been provided with ads and movies from CMS ingest server.

Profiling Engine: must be able to identify the STB/household or single user to enable the targeting system to track viewing behavior and set up an interest profile. It may have access to an existing profile from previous viewing sessions. Enhanced profile information from OSS/BSS/CRM systems has been integrated.

Campaign Management: The Ad Marketer has set up policies for the ad campaigns of his customers that are translated into rules applied by the Campaign Management. The Campaign Management system must support the inclusion of target group recommendations in its ad selection process in addition to content and contextual targeting.

Post-Conditions

TV/STB: has received a VoD program framed/interrupted by targeted ads.

VoD/Ad Spot Server: has delivered ad spots and VoD program according to a playlist generated by the VoD Management.

Profiling Engine: If targeting is done on household or user level the STB has identified the user's STB or the user herself and set up or updated the interest profile according to her watching behavior. The user profile has been synchronized with subscriber data provided by OSS/BSS/CRM systems.

Targeting Intelligence: has derived target group recommendations and delivered them to the Campaign Management.

Campaign Management: has selected ads based on content targeting, contextual targeting and on targeting information from the Targeting Intelligence.

Main Flow (A Numbers)

A1. User has chosen an ad funded VoD movie from the on demand portal. The STB requests the delivery of the selected VoD movie.

A2. VoD Management/Scheduling sends movie ID to Campaign Management and requests ad selection. The number of ads that are needed is predefined in the playlist composition rules.

A3. Campaign Management requests target info from Targeting Intelligence in order to include it into the ad selection process.

A4. Targeting Intelligence requests user profile from Profiling Engine.

A5. Profiling Engine delivers current user profile to Targeting Intelligence.

A6. Targeting Intelligence analyzes user profile and matches appropriate target group attributes.

A7. Targeting Intelligence sends target group recommendation to Campaign Management.

A8. Campaign Management matches content, context and target group recommendation to campaign policies and submits ad choice to VoD Management/Scheduling.

A9. VoD Management/Scheduling creates a playlist of ads and movie content according to the predefined playlist composition rules.

A10. VoD Management/Scheduling initiates play-out of pre-roll ad by VoD/Ad Server. In case of several scheduled pre-roll ads, for mid-roll and for post-roll ad delivery the process is repeated according to the playlist.

A11. VoD Management/Scheduling initiates movie play-out by VoD/Ad Server.

A12.   VoD/Ad Server delivers pre-roll ad to the STB. In case of several scheduled pre-roll ads and for mid-roll and post-roll ad delivery the process is repeated.

A13.   VoD/Ad Server delivers movie to the STB.

Parallel Flow (B Numbers)

B1.   STB pushes information about movie choice to Profiling Engine. In case the
user aborts the VoD play-out, the Profiling Engine is informed. For reporting
purposes this information is shared with the Campaign Management.

B2.   Profiling Engine updates the user profile according to the user's movie
choice. The Profiling Engine can derive information about the user's interests
from her viewing behavior. The user profile is enriched by data from other
sources like subscriber information about the previously watched movies
provided by the OSS/BSS/CRM systems including demographic data.

Technical Use Case Analysis

VoD scenarios can be distinguished from linear TV by one essential technological characteristic that can be exploited for advertising purposes. The content
stream is delivered to the user in form of a unicast transmission meaning that each
VoD stream is received by one distinct STB. Hence, targeted advertising on user
or at least household level can be achieved easily. And since the user actively
selects to watch a certain movie he may be more receptive and perhaps more
open-minded for advertisements, especially if they are matched to her interests.
VoD advertising thus promises to be quite efficient in reaching the desired audiences.

Operators have been experimenting with VoD ads varying in length, for example
so-called long form infomercials. They found out that relevance and information-
richness seem to have more impact on viewership than duration confirming the
statement enunciated above [111]. The most interesting advertising scenarios in
VoD are interstitial advertising and ad telescoping. Interstitial advertising means
that ads are placed before (pre-roll), in the middle of (mid-roll), or after the program (post-roll). Studies reveal that interstitial advertising is already highly accepted in the Web world [114]. They are for example used on the WebTV portals
Hulu and 3min.de and most other sites that offer free Web clips and seek to create
their revenue through advertising.

The Dynamic Ad Insertion Process

As illustrated above, the basic principle of VoD ad insertion is to use actually the
same infrastructure for ad delivery that is needed for regular on demand movie
delivery. The core of the system consists of the VoD/Ad Server and the VoD
Management that has the additional task of scheduling and managing the ad insertion process. This is best realized using an ad/movie playlist generated according

to predefined composition rules in terms of how many ads shall be delivered before and after the actual content. If mid-roll ads shall be included into the content, the movie must be split up into two parts. This must already be considered and prepared when ingesting the movies into the VoD/Ad Server. Another opportunity would be to insert cue tones inside the stream as described in the previous case. Though, this requires additional ad insertion equipment that is not illustrated above.

As soon as the user has selected to watch a movie the playlist must be set up. To know which ads to insert, the VoD Management requests the Campaign Management to select appropriate ads. The Campaign Management chooses ads that are targeted according to the movie content, contextual data like time and location, and the target group recommendation from the Targeting Intelligence. The user profile based on which the recommendation is made, is enriched by BSS data about the subscriber's previously watched movies. In order for the Campaign Management to know which ads are available, it must always be synchronized with the VoD/Ad Server's ad inventory. Hence, when new ad spots are delivered to the VoD/Ad Server, at the same time, ad metadata must be provided to the Campaign Management.

When the Campaign Management has sent the ad selection back to the VoD Management, the playlist can be completed in order to initiate the delivery process. After having finished the play-out, the VoD Management reports to the Campaign Management, if all ads have been delivered. The user could e.g. have quit watching the movie or have skipped the post-roll ad. This reporting data is shared with the Profiling Engine that verifies it against respective STB controlling information to further improve the user profile.

Challenges of VoD Ad Insertion
In order to address viewers with targeted ads, it is important to realize a dynamic ad insertion process. The simplest case of VoD advertising would be to deliver pre-packaged ads and movies and keep them stored as a package on the VoD/Ad Server. In this approach ads may be targeted according to the content they are delivered with. However, it is not possible to include personal targeting recommendations. Moreover, the ads included in the program packages will expire soon so that advertising will become obsolete. VoD advertising should thus follow a live insertion approach that comprises the individual selection of ads matched to targeting recommendations. However, in this case the same problem of obsolete ads can arise due to a shortage in ad inventory on the combined VoD/Ad Server. It is therefore essential that the VoD/Ad Server does not treat the entire video asset as one, meaning not distinguishing between programming and advertising. In the latter case, it can happen that ads must be ingested weeks earlier. Therefore, the Ad Marketer respectively the one who delivers the ad spots must be

enabled to refresh the ad inventory dynamically without completely reloading the programming [111, 186].

Another challenge in VoD advertising is that viewers might want to fast-forward through the ad. In the case of post-roll ads, there is no chance to prevent the consumer from just stopping the whole play-out. As for pre-roll and mid-roll ads, the capability of fast-forwarding should be disabled in order to improve the advertising impact [111, 186].

Ad Telescoping
A completely different approach to VoD advertising is ad telescoping that links the concept of iTV/ETV with VoD. Here, a consumer initially watches linear TV and views a short commercial that includes an iTV/ETV trigger. She is prompted by an overlay message to press a button on the RC to receive more information on the advertised product. Initiated by the pressed button the program being viewed is stopped. Simultaneously, a VoD session is initiated and the long format video stored on the VoD Server in the network is played out. Alternatively, the telescoped ad could be stored on a local DVR and be played out from there. At the end of the ad, the viewer is redirected to the original programming.

The ad telescoping approach can be improved by applying time-shift functionality. In this case, the linear TV stream is automatically recorded on the DVR, when the user switches to the long form VoD ad. Thus, she can continue viewing the original programming after having consumed the ad. As Sun [40] remarks, this helps to avoid the problem that the user is towed away from the program content, which might be criticized by the broadcaster whose content would be interrupted. Another option is to use a picture-in-picture feature to follow the running show while watching the longer commercial. Yet another possibility is the so-called "green button" advertising that initially works similar like the red button initiated ad telescoping. But instead of interrupting the broadcast pressing the green button records the long form ad on the local DVR. Later, the customer is reminded of the ad that she might want to see now [190].

4.2.5 EPG Advertising

Advertising in the context of an EPG offers good targeting possibilities, as the scenario is very similar to the Web advertising case described in section 4.1. However, the EPG environment causes additional challenges in terms of user identification that have to be considered. More advanced implementations can also include enhanced portal scenarios with further improved personalization options.

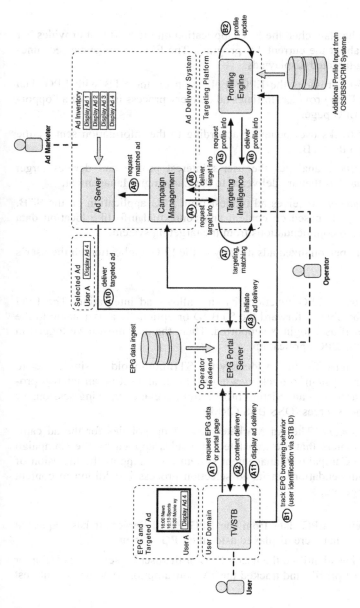

Figure 52: Targeted advertising in a Web-based EPG (source: own illustration)

Actors

TV/STB: The user has launched the EPG application on the STB that provides her with information about the current TV program. The EPG offers enhanced functionality including targeted display ads.

EPG Portal Server: provides the EPG application on the STB with EPG data delivered from an EPG provider. Initiates ad delivery process in case of ad opportunities within an EPG page.

Profiling Engine: tracks user behavior according to the information sent by the EPG application on the STB.

Targeting Intelligence: analyzes the user's interest profile and derives target group recommendations that are delivered to the Campaign Management.

Campaign Management: receives ad request from EPG application on the STB. Selects appropriate ads based on content and contextual info like location data and on target group recommendations from the targeting system.

Ad Server: delivers personalized ads directly to the EPG application on the user's STB.

Pre-Conditions

TV/STB: must provide EPG functionality that allows ad integration. The EPG application must be able to forward the STB ID or optionally a user name to the EPG Portal Server if user login is supported. Then, the user must have logged in before launching the EPG application.

Profiling Engine: must be able to identify the STB/household or single user to enable the targeting system to track viewing behavior and set up an interest profile. It may have access to an existing profile from previous viewing sessions or provided from other sources (OSS/BSS/CRM).

Campaign Management: The Ad Marketer has set up policies for the ad campaigns of his customers that are translated into rules applied by the Campaign Management. The Campaign Management system must support the inclusion of target group recommendations in its ad selection process in addition to content and contextual targeting.

Post-Conditions

TV/STB: has received EPG data from the EPG Portal Server. It has requested targeted display ads that were displayed aside the EPG content.

Profiling Engine: has identified the user's STB or the user herself. It has set up or modified an interest profile and tracked the TV consumption to adjust the interest profile.

Targeting Intelligence: has derived target group recommendations and delivered them to the Campaign Management.

Campaign Management: has selected ads based on content targeting, contextual targeting and on target group information from the Targeting Intelligence.

Ad Server: has delivered targeted ads upon requests from the Campaign Management.

Main Flow (A Numbers)

A1. STB requests EPG data for page the user has selected.

A2. Web/Portal Server delivers content data to the STB. Depending on the EPG implementation this may be complete pages or just the pure programming data.

A3. Web/Portal Server detects ad opportunity in current EPG page and initiates ad delivery process through a request directed to the Campaign Management.

A4. Campaign Management requests target info from Targeting Intelligence in order to include it into the ad selection process.

A5. Targeting Intelligence requests user profile from Profiling Engine.

A6. Profiling Engine delivers current user profile to Targeting Intelligence.

A7. Targeting Intelligence analyzes user profile and matches appropriate target group attributes.

A8. Targeting Intelligence sends target group recommendation to Campaign Management.

A9. Campaign Management matches content, context and target group recommendation to campaign policies and triggers ad delivery through the Ad Server.

A10.   Ad Server delivers targeted display ad to the Web/Portal Server.

A11.   Web/Portal Server delivers targeted ad to the STB. The ad is then displayed in the designated ad space on the recently requested EPG page.

Parallel Flow (B Numbers)

B1. EPG pages i.e. program information the user is browsing are tracked by the Profiling Engine. Depending on the EPG implementation the tracking request is initiated by a tracking pixel integrated in EPG pages or alternatively by the EPG Portal Server. User identification is realized using a cookie emulation based on the STB ID, if cookie storage is not possible.

B2. Profiling Engine generates or updates user profile if already existing. The profile contains information about the user's interests and her past browsing behavior. Additional profiling information from OSS/BSS/CRM systems is integrated if available.

Technical Use Case Analysis

The middleware defines the look and feel of the user interface and the different applications, which are offered to the user including aspects and possibilities of the EPG. The diversity of services potentially provided by an STB (e.g. linear TV, VoD, EPG, Web browsing, gaming) make it a hybrid device. This means that advertising in these different services necessarily differs in terms of the underlying technology. All approaches of targeted advertising discussed until now have in common that they focus on the IPTV core service, that is to show ads in the context of a streamed video. The EPG provides on screen access to program information in a portal like presentation [96], meaning that ads do not need to be inserted into the stream. They are rather displayed on portal pages like banner ads on a Web page. As will be shown, the EPG scenario analyzed here has indeed a lot of similarities with targeted Web advertising.

The Different Implementation Approaches of EPGs

Generally, the realization of an EPG requires a specific client and server side software integrated with the middleware. The STB provides a portal framework that needs to be filled with programming information. As the EPG is an interactive service, there are basically two realization methods that have already been mentioned in the interactive advertising case (see 4.2.3.3). One option is to follow the carousel approach implying that the program data is continuously pushed to the STB and reconstituted in a virtual file system. This has the advantage that once the data has been pushed to the STB, it is available for immediate access. Thus, there is almost no delay until EPG pages can be displayed, when the user has started the guide. An important drawback of carouseling is that there is often not an opportunity to react to recent program changes; another is that the concept does not include a back channel for client requests. Since targeted advertising requires a feedback channel to track behavior and update user profiles, and includes the delivery of single and specific ads, it is difficult to realize based on the carousel approach.

The second realization option for EPGs on an STB is to capitalize on the bidirectional architecture of IPTV networks. Here, the EPG server delivers data upon a request from the STB that is initiated as soon as the user activates the EPG. This allows providing most recent data and enables targeted advertising. Within this option it can be further differentiated between browser-based and data-driven solutions. The browser-based solution uses an embedded browser within the STB, hence applying standard HTML and/or JavaScript to control the EPG. Data-driven systems use lower layers of the EPG software to more directly transfer commands and data to the EPG [24].

Data centric EPGs can communicate with the STB using its fundamental language. On the one hand, this results in a reduction in the amount of processing steps that the STB must perform, as it does not need to receive and decode the HTML or JavaScript commands into native EPG commands. On the other hand, such systems mostly rely on proprietary implementations that complicate the integration of existing Web technology. Browser-based EPGs use high-level commands (HTML/JavaScript) that must be received, parsed, decoded, and processed. The entire process lasts longer than in data centric approaches, however it is possible to integrate prevalent Web technology without needing to adapt it. The performance in Web-based EPGs can be improved by using more sophisticated techniques that reduce the amount of transferred and processed data like e.g. Asynchronous JavaScript and XML (AJAX) [24]. AJAX allows updating Web pages without needing to reload the complete document. Hence, it is possible to keep the page structure and only refresh the programming data if a user browses through different TV channels. This can for example be realized using XMLTV[28], a popular XML-based file format for describing TV listings.

Advanced browser-based EPGs allow the integration of existing Web technologies. Using up-to-date Web standards, they can be designed to be sufficiently fast for satisfying customers' needs. Concluding, it can be stated that it is a promising approach to realize targeted advertising in a browser EPG, based on targeted advertising technologies from the Web.

Integrating Targeted Web Adv. Technologies with Browser-Based EPG Scenarios
The typical process of browsing through an EPG begins with the user initiating a page request by activating the EPG button on her RC. The STB browser is launched and the request for the EPG start page is forwarded to the EPG Portal Server that is a modified Web server. The server delivers the requested page containing channel listings to the STB EPG browser. The whole communication is based on HTML and possibly AJAX and XMLTV files. As illustrated in the use case description in section 3.2.3, EPG pages can include display ads. Concerning the fundamental elements, this use case is basically similar to targeted advertising in the Web. However, the user identification possibilities differ in the EPG scenario, which causes some changes in the use case flow.

The general problem about EPG advertising scenarios even if they are browser-based is the mostly insufficient cookie support. In the targeted Web advertising scenario user identification is based on two cookies that are stored on the user's computer. One cookie allots an ID to the user and is needed to identify her whenever she comes back to the website. Hence, this cookie needs to be stored perma-

---

[28] http://xmltv.org/

nently on the local device. Otherwise, it will not be possible to assign an existing profile. A second cookie is used to store the target group recommendations on the local computer. The Campaign Management reads out this cookie when a targeted ad is requested.

If the STB browser environment does not support cookies at all, a workaround must be found that realizes the functionality of these cookies otherwise. A possible solution is illustrated in the above use case model. The user ID cookie is emulated based on the unique STB ID that was already used for identification purposes in the other IPTV advertising scenarios. A necessary condition for this approach is that the STB ID can be read out in the EPG browser. Apart from that, tracking requests can be processed like in the Web scenario or alternatively also via the EPG Portal Server.

A recommendation cookie is not necessary as the EPG Portal Server triggers the ad delivery process. This means that the EPG pages do not include direct links referring to the Campaign Management. When the STB browser requests the delivery of an EPG page containing potential ad space, the Web Portal Server detects this advertising opportunity. It initiates the recommendation and ad selection process through a request directed to the Campaign Management. The Campaign Management requests a target group recommendation from the Targeting Intelligence and selects appropriate ads. Finally, the Ad Server delivers the targeted ads to the Web Portal Server that forwards the data to the STB.

Nevertheless, some STB browser environments allow at least the storage of cookies that are deleted when the session is over. In this case, the use case can be implemented almost entirely like in the Web scenario. Again the user ID cookie must be emulated using the STB ID as it has to be permanent. However, the recommendation cookie does not cause a problem because it can be newly generated in each session and will still fulfill its function. It can thus be referred to the description of the Web scenario in section 4.1 and the detailed analysis that follows in section 5.1.

Advanced Portal Solutions

EPGs provide a good opportunity for providers to differentiate their IPTV offering from others. Operators can for example implement more complex browser environments into the STB and replace the standard EPG by a compelling personalized multimedia portal with jumping points into linear TV. This can include email, TV over Web (TVoW), User Generated Content (UGC), sports fan pages, and other features to make the usage of the portal attractive. The setup process must be defined in a way that the end user can customize the interface. By offering such an advanced portal the operator can solve two problems at once. First, due to legal constraints the standard EPG of an IPTV service allows only very limited advertising (see section 6.2). With an enhanced service that the customer chooses to use voluntarily, this issue can be avoided. Second, to use the additional services like email or chatting, the user must necessarily login. Thus, the operator can identify and also target the single user and not only the STB/household.

Another interesting approach to advanced TV portal services are widget solutions that can bring Web services including targeted advertising directly to the TV. One example is the Yahoo! TV Widgets[29] service that offers overlays and banners delivering customer specified, interactive Web features directly to the TV screen. The service is based on Yahoo!'s Widget Engine that has been adapted for TV. It is a runtime environment, which can be used by developers to produce applets. Current widgets provide access to personalized content like weather forecasts, email, stock prices or Flickr[30] pictures and can in future also be used to deliver targeted advertising.

4.2.6 Personal TV Channel Advertising

As described in section 3.2.4 personal TV channel advertising can be realized using individually created channels based on special content characteristics a user likes or adapting the "barker channel" approach normally used for promotion purposes. In the following two subsections, the underlying technology and corresponding issues of both implementation scenarios will be discussed.

4.2.6.1   Personal TV Channels

Personal TV channels provide the customer with immediate access to relevant content with the same look-and-feel like live TV watching but without needing to browse different channels or sources. Introduced by APRICO Solutions[31], the personal TV channel concept tackles the problem of user identification through the creation of channel profiles instead of user profiles. As the virtual channels are created around a special user chosen topic, the recommendation system can incorporate the context of the personal channel into its decisions leading to accurate recommendation results right from the start. As will be shown the same technology can be used to realize very promising targeted advertising scenarios.

---

[29] http://connectedtv.yahoo.com/
[30] http://www.flickr.com/
[31] http://www.aprico.tv/. See http://www.watchmi.tv/ for an implementation example.

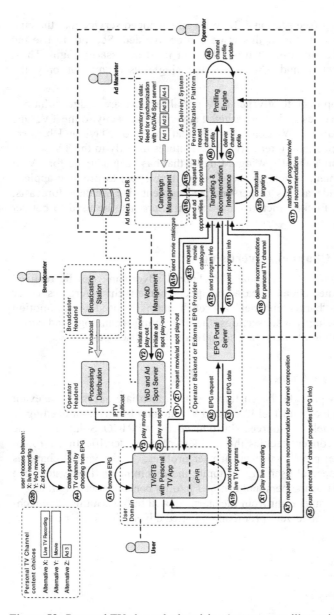

Figure 53: Personal TV channel advertising (source: own illustration)

Actors

TV/STB: incorporates personal TV application and associated EPG that are integrated with IPTV middleware. The personal TV application provides personalized TV channels including recorded live broadcasts, VoD programs, and advertising spots that are selected according to the channel profile. The STB provides client PVR capabilities for live TV recordings.

Broadcasting Station: see basic actor definition

Processing/Distribution: see basic actor definition

VoD Management: manages the VoD and ad delivery according to STB requests generated by the personal TV application.

VoD/Ad Spot Server: see description in dynamic VoD ad insertion use case.

EPG Portal Server: see description in EPG advertising use case. The EPG Portal Server provides an interface to the Targeting/Recommendation Intelligence.

Profiling Engine: tracks updates of personal TV channel properties.

Targeting/Recommendation Intelligence: builds network counterpart of personal TV application on STB. Analyzes the channel profile and derives contextual targeting information. Aggregates information about possible matches (live TV recording/VoD movie/ad spot) and recommends selected content to personal TV application on STB.

Campaign Management: manages ad campaigns provided by ad agencies/advertisers. Compares ad campaigns to content and contextual information delivered by Targeting/Recommendation Intelligence in order to select matching ad spots.

Pre-Conditions

TV/STB: is compatible with IPTV middleware. The personal TV application and EPG must be integrated within the client software.

VoD/Ad Spot Server: must have been provided with movies from CMS ingest server and ad spots from Ad Marketer.

Profiling Engine: must be able to create and manage personal TV channel profiles in place of user profiles.

Campaign Management: Ad Marketer has set up policies for the ad campaigns of his customers that are translated into rules applied by the Campaign Management. The campaign database is synchronized with the ads stored on the VoD/Ad Spot Server.

Post-Conditions

TV/STB: Personal TV channel has been created according to user's choice from EPG. Client PVR has recorded recommended live TV broadcasts. Content was played out according to the user's selection.

VoD/Ad Spot Server: has delivered ad spots and VoD program as selected from channel list by the user.

Profiling Engine: Channel profile has been generated corresponding to user's choice from EPG and updated according to her viewing behavior.

Targeting/Recommendation Intelligence: has requested information about content matching the channel profile and derived recommendations to build up a personal TV channel list.

Campaign Management: has selected potential ad spots matching the personal TV channel properties and has delivered these opportunities to the Targeting/Recommendation Intelligence.

Main Flow (A Numbers)

A1. User has launched EPG on the STB that is integrated with the personal TV channel application.

A2. EPG data is requested from EPG portal server.

A3. EPG data is delivered to STB.

A4. User initiates creation of a personal TV channel based on program information of the selected TV show.

A5. Personal TV app on STB pushes EPG metadata about selected "seed program" to the Profiling Engine.

A6. Based on the seed program's metadata the Profiling Engine creates a channel profile that is later used by the Targeting/Recommendation Intelligence to filter matching content including advertisements.

A7. Personal TV app on STB requests program recommendation for channel creation from Targeting/Recommendation Intelligence.

A8. Targeting/Recommendation Intelligence requests channel profile from Profiling Engine.

A9. Profiling Engine delivers channel profile information to Targeting/Recommendation Intelligence.

A10. Targeting/Recommendation Intelligence creates a targeting/personalization filter from the channel profile that is used to find similar programs.

A11. Targeting/Recommendation Intelligence requests information about available live TV programs that match profile filtering criteria from the EPG Portal Server.

A12. EPG Portal Server delivers program information according to filtering criteria.

A13. Targeting/Recommendation Intelligence requests catalogue of available VoD movies that match profile filtering criteria from VoD Management.

A14. VoD Management delivers filtered VoD catalogue.

A15. Targeting/Recommendation Intelligence requests ad opportunities in the context of the profile filter from the Campaign Management.

A16. Campaign Management delivers ad opportunities according to filtering criteria.

A17. Based on the channel filter and user ratings of previously consumed items the Targeting/Recommendation Intelligence computes potential ratings of the available program/movie/ad content and creates a channel list of best matching items.

A18. Targeting/Recommendation Intelligence delivers channel list including recommended programs/movies/ad spots to the personal TV app on the STB.

A19. Personal TV app triggers recording of recommended live TV programs by the PVR integrated in the STB.

A20. User is presented with personal TV channel list and chooses from the recommended items (live TV recording/VoD movie/ad spot, see play-out alternatives X, Y, Z).

Play-Out Flow (Alternatives X, Y, Z)

X1. STB initiates play-out of live TV recording selected by the user.

Y1/Z1. STB requests play-out of selected VoD movie/ad spot.

Y2/Z2. VoD Management initiates movie/ad spot play-out.

Y3/Z3. VoD/Ad Spot Server delivers requested movie/ad spot to the STB.

Technical Use Case Analysis
The personal TV channel concept is a content management, control, and usage concept for video recorder (PVR) technology that provides a user interface (UI) allowing to watch pre-recorded content with the same look-and-feel like live TV watching and that inherently supports multiple users [163].

The Personal TV Channel Concept

The personal TV channel concept is based on the idea of virtual channels combined with recommender technology. Each virtual channel represents a distinct topic the user is interested in, e.g. the news channel, the soccer channel, or the romantic movie channel. A user can define one or more channels. Multiple users can each define their own channels and also share them to other users. The concept tackles the shortcomings that come along with recent developments in the broadcast and PVR environment. The number of broadcast channels per region or country has strongly grown over the last years. PVRs become increasingly common and allow storage of live content for later viewing. In addition, video content from VoD services and more recently from the Internet can be accessed from the user's terminal. These new technical possibilities lead to a higher complexity concerning the content access by the TV user. The goal of personal TV channels is to enable the user to immediately access relevant content from all these sources without the need to browse through the massive amount of shows and movies that are available [163].

Creating Personal TV Channels

A personal TV channel is characterized by a filter that is a set of criteria indicating which programs fit the channel and which do not. The filter operates on the metadata associated with each program provided by the EPG. Programs that pass the filter are considered for recording and made available in the corresponding virtual channel [163].

Typically, a "seed program" chosen from the EPG or selected while watching is used to create a channel. The metadata associated with this program is then used to create a channel profile. This means that an appropriate filter is defined which allows to automatically find similar programs. The filter can be expanded by selecting additional seed programs that are suggested for inclusion into the channel. A personal channel can also be created by entering specific characteristics like genre or actors that are analyzed in order to suggest programs. In addition, users can choose existing channels from a gallery or such that are shared by other users and further adjust them according to their taste by accepting or dismissing suggestions from the system [163].

Once a personal channel is created, the selected programs must be recorded. This task is realized by a recording scheduler that manages the recordings of the different programs being part of the multiple virtual channels on the STB. This functionality includes a priority management and auto-deletion functions that are necessary to free up sufficient space for the recordings.

Recommender Technology for Channel Personalization

Filters of recently created channels may be too broad to provide accurate person-alization. In order to improve the results, a content-based recommender technol-ogy (see section 5.3.3.1) is applied that relies on user-weighed EPG metadata of programs. The user can rate ("like"/"dislike") items individually. These ratings are translated to ratings on individual features in the metadata and can be used to predict the rating of a new item based on the rating information available on the individual features of this new item. This kind of like/dislike rating helps to re-duce the cold-start problem that is common for most recommendation algorithms [163]. A cold-start problem appears if the system does not have enough informa-tion about the user's taste (see section 5.3.3.2).

As the recommender system operates in the context of a virtual channel, the sys-tem can learn faster than traditional recommender systems without context infor-mation (compare section 5.3.5 on context-aware recommender systems). A chan-nel profile is already implicitly defined in terms of the virtual channel. Another advantage of the content-based approach applied here is that the recommender only has to learn the taste of the single user who created the channel [163]. In collaborative filtering approaches that are based on the similarity between users, the quality of the recommendation depends on the number and quality of other user profiles (see section 5.3.3.2).

In addition to the user ratings, the channel profile is further improved by analyz-ing the way the user interacts with the content and by associating these interac-tions with appropriate ratings. Typical types of interaction are the watching be-havior, skipping, etc. The user's interaction is translated in terms of likes and dislikes and thus enhances the channel profile implicitly [163].

Implications for Targeted Advertising

The particular relevancy of the personal TV channel approach for targeted adver-tising lies in the inherent multi-user support and context awareness of the virtual channels. As already mentioned, some kind of user identification is required to target the possibly changing TV watching audience of one STB on a user level. One opportunity is to require users to login before watching TV, in order to target them based on a personal profile. The personal TV channel concept though does not need to identify individual users. It rather distinguishes single channels build-ing the basis for personalization and recommendation services. Instead of user profiles, personalization is realized based on channel profiles that automatically deliver context information since they are closely related to special topics. This accelerates the learning process and leads to a good recommendation quality i.e. targeting quality from the start. Advertising in personal TV channels thus enables to better address single users without the need for login.

Provided that metadata are available for commercials, the personalization concept described above is directly applicable for targeting in virtual channels [163]. Targeted commercial spots can easily be integrated into the sequence of programs. As each individually created personal TV channel represents part of the taste of single viewers, they will be more likely to watch ad spots that are integrated as part of the channel programming. The behavior of the user while watching the channel, e.g. if she skips a spot, is used to profile her likes and dislikes of certain commercials. This information can be used by the Campaign Management to create reports that are provided to ad agencies/advertisers. In addition, the business model includes the concept that an advertiser has only to pay for the time that a consumer has effectively watched the ad.

Besides the integration of ad spots into existing personal channels, the personal TV channel approach offers advanced advertising options. The technology can for example be used to create a branded channel of an advertiser that combines relevant information about a product with explicit advertising. An example would be a branded channel of a car manufacturer that includes long form ad spots about recent models in a sequence with recordings of car savvy programs from broadcast channels. In addition, it is possible to create specific promotion channels that feature special offers of new movies in the VoD portfolio or of titles that are about to be taken out. Finally, the personal TV channel concept can be used for cross-selling of the IPTV operator's products and services via an info channel.

4.2.6.2   Personalized Barker Channel

Barker channels are traditionally used for promotion and advertising purposes. The concept is to broadcast a channel containing a sequence of short preview clips of movies whose full version can be viewed on a separate pay TV channel.

In IPTV the service can be realized based on the VoD infrastructure described above. The VoD Management sets up a personal barker channel playlist based on target group information from the Targeting Intelligence. The VoD Management must have its own interface to the Targeting Intelligence in order to be able to directly request movie clip recommendations. Alternatively, the Campaign Management must be provided not only with metadata about ads, but also with information about the clips that are available. Then, it can select movie clips and ad spots based on the target group information from the Targeting Intelligence.

As soon as the user switches to her personalized barker channel, the VoD Management initiates the play-out of the movie previews and ad spots of the playlist. The user is then presented with the personalized sequence of new interesting shows that are available. She will follow the spot sequence with a higher attention than in traditional barker channels because it is targeted on her personal viewing behavior. This is also valid for ad spots included in the channel loop. Using her RC, the user can interact with the system to select an advertised movie and watch the full-length version on demand or request more information about a product that is advertised.

Another approach to the barker channel concept would be a kind of preview extension of the personal TV channel use case described in the previous section. In this scenario, a barker channel could be used to provide the user with a sequence of previews or trailers of movies that are available in her personal TV channel including targeted ad spots. This could be a lean back alternative to reading the EPG descriptions of the programs.

4.3   Targeted Advertising in the Mobile Environment

The technological analysis of targeted advertising in the mobile channel is another main focus of this book. Especially the characteristic of being a very personal device promises excellent targeting opportunities on mobile phones. As described in section 3.3 the most interesting use cases include on- and off-portal mobile Web targeting, in-message advertising and direct message marketing, on-device advertising, and advertising in mobile TV and video scenarios. Like in the Web and in IPTV the use case analysis will start with the definition of important players in the mobile advertising environment.

4.3.1 Players in the Mobile Advertising Environment

Like in the case of IPTV the stakeholders involved in the value chain of mobile advertising have been described in section 2.1.3.3. Based on this overview it is possible to determine the players that are relevant for the below discussed use cases. These include the User, the Mobile Network Operator, the Content Provider or Publisher, and again the Ad Marketer. The roles of these stakeholders are described below.

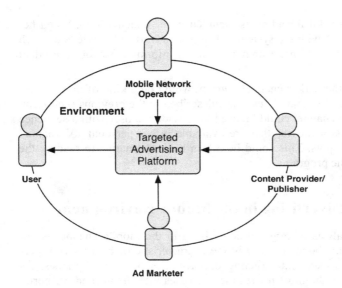

Figure 54: Players in the environment of a targeted advertising platform in mobile networks (source: own illustration)

User
A subscriber of mobile services offered by the mobile network operator. She owns a mobile phone that besides voice is capable of messaging and GPRS or 3G data services enabling mobile Web usage, and mobile TV and video.

Content Provider/Publisher
A provider of media content related services. This can include publishing of mobile websites, offering of messaging services, distribution of mobile applications running on the mobile phone, or providing TV and video related services.

Mobile Network Operator
The Mobile Network Operator maintains the network infrastructure and provides GSM voice, messaging and data services. He also hosts the different components building up the targeting platform. This includes similar functional units and concepts as introduced in the Web and IPTV cases that are adapted to the requirements of the mobile environment but also mobile specific components. Depending on the scenarios ad insertion may be realized in the network or on the mobile device.

Ad Marketer
Like in the Web and IPTV scenarios the Ad Marketer sells ad opportunities to advertisers or ad agencies. Due to the variety of mobile services this includes multiple different ad formats. He operates the ad delivery system comprising campaign management and ad serving capabilities. Campaign management includes organizing the ad delivery according to campaign rules and scheduling information, and based on target group recommendations delivered by the targeting platform.

4.3.2 Use Case Actors in the Targeted Mobile Advertising Process

Following the proceeding in the IPTV section, the functional components in the responsibility of the above-described players are now introduced generally in order to avoid redundancies. More detailed and use case specific descriptions of the actors' roles will be given at the beginning of each use case analysis.

User Domain
Mobile Device: provides the environment for multiple different applications that can potentially be exploited for targeted advertising. The phone supports messaging services (SMS, MMS) and data connections via GPRS or UMTS, which are the basis for all targeting scenarios.

Content Provider/Publisher
CMS: facilitates the publication of content and may occur in different scenarios in each case performing different tasks. In the mobile Web use case it is used for creating and managing HTML content that is optimized for the mobile environment. In video scenarios the CMS manages the delivery of content to the video servers.

Targeting Platform Operator
Profiling Engine: tracks the user's behavior and aggregates this information to user-specific interest profiles. The identification of individual users depends on the use cases scenario. As in the mobile Web cookie storage on the device cannot be guaranteed, the identification must be performed using mobile specific IDs like the Mobile Subscriber Integrated Services Digital Network Number (MSISDN, see section 4.3.3). The MSISDN is also used in other scenarios e.g. messaging. Like in the Web and in IPTV user profiles may be enriched by information from other profile databases like OSS/CRM systems and especially location provisioning systems that determine the location the user currently resides in. Moreover, the diversity of mobile phones requires sophisticated device targeting.

Targeting Intelligence: analyzes user profile data that it receives from the Profiling Engine. It then sends matched target group recommendations to the Campaign

Management (definition below). Due to the lacking cookie support of most mobile devices, the target group recommendation often cannot be stored in a recommendation cookie on the phone and must thus be directly transmitted to the Campaign Management.

Ad Marketer
Campaign Management: manages ad campaigns of Ad Marketer's customers who are offered to book different advertising opportunities, especially including the delivery of device-targeted ad formats. Information about delivered ads is stored in a campaign report.

Ad Server: delivers different ad types (banner ads, in-message text ads, complete ad messages, interstitial ads) to the Web/portal server, an ad insertion unit in the network, or directly to the mobile device.

4.3.3 Mobile Web Advertising

Like EPG advertising in IPTV mobile Web advertising is another use case basically extending the targeted Web advertising scenario. Hence, the advertising opportunities in terms of ad formats and the underlying technology design are quite similar. Due to the specific properties of the mobile environment, some crucial points have to be considered that require adaptations in the implementation. The below depicted use case model describes an on-portal mobile advertising scenario. Architectural differences in off-portal scenarios will be examined in the technical analysis following below.

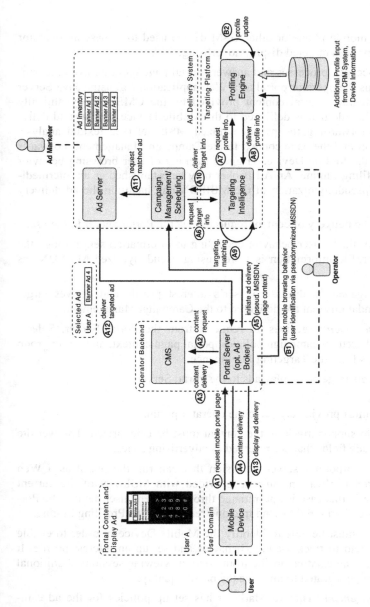

Figure 55: On-portal mobile Web advertising (source: own illustration)

Actors

Mobile Device: mobile phone or other GSM device used to browse an operator portal that incorporates targeted display advertising.

Portal Server: accepts, processes and answers portal page requests from the Mobile Device. Runs the operator portal as a Web application e.g. using Java Server Pages (JSP). Integrates portal content provided by the CMS into dynamically generated HTML code that is delivered to the Mobile Device. Initiates ad delivery process by forwarding the pseudonymized MSISDN (see textual analysis below) of the user and the page context to the Campaign Management. Forwards received ads to the Mobile Device. Triggers tracking of user browsing behavior through the Profiling Engine. An Ad Broker may be established as an intermediary performing pseudonymization of the MSISDN and handling the ad delivery process.

CMS: manages the delivery of content requested via the Portal Server to the user.

Profiling Engine: tracks user behavior according to information sent through the Portal Server. Profile information is stored using pseudonymized MSISDNs as identifiers.

Targeting Intelligence: analyzes the user's interest profile and derives target group recommendations that are delivered to the Campaign Management.

Campaign Management: receives ad requests from the Portal Server. Selects appropriate ads based on campaign policies, portal page context, and target group recommendations from the Targeting Intelligence.

Ad Server: delivers targeted display ads to the Portal Server.

Pre-Conditions

Mobile Device: must provide access to the operator portal.

CMS: In order to support tracking the content must be categorized. The website layout must include fields that are reserved as advertising space.

Portal Server: incorporates server extension that can run the portal as a Web application. Portal application must be provided with MSISDN of the current user. As tracking in this case is not initiated through the end user device, the Portal Server must be configured to send tracking requests to the Profiling Engine.

Profiling Engine: must be able to identify the Mobile Device in order to enable the targeting system to track viewing behavior and set up an interest profile. It may have access to an existing profile from previous viewing sessions. Additional CRM data may be integrated to improve the profile quality.

Campaign Management: The Ad Marketer has set up policies for the ad campaigns of his customers that are translated into rules applied by the Campaign

Management. The Campaign Management system must support the inclusion of target group recommendations in its ad selection process in addition to content targeting.

Post-Conditions

Mobile Device: has received portal pages including targeted display ads.

Portal Server: has delivered portal content and targeted ads to the Mobile Device.

Profiling Engine: has identified the Mobile Device, set up or modified an interest profile, and tracked the user's online behavior to adjust the interest profile.

Targeting Intelligence: has derived target group recommendations and delivered them to the Campaign Management.

Campaign Management: has selected ads based on page context information and on target group recommendations from the Targeting Intelligence.

Ad Server: has delivered targeted ads to the Portal Server.

Main Flow (A Numbers)

A1. Mobile Device requests mobile portal page from Portal Server.

A2. Portal Server requests content data from CMS.

A3. CMS delivers portal content to the Portal Server.

A4. Portal Server generates HTML page and delivers it to the Mobile Device.

A5. Portal Server detects ad opportunity in current portal page and initiates the ad delivery process through a request directed to the Campaign Management. The ad handling can be managed by an intermediary Ad Broker that transmits the pseudonymized MSISDN and the page context (e.g. sports) to the Campaign Management.

A6. Campaign Management requests target info from Targeting Intelligence in order to include it into the ad selection process.

A7. Targeting Intelligence requests user profile from Profiling Engine.

A8. Profiling Engine delivers current user profile to Targeting Intelligence.

A9. Targeting Intelligence analyzes user profile and matches appropriate target group attributes.

A10. Targeting Intelligence sends target group recommendation to Campaign Management.

A11. Campaign Management matches page context, further contextual data like time or user's location, and target group recommendation to campaign policies and triggers ad delivery through the Ad Server.

A12.   Ad Server delivers targeted display ad to the Portal Server.

A13.   Portal Server delivers targeted ad to the Mobile Device. The ad is then displayed in the designated ad space within the previously delivered portal page.

Parallel Flow (B Numbers)

B1.   Profiling Engine tracks portal pages the user is browsing. The Portal Server initiates the tracking request. User identification is realized using the pseudonymized MSISDN of the user.

B2.   Profiling Engine generates or updates user profile if already existing. The profile contains information about the user's interests and her past browsing behavior. Additional CRM data from the subscriber database is integrated.

Technical Use Case Analysis
At first sight, the mobile Web advertising scenario might be considered to be a copy of the Web advertising scenario incorporating only slight changes. This impression is not completely wrong as the whole purpose is to browse ad financed or supported websites like in the regular Web. However, the special characteristics of the mobile environment cause some fundamental differences that have to be considered in the use case analysis.

Opportunities and Challenges of Mobile Web Advertising
Compared to the customer premises in the regular Web and in IPTV, mobile devices have the unique feature of being very individual devices. As such, they allow advertisers to target users on a really personal level. Mobile phones are owned and used by one single person allowing to create detailed customer profiles and targeting users with very customized ads according to their interests and behavior resulting in increased campaign effectiveness [112].

An important characteristic of mobile advertising is that mobile phones provide a completely different browsing experience compared to PCs. Mobile phones have a broad range of different form factors, screen sizes and resolutions representing a challenge for the display and optimal viewing of content and advertising. In addition, mobile phone displays are much smaller than PC screens and the bandwidth of data connections is still restricted. This may have implications on the applicability of targeted advertising solutions from the Web in the mobile environment.

HTML vs. WAP

Recently released mobile phones offer a good Web experience due to their large and high resolution displays. Many of these devices provide browsers for the regular Web like e.g. the iPhone that uses an adapted version of the Safari browser. In these cases, one must be aware that users in fact browse regular Web pages based on HTML meaning that they hit the same technology points. Hence, the regular Web advertising scenario as described in section 4.1 must be applied. However, the question is in how far the technology considerations of the static PC browsing environment match the requirements of mobile devices for example in terms of user identification. The regular Web advertising scenario will only work on mobile devices, if it is completely supported without modifications from the server-side. This means that the mobile device must support cookies in order to identify a device, track the browsing habits, and make recommendations. If a website publisher wants to target mobile users explicitly, he cannot rely on regular targeted Web advertising.

In addition to regular Web pages, most publishers thus provide a parallel mobile Web world optimized for mobile usage to offer a better user experience. This makes even more sense as some mobile phones may only support browsing of specially optimized mobile pages e.g. based on the Wireless Application Protocol (WAP) standard. The recent version WAP 2.0 is based on XHTML Mobile Profile (XHTML MP) and in consequence supports basically similar Web offerings and advertising possibilities like the regular Web. However, the websites are optimized for smaller screens and lower bandwidths resulting in limitations concerning rich-media display capabilities. But what is crucial, is that in these cases the underlying technology can be adapted to better support the specifications of mobile scenarios including better targeting conditions.

Device Targeting Opportunities

It has become clear now that mobile device targeting plays an important role in mobile Web scenarios, as diverging form factors and screen sizes may require the delivery of device-specific websites and ad formats (compare for example the different banner ad sizes described in section 2.5.3.1). An example for such customized Web offerings is the T-Online Web'n'Walk[32] portal that is available in a customized iPhone version. However, the dynamic adaptation to different devices requires sophisticated device identification methods.

In most cases the identification of the device type is performed using HTTP header data that is sent to the Web server when a mobile device requests a Web page. The HTTP header comprises several fields that may be relevant for this

---

[32] http://www.t-mobile-favoriten.de/ (mobile-optimized website).

purpose. The *user-agent* header field for example contains a line of text, which typically includes the device model and manufacturer and may also contain information such as the client device's Operating System (OS) version, browser version, Java capabilities, etc. In addition, the header may include a field called *x-wap-profile* that provides a link to the so-called User Agent Profile (UAProf), which is an XML document containing information about the features and capabilities of a mobile device. UAProf is a WAP Forum/OMA specification [148] concerned with capturing capability and preference information for wireless devices. The XML file typically holds data such as the vendor, the device model, the screen size, multimedia capabilities, character set support, and more. UAProf production is voluntary and usually provided by the vendor of the device or by the telecommunications company. More information about the detection of user agent types and client device capabilities can be found in [56]. In order to enable device or client type specific ad delivery, the HTTP header data must eventually be made available to the targeting system. As the client specifications are usually already extracted in the context of device-specific content delivery (e.g. screen size), the relevant information must just be forwarded as an additional input source for the Profiling Engine. In cases where the targeting system is also used for device-specific content customization, the HTTP header could be forwarded to the Profiling Engine in raw format. Then the Profiling Engine must provide respective capabilities enabling the extraction of device data from the HTTP header.

On-Portal vs. Off-Portal Mobile Advertising
The T-Online use case scenario chosen to examine targeting opportunities in the regular Web is an example for a typical portal page on the Web. What makes it special to some extent is that is operated by Deutsche Telekom that may at the same time be the Internet access provider of some of the users browsing the site. As mentioned in the use case analysis this offers enhanced targeting opportunities by integrating customer data from the subscriber database. However, this is an asset that most Web page operators cannot integrate in their targeting efforts. They must rely on profiling data information derived from user behavior or explicitly provided by the user through a community profile. This gives a feeling of what off-portal and on-portal advertising can mean in terms of targeting options.

The situation in today's mobile Web can be compared to early times of the regular Web, when online providers like Compuserve, AOL, or even T-Online provided Internet access via a proprietary community-like online platform. These providers offered a kind of portal that was the central starting point for all online activity. In the mobile world operators similarly initiated the first content-based services made available through self-contained portals (or "decks") that can effectively be considered to be some kind of homepages for the mobile Web. These portals have been and still are for most users the gateway to the mobile Web. They are usually integrated with the subscribers' browsers and provide a variety of links to branded, mobile specific external sites. Similar to the T-Online Web portal such mobile operator portals offer best "on-portal" targeting opportunities, as the operator can access mobile subscriber data. However, mobile users increasingly browse outside the operator portal. These "off-portal" sites are becoming important destinations for mobile Web browsing offering "direct-to-consumer" advertising opportunities. Hence, publishers do not anymore depend on carriers integrating their services into the portal. Eventually, both channels are complimentary drivers to the overall growth in mobile data usage [112].

User Identification Opportunities in Mobile Web Scenarios
As mentioned above "traditional" targeted Web advertising can only work in mobile scenarios if the targeting system is able to identify the mobile device, which in mobile scenarios is equivalent to user identification. Therefore, a mobile phone must support the local storage of cookies. If this is not the case again a workaround like in the EPG case must be found. Instead of integrating additional identification methods beyond the cookie approach into regular Web portals, it makes more sense to integrate the requirements for targeting of mobile devices into specifically adapted solutions for the mobile space. The background of this idea is the above introduced consideration that most content providers interested in offering mobile services will anyway operate special mobile sites to achieve a better user experience through e.g. optimized content presentation. It is then a logical step to tackle the problem of user identification in these customized mobile Web services.

In principle, there are three identities that could be used for identification purposes: The International Mobile Equipment Identity (IMEI), the International Mobile Subscriber Identity (IMSI), and the Mobile Subscriber Integrated Services Digital Network Number (MSISDN). The IMEI is the mobile phone's identity stored in the phone itself. The IMSI is the identity of the Subscriber Identity Module (SIM) card while the MSISDN is the phone number. A SIM is uniquely associated to an IMSI, while the MSISDN can change in time (e.g. due to number portability), i.e. different MSISDNs can be associated to the SIM. One of these identities must be made available to the targeting system implemented in the website that wants to display targeted ads.

Implementation of On-Portal Mobile Advertising
The on-portal mobile advertising scenario is depicted in the above use case model. As the network operator also controls the mobile portal the provision of one of the unique identifiers for internal usage does not cause a problem. The basic idea is that the portal is realized as a Web application (e.g. using JSP) running on the Portal Server that is provided with the MSISDN as soon as the user

goes online. When the user starts the portal application, the actual content oft the portal page is delivered to the device. At the same time the Portal Server triggers the ad delivery through the Campaign Management. Due to privacy restrictions the MSISDN must be pseudonymized before initiating the targeting process (see section 6.2.2.2). At no point during the targeting process the MSISDN must be associated with profiling data. The pseudonymization could for example be realized through an Ad Broker operating as an intermediary that may also be used for ad delivery handling including ad caching in order to achieve minimal latency. Hence, the Campaign Management receives an ad request from the Portal Server including the pseudonymized user ID and the page context (e.g. sports). According to this content information and the target group recommendation it requests from the Targeting Intelligence, the Campaign Management selects an appropriate ad that is delivered by the Ad Server.

Tracking can be realized via the Portal Server using the pseudonymized MSISDN. The Portal Server forwards information about content categories browsed by the user to the Profiling Engine. In contrast to off-portal targeting the on-portal solution has the advantage that targeting can even be realized when no tracking is done. In this case the user profile would only consist of customer data from the subscriber database (e.g. age, gender, home location). Before the subscriber data is made available to the Profiling Engine, the same pseudonymization process has to be applied.

Implementation of Off-Portal Mobile Advertising
Off-portal advertising requires a targeting provider that realizes the profiling and recommendation work and provides his services for integration into a website. As usually none of the above-mentioned identities is directly accessible by Web applications, the targeting provider will have to agree with the mobile operator on some interface via which he can access one of the identifiers. Similar to the transmission of user agent metadata, the operator may for example add an additional MSISDN field (typically called *x-msisdn*) to the HTTP header when a user initiates a WAP connection through his WAP gateway. The targeting provider thus must ask the operator to enable this kind of MSISDN forwarding for his destination site. As in these cases the user ID is not provided by the mobile device itself but through the network operator, targeting will only work if the device is connected via a WAP gateway. If the user accesses the Internet via a Wireless Local Area Network (WLAN or Wi-Fi) access point, user identification will remain impossible. Another drawback is that a targeting provider will have to make the above described agreements with several network operators to enable targeting for subscribers no matter which operator they are subscribed to. Hence, off-portal targeting requires a lot of organizational and contractual efforts that have to be tackled by the targeting provider. It is imaginable that large ad net-

works can conclude agreements with several operators and offer targeted advertising to the publishers as an integrated service including campaign management and ad serving. This has the additional advantage that as long as user data is kept anonymized a large profile database can be built leading to improved targeting results.

4.3.4 Message Advertising

Messaging is currently the most important advertising format in mobile advertising generating almost 90 percent of the revenues in this field [112]. As described in the use case introduction in section 3.3.2, message advertising can be differentiated into the two types of in-message advertising (Application-to-Person/Person-to-Person, A2P/P2P) and direct message marketing. While direct message marketing accounts for the majority of today's message advertising implementations, in-message advertising especially promises to generate substantial new revenue and increase customer loyalty through highly targeted advertising. The following two sections will examine how message advertising can be realized in both cases and which issues have to be considered.

4.3.4.1 In-Message Advertising

The use case model below depicts an A2P scenario where a user has opted in for a SMS news service. Thereupon, she receives information messages including text ads that are targeted according to demographic information, user interests and the message context. Advertising in P2P messages can be realized in a similar way.

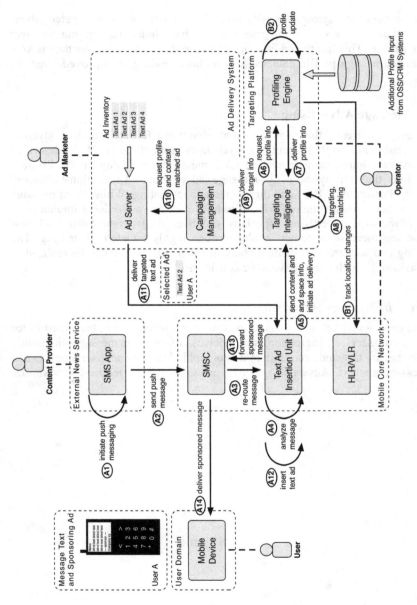

Figure 56: In-message advertising in a news push scenario (source: own illustration)

Actors

Mobile Device: mobile phone or other GSM device enabled to receive text messages (SMS).

SMS Application: SMS news service installed on 3rd party server.

SMSC: Short Message Service Center, network element in the mobile telephone network, which delivers SMS messages. Receives a Mobile-Terminated (MT) message from the SMS application for further processing.

Text Ad Insertion Unit: receives incoming MT message from SMSC and triggers text insertion process. Analyzes the content and delivers a content describing vector to the Targeting Intelligence.

HLR/VLR: The Home Location Register (HLR) is a database within the mobile phone home network that provides routing information and is responsible for the maintenance of user subscription information. The Visitor Location Register (VLR) contains all subscriber data for visiting mobile subscribers currently located in the area controlled by the VLR.

Profiling Engine: tracks location data provided by HLR/VLR and adds changes to the user profile. This can also include information like the most frequently visited locations of the user. Integrates subscriber information from OSS/BSS/CRM systems and optionally behavioral information based on user's Web browsing behavior into the user profile. Profile information is stored using the pseudonymized MSISDN as identifier.

Targeting Intelligence: analyzes information about the message delivered by the Text Ad Insertion Unit and derives a content category recommendation. Makes a target group recommendation incorporating user profile data delivered by the Profiling Engine.

Campaign Management: Selects appropriate ads based on content category and target group recommendations info provided by the targeting system.

Ad Server: delivers personalized text ads for insertion to the Text Ad Insertion Unit.

Pre-Conditions

User: must opt-in for ad sponsored SMS news service, either via message or Web sign-in.

SMSC: is configured to re-route SMS that match certain criteria (e.g. MSISDN that identifies recipient as member of in-message advertising group).

HLR/VLR: provides interface for subscriber data exchange to Profiling Engine.

Campaign Management: The Ad Marketer has set up policies for the ad campaigns of his customers that are translated into rules applied by the Campaign Management.

Post-Conditions

Mobile Device: has received SMS with ad enhancement.

Text Ad Insertion Unit: has inserted targeted text ad into news SMS.

Profiling Engine: has updated user profile according to subscriber information delivered by HLR/VLR.

Targeting Intelligence: has derived content and target group recommendations and delivered them to the Campaign Management.

Campaign Management: has selected ads based on content, demographic and geographical targeting methods.

Ad Server: has delivered text ads to Text Ad Insertion Unit.

Main Flow (A Numbers)

A1. User has opted in to receive ad sponsored news messages. The SMS application of the news provider initiates the delivery of a news message.

A2. SMS application sends news SMS to the SMSC of a mobile operator who supports ad insertion into short messages.

A3. SMSC detects that incoming message requires ad insertion and re-routes it to the Text Ad Insertion Unit.

A4. Text Ad Insertion Unit analyzes message to determine available space and computes a content describing vector.

A5. Text Ad Insertion Unit sends information about available space in the message and content describing vector to the Targeting Intelligence thus initiating the ad delivery process.

A6. Targeting Intelligence requests user profile from the Profiling Engine.

A7. Profiling Engine delivers current user profile to Targeting Intelligence.

A8. Targeting Intelligence computes matching content category and target group recommendation based on the user profile previously delivered by the Profiling Engine.

A9. Targeting Intelligence sends content category and target group recommendations to the Campaign Management.

A10.   Campaign Management matches content and target group recommendation to campaign policies and triggers text ad delivery through the Ad Server.

A11.   Ad Server delivers targeted text ad to the Text Ad Insertion Unit.

A12. Text Ad Insertion Unit appends text ad delivered by the Ad Server to the original message.

A13. Text Ad Insertion Unit forwards sponsored message to the SMSC.

A14. SMSC delivers sponsored ad message to the Mobile Device.

Parallel Flow (B Numbers)

B1. Profiling Engine periodically tracks location changes of the user by requesting the HLR. User identification is realized using the pseudonymized MSISDN of the user.

B2. Profiling Engine generates or updates user profile if already existing. The profile contains information from OSS/BSS/CRM systems, location information, and optionally information about the user's interests derived from her past Web browsing behavior.

Technical Use Case Analysis

As was already pointed out in the analysis of the on-portal advertising scenario in the previous section, mobile operators own a very unique asset: they have access to demographic and behavioral data of mobile subscribers on a user level. In combination with location awareness this enables them to offer personalized and relevant advertising that will lead to a high acceptance level of ads among the users thus increasing ad efficiency. Another major benefit of message advertising is that, unlike the situation for example in the TV world, operators do not need to cope with the integration into an existing value chain and can choose themselves which advertising partners they select.

General Short Message Delivery Flow

The above depicted use case model implements the A2P scenario of an ad sponsored push service. This can be a news service the user has to subscribe to in order to receive updates about important events in e.g. politics or sports. It should though be noted that potential P2P scenarios look quite similar with the only difference that the SMS App would be replaced by a second Mobile Device. In this case, the external news provider i.e. the Content Provider schedules the messaging meaning that he initiates the whole delivery process by submitting a message to the SMSC. The SMSC is responsible for the relaying, storing and forwarding of a short message between Short Messaging Entities (SME) like in this case the Content Provider and the Mobile Device.

Usually, the SMS delivery process of Mobile-Terminated (MT) messages, i.e. that are directed towards a Mobile Device, works as follows. The short message is submitted from the SME to the SMSC. After completing its internal processing, the SMSC interrogates the HLR and receives the routing information for the mobile subscriber. The SMSC sends the short message to the Mobile Switching

Center (MSC) using the *forward short message* operation. The MSC retrieves the subscriber information from the VLR. The MSC transfers the short message to the Mobile Device. The MSC returns the outcome of this operation to the SMSC and if requested by the SME, the SMSC returns a status report indicating delivery of the short message. As already described in section 2.3.2 the wireless network signaling infrastructure is based on Signaling System #7 (SS7) [95].

Ad Insertion Process
In this use case scenario the message delivery process must be adapted insofar as at some point the insertion of the targeted ad must take place. Therefore, effectively each SMS must be analyzed whether it is a candidate for ad insertion or not. This can basically be realized in two different ways. The first and above illustrated solution requires a modern SMSC that possesses a "re-routing feature" for forwarding messages according to pre-defined routing rules. In this case the SMSC can be configured to check all incoming messages for certain criteria (e.g. originator offers service that requires ad insertion, recipient that is subscribed to the ad sponsored service) and forward them to a distinct Text Ad Insertion Unit. The second opportunity must be applied in case of legacy SMSCs without re-routing possibilities. Here, a multifunctional ad insertion center is required that combines filtering functionality on the one hand and text insertion capabilities on the other. This unit would need to be interconnected as a proxy into the SS7 communication flow in order to scan literally each message as soon as the SMSC initiates the forwarding to the MSC and if necessary perform ad insertion. Certainly, the first of these two solutions is preferable as it helps to avoid performance problems that might arise in the other case since each SMS would need to be cached in the SS7 proxy waiting for further processing.

Nevertheless, the actual ad insertion procedure is the same in both alternatives. If the message meets provisioned conditions the text insertion process is triggered. The first step is to analyze the message in order to find out if enough space for ad insertion is available in the message. This requires prior coordination with the Campaign Management about the minimum of free text space that must be available and a strategy to avoid correlated issues. One option is to predefine a couple of ad categories according to the required length. The Text Ad Insertion Unit would then determine the available space and assign one of the agreed length categories. Another possibility is to have only one text ad length category and upgrade the message to a concatenated message containing the original message text and the ad text, when the text to be inserted does not fit.

If content targeting shall be implemented, the next step to accomplish is to analyze the actual content of the message in order to define the context that is needed to select appropriate ads. This can for example be realized using an algorithm to determine the so-called Term Frequency-Inverse Document Frequency (TF-IDF) weight, which is a statistical measure used to evaluate how important a word is to a document. The result of this algorithm is a metadata vector describing the content of the news message. Finally, a data record containing the recipient's MSISDN serving as identifier, the content describing vector, and information about available ad space is forwarded to the Targeting Intelligence.

The Targeting Intelligence has basically two different tasks in in-message advertising scenarios. First, it must determine the news message's content category that is required by the Campaign Management to assign ads that are booked for special contents. This can be realized using a classic Content Based (CB) filtering method that matches the metadata vector against content category vectors (see section 5.3.3.1). The inventory of available content categories must be defined in agreement with the Campaign Management.

Secondary, the Targeting Intelligence has to make a target group recommendation incorporating user profile data delivered from the Profiling Engine. Profile input comes from the operator's OSS/BSS/CRM systems and the Home Location Register (HLR). This includes socio-demographic data derived from the subscriber database, and continuously updated data about the user's current Location Area (LA) respectively the cell ID allowing to determine the approximate user location. The incorporation of location-awareness into the targeting process is discussed in more detail in the context of location-based couponing in the next subsection.

In addition, behavioral information can be included into the targeting process. Though, it should be noted that in the above depicted case the Profiling Engine cannot track the user behavior. This may be different in interactive messaging scenarios where user preferences could be derived from the interaction dialogue (e.g. if a user requests more information about an ad or not). However, here it is assumed that the customer also uses the Mobile Device for mobile Web browsing. Hence, the Profiling Engine has access to user interest data based on her prior browsing behavior. As in both cases, Web and messaging, user identification is realized using the MSISDN as an identifier, profile information can be collected in one common database without additional efforts. If the profiling data shall be enhanced by behavioral information from other channels, e.g. IPTV, additional challenges in terms of identity management have to be tackled (see section 4.4.1 and 5.2.4). Attention has to be paid to the fact that the profile data, which is stored in the database of the Profiling Engine, is assigned to pseudonymized MSISDNs. Thus, the Text Ad Insertion Unit must able to effectuate a similar pseudonymization as is performed by the Ad Broker in the Web case. Due to privacy restrictions this functionality is essential anyway. The fact that the message content is analyzed may raise additional privacy concerns especially in the context of P2P scenarios and must be taken very serious, as otherwise the whole business model may be questioned.

Finally, the Targeting Intelligence delivers a content category recommendation, a target group recommendation and the information about the text length available for ad insertion to the Campaign Management. The Campaign Management selects appropriate ads and delivers them to the Text Ad Insertion Unit that performs the actual ad insertion process. To create a clear and consistent end-user experience, the Text Ad Insertion Unit also inserts a text separator to differentiate between original and inserted text. Eventually, the delivery of the composed message is continued as usual.

It should be noted that if behavioral data is not incorporated into the targeting process, meaning that the subscriber database and the HLR are the only sources of user information, one might want to drop the Targeting Intelligence as a distinct unit. The reason for this consideration is that the subscriber data is static and does not include information dynamically changing and thus requiring the real-time computation of recommendations. It usually comes in a format (e.g. gender, age) that can be directly processed by the Campaign Management. The same is true for the location area information from the HLR that could be directly accessed by the Campaign Management. The content category recommendation technology could be integrated into the Text Ad Insertion Unit.

Issues in Inter-Operator Messaging and Roaming Scenarios
As already described the message transfer in GSM networks is managed by the SMSC. In cases where sender and receiver are subscribers of different mobile network operators the message must be transferred from one network to the other, which is the task of the MSCs. Special attention must be paid to the fact that typically the SMSC of the sender's network effectuates the delivery process. This causes some peculiarities affecting the targeting opportunities especially in P2P scenarios. Due to the fact that the SMSC in the message originator's network triggers the ad insertion process, targeting and ad delivery are performed there, too. As the operator of the source network does not possess any information about the subscribers of the destination network (neither socio-demographic nor location data), the only remaining targeting opportunity is content targeting. An approach that would allow ad insertion anyway is to implement a message proxy in the destination network that intercepts all incoming messages from foreign networks and triggers the ad insertion process. However, this solution certainly lies in the responsibility of the foreign operator and thus is absolutely independent of targeting implementations in the source network. In A2P scenarios like the above depicted news service this issue can cause that subscribers of a network which implements targeted advertising receive ads in their news messages, while subscribers of a network that does not include targeted advertising receive the plain

message without sponsoring ad. It should be noted that the provider of the news service and the mobile operator will have to agree on a deal about how to share the advertising revenues if in-message advertising shall be realized.

In addition to the described issue when transmitting messages between different mobile networks inside one country, in-message advertising also has consequences for international roaming. As ad insertion may cause concatenated messages the operator may incur additional roaming costs. He should thus perform a roaming check before inserting ads in order to find out whether a subscriber currently stays abroad and if yes cancel the process.

4.3.4.2 Direct Message Marketing

Direct message marketing is the most mature mobile ad delivery channel and occurs in several different forms. It can be used to provide the user with product information, incentives, or reminders and updates about special events. A basic feature of direct message marketing campaigns is to offer the user interaction opportunities through SMS, MMS or mobile Web [201]. The most interesting targeted advertising use case scenarios that incorporate direct message marketing activities are ad funded mobile communications, location-based couponing, and subsidized P2P messaging services, which will be introduced in the following.

Ad Funded Mobile Communication
The first operator who started offering mobile communications financed by advertising was the UK-based Blyk[33]. Blyk was founded as a Mobile Virtual Network Operator (MVNO) who markets its services under its own brand though using the wireless network of other carriers. The business model was to give users free text messages and minutes in exchange for receiving messages from brands. Blyk quickly gained a huge number of customers, but after a while advertisers stopped booking campaigns. The main reason for this development was obviously that customers unwilling to pay for mobile services tend to be less interesting to advertisers [165]. As the business model of acting as an independent MVNO did not work out, Blyk moved towards an operator partnership with Orange UK aimed at positioning targeted advertising as a complementary revenue source [154]. E-Plus in Germany followed a similar approach with their Gettings[34] service. Here, the user could opt-in for one of three different packages comprising the delivery of a distinct number of ad messages and received in exchange a credit on her mobile account. Meanwhile Gettings was relaunched and now offers carrier independent mobile couponing services (see below) [109].

---

[33] http://www.blyk.com/
[34] http://www.gettings.de/

From a technical point of view, ad funded mobile communication is not a very complex use case scenario and can basically be implemented based on targeting technology as described in the previous subsection. The main difference lies in the fact that ads are not inserted into existing text messages but rather are a message on their own. Thus, the Ad Server acts as a messaging application that itself initiates the transmission of SMS/MMS messages or emails. In the Gettings case targeting was based on information from the subscriber database and explicit interest declarations of the user in combination with behavioral targeting technology by Wunderloop[35] [131]. The Wunderloop approach serves as a basis for the generic description of targeting platforms in section 5.1 and will thus not be discussed here.

Location-Based Mobile Couponing
As was already explained mobile devices are not only individual devices, they travel with the user wherever she goes. This is a true benefit for advertisers as it enables them to target subscribers based on their current location. Besides recently emerging location-based communities, especially messaging services can profit from this opportunity. On the one hand location awareness can improve the targeting quality by incorporating such data as an additional targeting criteria as described in the previous subsection. On the other hand it opens up additional opportunities by using the location information itself as an advertising trigger. One of the most interesting examples for this approach is location-based couponing, where coupons or discount messages are sent to the user when she comes close to advertising businesses like restaurants or movie theatres. In this case the Campaign Management respectively the Campaign Scheduling must be provided with information about users currently visiting a distinct location in order to be able to initiate the message ad delivery. As the Campaign Management knows for which locations campaigns are booked, one implementation possibility would be to periodically request the Targeting Intelligence for recommendations about relevant users. In this request the Campaign Management must send the locations and target groups addressed by the campaigns to the Targeting Intelligence. Upon this trigger the Targeting Intelligence queries the Profiling Engine for profiles of users in these areas. The Profiling Engine continuously tracks location changes of all users in the network and thus always holds recent data. The tracking can be performed via direct access to the HLR of the network or through a distinct location server that may incorporate enhanced methods in order to achieve more accurate location identification (see below). Based on the result of the profile query

---

[35] In 2010 Wunderloop was acquired by the U.S. targeted advertising company AudienceScience and Wunderloop's targeting technology was integrated into AudienceScience's targeting solution [220]. See http://www.audiencescience.com/.

and the target group information from the Campaign Management, the Targeting Intelligence can derive, which subscribers match best and should be provided with ad messages. These recommendations are then sent back to the Campaign Management, in order to initiate message ad delivery to the recommended users. For privacy reasons the whole process must be performed using pseudonymized MSISDNs.

As mentioned the Profiling Engine can track the location of users by directly accessing the HLR or through a distinct location server. The location determination by querying the HLR is done using the base station network and thus is called network-based positioning. This method leverages the fact that the HLR is always updated with information about the Location Area (LA) a user currently resides in. An LA consists of a varying number of radio cells that may also be identified by the network operator. However, a cell can still cover a radius of several km. Using a table that associates the LAs or cell IDs to geographic coordinates, the location of the user can be broadly identified. The HLR stores the subscriber data including location information in data records that can be directly accessed by the Profiling Engine making the implementation quite simple. A general advantage of network-based techniques from a mobile operator's perspective is that they can be implemented without having to affect the handsets making it easy for an operator to incorporate location awareness into services. More accurate location identification can be achieved using triangulation (based on measuring angles from known points to the unknown location) or multilateration (based on measuring the Time Difference Of Arrival (TDOA) of a signal emitted from the respective object to three or more receivers). However, the implementation of these methods requires an additional location server that can perform the computing and eventually provide the Profiling Engine with the results. A mediating location server is also required if the user location shall be determined using handset-based positioning meaning that the location is calculated by the user device itself using locally installed client software. This implies that user cooperation is required if the location server shall be able to access the data. Most handsets allow the local software to request the cell ID or Global Positioning System (GPS) data if a GPS module is available, whereas in this use case scenario only the GPS data is relevant as the cell ID can also be determined network-based. The most sophisticated locating results can be achieved by implementing a location server based on hybrid positioning systems like Assisted GPS (A-GPS) that integrate network-based and handset-based technologies [196].

Subsidized Person-to-Person Messaging
One variant of subsidized P2P messaging has already been introduced in the previous subsection, where ads were inserted right into the actual message in order to finance the service. A conceptual drawback of this approach is that the

receiver is provided with advertising without being asked while the initiator of the messaging process remains spared. Alternatively, the subsidized messaging business case could also be implemented based on direct message marketing. Instead of inserting ads into the message, the operator could push a complete targeted advertising message to the sender in return for each message sent. The underlying technology would be the same as described above in the context of ad funded mobile communication. Compared to subsidized P2P messaging based on ad insertion, the direct message marketing approach allows better targeting opportunities in cases where sender and receiver are subscribers of different mobile operators. This is due to the fact that ads are always sent to the originator of the message whose subscriber data is known by the operator.

4.3.5 On-Device Advertising

As described in the short description of the on-device advertising use case in section 3.3.3, mobile applications can basically be differentiated according to their network connectivity while they are used. So-called "connected mobile applications" require network connectivity in order to perform the majority of their tasks. Without permanent Internet connection the utility of such applications is largely diminished. Examples include chat clients or streaming media applications. "Intermittently connected mobile applications" such as Active Idle Screen (AIS) or On-Device Portal (ODP) solutions, and applications like email clients or newsreaders require occasional network connectivity in order to perform some of their tasks. In most of these cases data caching functionality is implemented to enable appropriate application usage. However, occasional Internet connection is unavoidable in order to keep the data fresh. "Non-connected mobile applications" finally do not require network connectivity. Examples of this category include for example non-multiplayer games or productivity applications like word processors [137].

Ad Serving Opportunities in Mobile Applications
The functionality of targeted advertising implementations in mobile applications that are not always connected to the Internet is affected in terms of ad supply, ad display and tracking, as well as ad reporting. In principle, the possible realization approaches can be categorized similar to the above differentiation in terms of connectivity. Depending on the desired capabilities four different ad serving scenarios could be implemented: non-ad refresh, connect time ad refresh, independent ad refresh, and an ad engine approach [137].

In the "non-ad refresh" scenario the ad is supplied to the application at the time of the download. Subsequent ad refreshment does not take place and user tracking or ad reporting are usually impossible disqualifying this scenario for any targeting approaches. "Connect time ad refresh" means that ad supply and reporting are effectuated as soon as the application connects to the network, so that at this time potential targeting information may be exploited. "Independent ad refresh" follows the concept to deliver and cache ads according to advertising needs, track user behavior and report ad exposure independently from application connect, for example once a day at off-peak carrier hours. Another approach is to implement an "ad engine" as a central software function residing on the mobile phone in order to enable multiple mobile applications installed on the device to request ad delivery, track user actions, and report ad interaction. This ad engine has to receive and cache available ad units and provides them locally to mobile applications in real-time upon request in order to display them immediately in the context of the respective mobile application. Such an approach can avoid the repeated implementation of refresh functionality, guarantee consistent ad serving interfaces across applications and even platforms, and enable ad serving to mobile applications regardless of their app-specific core connectivity design [137]. In order to realize an ad engine approach a widely adopted standard is required that must be supported by the different stakeholders in the application development space. One suggestion comes from the OMA who has defined the Mobile Advertising (MobAd) enabler architecture [151] including network-side as well as device-side components, respectively network-side service provider and client-side advertising applications. Core functionalities of this specification comprise ad selection, ad delivery, and ad metrics data handling, as well as interfaces to external contextualization and personalization resources. The ad engine concept will be discussed in more detail in the context of converged scenarios in section 4.4.2.

Targeting Opportunities in Mobile Applications
The targeting opportunities in mobile application advertising heavily depend on the environment the application is running in. User identification is mostly easier than in the mobile Web scenarios described above in section 4.3.3. Many manufacturers of Java 2 Platform, Micro Edition (J2ME) compatible devices including Nokia, Samsung, Sony Ericsson, and Motorola allow the phone's IMEI or IMSI to be requested from within the Java application using device specific properties like *System.getProperty("com.nokia.mid.imei")* [145]. In the case of native applications the identification possibilities depend on the availability of respective methods provided by the application development environment. However, there is always the opportunity of implementing a unique application ID that may be used for identification purposes.

As described in section 4.3.4.2 geographical targeting using real-time location data can basically be performed following a network-based or a handset-based approach. Contrary to the messaging use case where ad insertion was realized in the network, in the case of mobile applications it makes more sense to realize the positioning terminal-based. The proceeding is similar to the determination of the IMEI/IMSI. J2ME applications can request the cell ID internally using specific properties as for example *System.getProperty("com.sonyericsson.net.cellid")* if the phone is able to read out the cell ID. Again this functionality is supported by many manufacturers and devices but not by all, and in addition, some phones only allow the cell ID to be read out by applications certified by the manufacturer. After having obtained the cell ID, it must be resolved into location data (latitude, longitude) by requesting a respective database operated by the mobile carrier. Similar databases are also provided by some open source projects like for example OpenCellID[36] [141]. Besides this cell ID based method many recent devices also support the Java Location Application Programming Interface (API) allowing to use GPS and even A-GPS positioning technology [22]. Applications in other platforms (e.g. iPhone, Symbian, Windows Mobile) are usually provided with comparable native libraries.

The detection of the device type is usually already done during the acquisition process, either implicitly when downloading from a brand specific app store or explicitly through self-selection when downloading from an arbitrary website. Moreover, the webstore may identify the device that initiates the download from the header information in the HTTP download request as described in section 4.3.3. In each case the device information can be stored within the application or together with a unique application ID in a server-side database in order to realize device targeting when the application later requests ad delivery. The same principle can be applied to any other targeting info that could already be accessed at the time of the application download (context of download, user id, user info) [137].

Implementation Approaches
In practice, the realization of targeted advertising in mobile applications follows different approaches depending on the application purpose and environment. Vendors of AIS and ODP solutions typically provide self-contained targeting solutions integrated with their application. The AIS provider Mobile Posse[37] for example offers a solution that can be pre-installed on the phone or downloaded later. The software allows the delivery of scheduled and targeted content respectively advertising while the mobile phone is not in use. Content and ads are transmitted in times with low network traffic, and in the same connection usage and reporting data are sent to Mobile Posse's targeting system. A detailed analysis of these solutions would lead too far at this point, more information on AIS and ODP can be found in [212] and [31].

---

[36] http://www.opencellid.org/
[37] http://mobileposse.com/

Other solutions are based on existing targeting and ad delivery systems already used in the context of mobile websites. The mobile advertising network AdMob[38] for example provides an iPhone specific advertising solution allowing the integration of advertising into iPhone Apps as well as mobile websites. Indeed, it is imaginable to adapt the on-portal case described in section 4.3.3 in a way that allows mobile applications to connect to the Portal Server respectively the Ad Broker based on HTTP communication. Instead of the MSISDN, the IMEI or IMSI could be used for user identification though again privacy concerns have to be respected. Special attention must be paid to the fact that mobile applications may not always be online, which concerns ad delivery and the transmission of user tracking data. In order to apply the on-portal scenario without major architectural changes, the mobile application would thus need to implement ad caching and local tracking functionality that must be kept transparent outwards eventually coming close to the above mentioned ad engine concept. From the business perspective such a scenario would make sense for the operator, as he could offer application developers to use his existing advertising delivery infrastructure via an API acting himself as a kind of advertising network.

4.3.6 Mobile TV and Video Advertising

Typical mobile TV or video scenarios comprise the delivery of content to the user over a mobile (UMTS) or a broadcasting network (e.g. Digital Video Broadcasting – Handheld, DVB-H). A basic introduction to these mobile TV technologies is given in section 2.3.2. Additional concepts include downloadable videos mostly realized in form of video podcasts. Correspondingly, three delivery methods must be differentiated that help to determine possible targeted advertising scenarios: TV or video streaming over mobile networks, TV broadcast, and video downloads [137].

Evaluation of Mobile TV/Video Delivery Methods for Targeted Advertising
In mobile networks either linear TV or VoD content is streamed to the mobile phone very much akin to IPTV and starts playing when the first bits of the video stream are received. The quality of the video differs based on varying network conditions. Due to the bidirectional architecture mobile network based streaming scenarios allow targeting systems to track the actual viewing behavior of the user in order to derive interest profiles and provide advertisers with statistic reports for example about what percentage of a video or ad has been viewed by the audience. The granularity of targeted ad delivery depends on whether a VoD or a linear TV service is offered, respectively if the transmission is effectuated in unicast or in

---

[38] http://www.admob.com/. In 2009 AdMob was acquired by Google [110].

multicast mode using Multimedia Broadcast Multicast Service (MBMS). Possible ad formats include linear ad breaks, non-linear ad breaks, and interactive ads as described in section 2.5.3.4.

In mobile phone optimized broadcast networks e.g. based on DVB-H or Digital Multimedia Broadcasting (DMB) linear TV channels are aired continuously. Each user receives all channels at once and can select which she wants to watch. Advertising opportunities exist within commercial breaks as well as with banner or overlay type of effects. However, due to the fact that each user receives the same programming targeted advertising is almost impossible. Limited geographical targeting may be realized in case of differing regional programming or generally by installing ad insertion units at the location of the broadcasting stations. As broadcasting inherently does not include bidirectional communication viewer tracking can only be realized through a hybrid solution using the mobile network as a backchannel. Such an approach could effectively be compared to an IPTV scenario where the STB includes an additional DVB-T tuner. Despite the limited personalization possibilities within the broadcast channels, this tracking data might be exploited for targeted advertising in mobile VoD services over the mobile network or even in other channels like the Web or IPTV.

The third method of delivering mobile TV or video to the customer is to provide the content as a file that is downloaded and stored on the mobile completely before starting to play. The most famous implementation of this approach are video podcasts for example accessible via the Apple iTunes Store or directly on websites of programmers. One big advantage of this concept is that the video quality is only dependent on the quality of the source file on the video server. Together with the increasing storage availability and multimedia capabilities of cutting-edge mobile phones this makes video podcasts a compelling media consumption channel for users and should be recognized as a valuable advertising opportunity. However, the realization of targeted advertising in these scenarios is challenging due to the fact that video download and consumption do not coincide and the video may even be consumed when not connected to the Internet. Crucial points emerging from this issue include the problem of tracking user viewing behavior, and the obsolescence of ads potentially enclosed within the podcast file be it linear (pre-, mid-, post-roll) or non-linear advertising (banners, overlays).

As can be derived from this description video podcasts are basically similar to other on-device applications and the implementation of targeted advertising consequently faces similar problems. Hence, it can be referred to the previous section where major opportunities and challenges of on-device advertising have already been discussed. In addition, the online/offline problem will be examined in more detail in the context of the converged scenario in section 4.4.2. Mobile TV based on broadcast networks enables linear TV scenarios very similar to "traditional" broadcast TV through terrestrial or satellite transmission. As mentioned targeting towards individual users cannot be realized due to the nature of the technology. Hybrid approaches that combine broadcast networks for content delivery and use the mobile network to provide a back channel may allow tracking the viewing behavior of users for usage in the context of other services like VoD. However, in these cases the underlying technology would be the same as in solutions exclusively based on mobile network technology. Therefore, mobile broadcast TV does not provide any additional targeting potential and thus will not be further discussed. Contrary, mobile TV or video streaming over mobile networks provides best targeting conditions owing to the inherently bidirectional data connection. As was pointed out earlier, the targeted advertising opportunities depend on whether linear TV or VoD services are offered. The underlying unicast and multicast technologies enable very similar targeted advertising scenarios as in IPTV. Hence, in the following the most relevant use cases of the IPTV domain will be analyzed in how far they can be transferred to the mobile environment and which differences occur. Though, before this analysis can be performed some basic considerations concerning the implementation of targeted advertising in the mobile environment must be made.

Technological Conditions for Targeted Advertising in Mobile TV Scenarios
The targeting opportunities in the mobile TV environment depend basically on two factors: the transmission mode (unicast vs. multicast) and the ad insertion point (network vs. device). Mobile VoD scenarios are based on unicast transmission, while linear mobile TV can be realized using MBMS based multicast transmission, as was already mentioned in section 2.3.2. It should though be noted that today MBMS implementations are still nascent. The point-to point character of unicast transmission allows individually targeted ads to be inserted at the mobile TV headend location. In MBMS multicast scenarios the insertion of ads may be effectuated at some network node between the headend and the Base Station Controller (BSC). However, the underlying technology of MBMS constrains the finest targeting granularity to radio cell level. This is due to the fact that the devices of all subscribers who currently reside in one cell area and want to watch a certain linear TV channel tune in to the same point-to-multipoint radio bearer [92]. Targeting of individual users is thus not possible in MBMS multicast scenarios. This could though be achieved by performing the ad insertion in the mobile device i.e. terminal-based. Again the similarities to the IPTV environment are obvious. Generally, targeted advertising implementations in the context of mobile TV must though take into account that the data connection may be temporarily unavailable, for example due to a lack of radio coverage. This may require architectural changes compared to targeted advertising in IPTV.

An important standard in the context of targeted advertising implementations in mobile TV is the OMA Mobile Broadcast Services Enabler Suite (BCAST) [150], which defines a technological framework and globally interoperable technologies for the generation, management and distribution of mobile broadcast services over different broadcast distribution systems. In this context the term "mobile broadcast services" refers to a broad range of services, which leverage the unidirectional one-to-many broadcast paradigm as well as the bi-directional unicast paradigm in a mobile environment, and covers one-to-many services ranging from classical broadcast to mobile multicast. This enabler suite amongst others specifies functions for the Electronic Service Guide (ESG, comparable to the EPG in IPTV), file and stream distribution, interactivity, personalization and support for user-based profiles and preferences, and location information.

Display Advertising in Mobile TV and Video Scenarios

Like in IPTV display advertising in mobile TV comprises scenarios where banner or overlay ads share the mobile display with the streamed content, which in MMA terminology is called non-linear ad breaks (see section 2.5.3.4). Depending on whether ad insertion takes place in the network or on the device enhanced display ad formats like wallpapers or splitscreen may in principle also be applied if the necessary computing power is available. But with respect to the limited screen size of mobile phones, these ad formats may not be appropriate.

Network-based banner ad insertion in linear mobile TV can be realized as described for IPTV (see section 4.2.3.1). An ad insertion unit can be placed in the headend or at decentralized locations down to the BSC allowing to target content, time, and regions. The major challenge in this context is that the display ad must be inserted into the MPEG compressed and potentially encrypted multicast stream requiring sophisticated ad insertion units. In terminal-based ad insertion scenarios the MBMS multicast stream remains untouched and the ad insertion must be performed within the mobile phone. The user identification problem of IPTV where usually only the household but not single users can be targeted (compare section 4.2.3.1) does not exist owing to the often emphasized fact that mobile phones are personal devices. The mobile user may be identified using the IMEI or IMSI of the mobile phone respectively SIM card that may be requested by the media player as described in the previous section on on-device advertising. Hence, tracking of individual viewing behavior is possible and can be used by a targeting system to derive target group recommendations. As depicted in the IPTV use case the actual targeting and ad delivery processes may be performed in real-time by centralized units in the headend. However, one might want to consider the implementation of a mediating ad broker as introduced in the context of mobile Web advertising or even following a decentralized approach for tracking and managing the ad insertion using a local ad engine for example based on the

OMA MobAd enabler architecture mentioned in the on-device advertising section. In this case, a catalogue of ads could be pushed to the user terminal's memory in advance (for instance via IP-Datacast) [209]. The reason for this consideration lies in the unreliability of wireless connections that can cause delays in the ad delivery leading to ad display in the wrong context. Moreover, the real-time ad delivery consumes additional bandwidth that may be lacking in content delivery although this point is more relevant in case of ad spot insertion, which will be examined below. A crucial point of terminal-based ad insertion is the limited computing power of mobile devices that in addition widely differs on different mobile phone types. Finally, the required computing activity causes increased power consumption leading to reduced battery lifetimes.

As described in the section on display advertising in IPTV, banner and overlay ad formats can be enhanced in order to offer interactive services giving the user the ability to interact with content and service providers. This is also true for display advertising in mobile TV where interactive response components (compare the part on RFI in section 4.2.3.3) such as "click to mobile Web" call-to-actions or "click to receive a message" may be implemented. Instead of implementing complex interactive advertising scenarios like DALs or microsites customers may simply be redirected to mobile Web pages offering a similar user experience. Interactive advertising scenarios may be implemented based on the OMA BCAST enabler specification that defines different types of interactions between mobile terminals and the service provider. This can for example include scenarios as offering the user to order a ring-tone matching the music that is just played in a show [150].

Ad Spot Insertion in Mobile TV and Video Scenarios

Similar to IPTV the mobile TV environment provides in-stream advertising opportunities in linear and on demand scenarios. As described in section 2.5.3.4 these linear ad breaks take over the full mobile display screen and replace the streamed video content for a given period of time. An alternative advertising scenario lying somewhere in between the classic linear TV "commercial break" and interstitial advertising known from VoD is to play short pre-roll video ads when mobile TV is started or mid-roll ads during channel changes [209]. Concerning the underlying technology the conceptual approaches developed in the use case analysis on linear TV and VoD ad insertion can be applied.

Since linear mobile TV is streamed using MBMS multicast, similar ad insertion technology as in IPTV multicast scenarios can be implemented. Ad splicing units based on SCTE cue tone signaling originally stemming from the cable industry may be installed at the mobile TV headend location, somewhere in the core network e.g. at the SGSN location or at the site of the BSC, enabling time, content and regional targeting. As described above placing an ad insertion unit at the BSC site anyway does not allow targeting of individual users, which is a difference to IPTV multicast scenarios where addressable advertising can be realized if ad insertion units are installed at the DSLAM location respectively at the multicast endpoint. It may however still make sense to effectuate ad insertion at the BSC site, namely in cases where BSCs are located around special event locations like soccer stadiums. MBMS multicast moreover provides the possibility of streaming a particular branded channel during the soccer game exactly to the BSC that covers the stadium [20]. As mentioned mobile VoD services provide similar opportunities for targeted advertising as IPTV VoD. Video and ad delivery can be implemented based on common serving infrastructure located in the mobile TV headend. The scheduling is realized by the VoD management that composes a playlist containing the actual content framed, respectively interrupted by pre-, mid-, and post-roll ads. As the mobile media player can read out the IMEI or IMSI of the mobile phone or SIM card, single users may be identified without the log-in requirement prevalent in IPTV and their viewing behavior can be tracked in order to perform individually targeted advertising.

Alternatively, ad insertion technology could in both scenarios be implemented terminal-based, which would enable individual targeting even in linear mobile TV. However, it must be kept in mind that this opportunity is constrained by possibly low-performing devices but mainly by interruptions due to mobile network unreliability if the ad spot that needs to be inserted is streamed in real-time. As proposed in the context of STB-based display ad insertion possible solutions include the implementation of a mediating ad broker or of a local ad engine that is in advance provided with a catalogue of potential ads. During interstitials, an advertising matching the user's interest is then run from device memory, selected through an on-device targeting intelligence.

A crucial point in the realization of mobile TV advertising besides the technological feasibility is that typical 30-second spots and 5 to 7 minute "commercial breaks" need to be reduced in time. This is due to the typical usage situations in which mobile TV is consumed. Assuming that users will tune in only for a short time when for example waiting for the bus or on their way to work, ad spots and ad breaks will most likely cause that the user stops watching. In VoD scenarios the insertion of shorter pre-, mid- or post-roll ads is unproblematic as the content is transmitted via unicast. From a technical point of view the same is true for linear ad insertion, albeit it will be difficult to maintain the same TV program as in "normal" TV. Therefore, the implementation of shorter ad breaks needs to be agreed by the various actors in the advertising value chain. It should though be noted that many TV channels currently available in mobile TV are anyway offered as special "made-for-mobile" channels half and half consisting of actual live TV transmissions and customized mobile TV programs. Contrary to IPTV, the chance that the different stakeholders may soon agree on a revenue sharing deal for targeted mobile TV advertising is much more likely than in IPTV. This is due to the fact that mobile TV is still nascent and mobile network operators will play a key role in delivering a seamless mobile TV experience and putting adequate network and device enablers in place [209].

ESG Advertising in Mobile TV
Being the mobile counterpart to the IPTV EPG, the ESG is an emerging portal for multimedia content offering display advertising opportunities for content related or general product and services advertising. As was already described in the IPTV EPG use case analysis in section 4.2.5 there exist two basic possibilities of implementing program guides, which may also be implemented in the context of mobile ESGs. First, ESG data can be continuously carouseled respectively broadcasted to all devices in the network. This approach is not limited to broadcast network-based mobile TV as MBMS also provides a broadcast mode that could be used for this purpose [20]. Second, the mobile device can actively request ESG content via a unicast pull mechanism as soon as the ESG portal is launched. While the carouseling approach pushes the same data to all viewers, the second variant allows the individual delivery of targeted ads. Concerning the realization in a browser-based scenario it can be referred to the respective IPTV section. User identification may be realized using the MSISDN as described in the context of on-portal mobile Web advertising in section 4.3.3.

It should be noted that as part of the BCAST standards framework the OMA has released a specification on service guides for mobile broadcast services [150]. The OMA BCAST ESG structure is made up of numerous so-called fragments represented as separate XML documents. The core fragments contain the program guide with information, which is meaningful to end users, such as a list of TV channels and programs on each TV channel. Beyond this pure program guide functionality, an OMA compliant ESG also contains data only aimed at the receiving application that is not rendered to end-users. This includes for example access fragments, which provide the mobile device with information allowing to select the most appropriate bearer in the current location meaning that multicast bearers may be prioritized over unicast bearers when both options are available. The ESG is thus a key feature for offering mobile TV services that seamlessly integrate unicast and broadcast delivery [92]. Service guide fragments can be delivered over broadcast as well as unicast channels allowing the implementation of both the carousel and the unicast pull based ESG approach. In addition, to these two realization alternatives, it is imaginable that only some basic ESG data is provided in broadcast mode with additional data including the delivery of targeted ads being accessed when necessary [209].

4.4   Targeted Advertising in Converged Scenarios

While the previous sections dealt with targeted advertising scenarios either in the Web, in IPTV, or in the mobile environment, this section will now focus on converged scenarios implementing targeted advertising across several ICT channels at the same time. The integration of these channels into a multiplatform targeting environment causes additional challenges. As described in section 3.4 two exemplary use cases will be analyzed. While the first use case more generally introduces into the characteristics of triple-play scenarios and resulting implications for targeting, the second case deals with the very complex scenario of dynamic ad replacement in pre-recorded content touching multifold aspects that may arise in a converged ICT world.

4.4.1 Targeted Advertising in a Triple-Play Environment

The depicted triple-play environment includes services in IPTV, Web, and mobile. The starting point of the scenarios lies in the IPTV domain, where the user watches a soccer channel. As a reaction to her watching behavior she is provided with targeted advertising in the Web and on her mobile phone. In order to manage tracking and targeting across the different domains, an Identity Management (IdM) system is introduced.

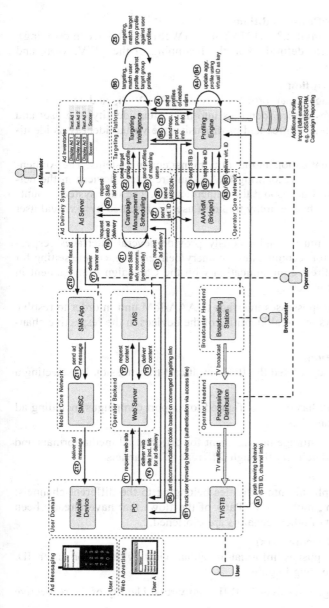

Figure 57: Targeted advertising in a triple-play environment (source: own illustration)

Actors/Pre-Conditions/Post-Conditions
See descriptions in sections 4.2.3.2 (IPTV), 4.1.3 (Web), and 4.3.4.1 (messaging), and respective basic actor definitions at the beginning of the IPTV, Web, and mobile use case sections.

Additional Actor Description
Profiling Engine: manages user profiles across IPTV, Web, and mobile. The Profiling Engine resolves device identities into the virtual identity of a user and stores behavioral data in an aggregated profile using the virtual identity as identifier.

AAA/IdM: bridged authentication and identity management systems. The Authentication, Authorization, and Accounting (AAA) unit registers devices in the network and notifies the IdM unit about the authentication. The IdM system mounts the device identities into the hierarchy tree of a user represented by a virtual user identity.

Targeting Intelligence: must simultaneously provide several interfaces respectively operating modes for recommendation query/delivery, e.g. cookie setting for Web advertising, and direct communication with the Campaign Management in case of direct message marketing.

Campaign Management: possesses interface to AAA/IdM unit in order to resolve virtual identities of users into real identities of the devices in the respective channel.

Additional Pre-Conditions
STB: The user has already started the IPTV multicast transmission by selecting a TV channel.

Campaign Management: has to be configured to support campaigns including ad delivery in different channels.

Ad Server: must provide storage management for different ad media formats and provide interfaces for ad delivery through different ICT channels.

Use Case Flow
The use case flow is split up into activities belonging to the different channels: IPTV = A, Web = B/Y, mobile = Z. Parts of the flows that have already been described in the context of other scenarios are shortened.

IPTV Tracking Flow (A Numbers)
A1. STB continuously pushes information about viewing behavior (user ID, channel info) to Profiling Engine.

A2. – A3. Profiling Engine resolves STB ID into virtual identity of the respective user.

A4. Profiling Engine updates the user profile according to the user's viewing preferences using the virtual identity as a key for storage in the database. The Profiling Engine can derive information about the user's interests from her viewing behavior. The user profile is enriched by OSS/BSS/CRM data. Besides the tracking data from IPTV the Profiling Engine can simultaneously integrate profile information from all three channels.

Web Domain Tracking Flow (B Numbers)

B1. As described in the Web case analysis (see section 4.1.3), user action on the portal page initiates a tracking request through a tracking pixel integrated in the code of the Web page. The Web user is authenticated through her access line.

B2. – B3. Profiling Engine resolves line ID into the virtual identity of the respective user.

B4. The browsing behavior is analyzed in order to further update the user profile, which is stored using the virtual identity as identifier. However, it should be kept in mind that in this case primarily IPTV usage behavior shall matter.

B5. User profile information is delivered to the Targeting Intelligence.

B6. Target group recommendations especially incorporating user information from IPTV are stored on the user PC using a recommendation cookie.

Web Domain Ad Delivery Flow (Y Numbers)

Y1. – Y4. PC requests delivery of portal page including an ad link that refers to the ad delivery system.

Y5. – Y7. The embedded ad reference initiates the delivery of a targeted ad through Campaign Management and Ad Server based on the target group information stored in the recommendation cookie.

Mobile Domain Flow (Z Numbers)

Z1. Campaign Management periodically requests Targeting Intelligence for recommendations about users that should be provided with an SMS ad for the mobile TV offering.

Z2. Therefore, it sends the corresponding target group profile to the Targeting Intelligence.

Z3. – Z4. Targeting Intelligence queries Profiling Engine for profiles of users with mobile phones.

Z5. Based on the result of the profile query and the target group information from the Campaign Management, the Targeting Intelligence derives the best matching subscribers.

Z6. Virtual identities of best matching customers are sent back to the Campaign Management.

Z7. – Z8. Campaign Management resolves virtual identities into MSISDNs of mobile subscribers that shall receive the ad message.

Z9. Campaign Management requests Ad Server to deliver direct marketing SMS.

Z10. – Z12. Ad Server sends text ad to SMS App that effectuates the SMS delivery process via the SMSC.

Technical Use Case Analysis
As the ICT space develops to an all-IP world new use case opportunities arise integrating services from the single channels. The above depicted model combines previously described scenarios from IPTV, the Web and mobile. To the user it may at first sight not be obvious that the advertising she receives is based on converged technology, as she actually does nothing more than watching a special programming provided over IPTV. The convergence in this case concerns primarily the advertising platform and less convergence of media content. Such a case will be described in the next subsection.

The whole scenario starts at home where the user watches a special programming over IPTV. In this case it is assumed that she consumes a premium soccer channel provided through the operator. She could also be watching an arbitrary TV show though the soccer channel is a catchy example. The crucial point is that the IPTV carrier operates a targeting platform that tracks her watching behavior in order to generate a user profile. The targeting system basically works as described for example in the network-based banner ad insertion or the linear ad insertion case. Thus, the user can of course also be targeted with IPTV advertising as discussed in the analysis of those cases. However, the added value in this case is that the operator's advertising opportunities are not restricted to the IPTV channel. Rather, he can particularly target the user via mobile and Web services assuming that she is also a mobile subscriber of the operator and frequently visits his Web portal.

Identity Management Challenges in the Triple-Play Advertising Scenario
In previous use case analyses it has already been stated that user identification is a necessary requirement for targeting solutions. However, in each of the channels (Web, IPTV, mobile) a different identifier was used for user recognition. The Web scenario used a cookie, IPTV the STB ID, and the mobile Web case the MSISDN for identification purposes. Though, in this converged case user profile data generated from tracking in all ICT channels has to be considered. If the operator wants to leverage his multi-channel customer relations, he must thus find a solution that allows addressing the user via one single identity and which can be implemented using identity management capabilities. Such an IdM system can for

example implement an abstraction layer that on the one hand mediates between systems using different identities, and on the other hand provides a unified interface via which a central access to all kinds of user information is enabled. Another aspect of IdM is the handling of profile data. The Profiling Engine must be provided with a unified view on user profiles no matter if they stem from user profiling in different channels, from the HLR of a mobile network or from a CRM database. Generally, two approaches are possible to tackle this problem. The first possibility is to keep the profile data of different systems stored in decentralized databases and use a federation system to create a virtual database. The second way is to move all data to a centralized profile database though requiring substantial consolidation efforts [87].

According to Sun [40] another problem in the context of IdM is the varying targeting granularity of the different scenarios. Mobile phones provide a fundamentally higher personalization level than IPTV services. As has become obvious in the use case descriptions in section 4.2.3 targeting of individual viewers is very difficult in IPTV. In most cases the maximum granularity that can be achieved is the household level meaning that single members of a family cannot be differentiated by the targeting system. In contrast, the mobile phone is always an individual device only used by its owner. The targeting granularity in the Web lies mostly somewhere in between the opportunities of IPTV and mobile. In each case, the IdM must be able to deal with this issue. In a scenario where several family members living in one IPTV household are also mobile subscribers of the same operator, wrong targeting results can emerge. This happens if the IdM just breaks down the profiling data of the entire household on each single user. Therefore, the Profiling Engine must apply intelligent rules to select which general household information can enrich the profile of a single user leading to better targeting results than could be achieved only with the mobile profile, and which information should better be skipped.

Implementation Considerations for IdM enabled Targeting
Typical IdM systems focus in general more on managing user identities on the service level. In order to leverage IdM functions in the context of a converged ICT scenario, a way must be found to connect device identities like MSISDN or STB ID to the IdM domain. This actually means that a bridging between the authentication (AAA) systems of the single ICT channels and the IdM has to be realized. A more detailed overview of these IdM issues is provided in section 5.2. In the following some important aspects of an implementation in the triple-play scenario will be discussed.

The initial situation of the triple-play use case is that a user starts watching a premium soccer channel on IPTV. In order to realize targeting her viewing behavior must be tracked. For reasons of simplification the Presence Engine has been omitted in the above illustration; it is assumed that tracking information is directly transferred from the STB to the Profiling Engine. When the user turns on her STB, it is registered with an AAA system that its usually realized as a distinct unit for IPTV, mobile, and Web, but may also be an integrated solution across the channels [87]. This aspect has so far not been emphasized, as it was sufficient to know that there was an identifier (MSISDN, STB ID, cookie) that could be used for targeting purposes. However, in this scenario the authentication process is important, since at this point a connection to the IdM system must be established. It should be noted that this connection must certainly be realized across all channels and eventually enables the mapping of identities via an abstraction layer managed within the IdM system (see Figure 58).

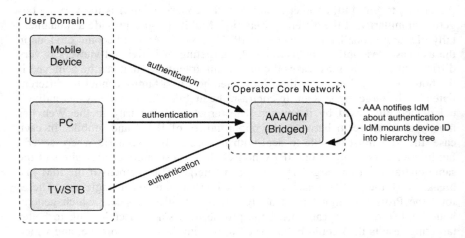

Figure 58: Device authentication and AAA/IdM bridging (source: own illustration)

After the STB has been registered in the network and the IdM system has been noticed about this authentication, the tracking process starts. There are generally two options concerning the profiling of user behavior in converged scenarios. First, the Profiling Engine may track and store usage data separately for each channel and later present a virtually merged profile towards the Targeting Intelligence. The second (and above depicted) option is to first resolve tracking requests of a device to a virtual master identity serving as an umbrella for all identities of a user and then use this identity as the key for storage of behavioral data across all devices/channels in one profile. While the first case may be more appropriate in case of existing legacy targeting systems in the single channels, the second approach is generally preferable as it promises a higher performance and an added value through the reusability of aggregated behavioral profiles for other services. However, in both cases the IdM performs the mapping of identities belonging to one person. Another aspect in terms of user profiling is the enrichment of profile information through other systems like OSS/BSS/CRM systems. In previous use case descriptions it was implicitly assumed that this data would have been integrated through some proprietary interface construction. Though in converged cases these systems should be equally connected to the central IdM system and thus be made available through a virtual identity.

Targeting Intelligence Flexibility Requirements in Converged Scenarios
The actual targeting process can be realized based on similar processes as described in previous cases and in the generic overview in section 5.1. However, attention should be paid to the fact that in order to enable targeted advertising through multiple channels, the Targeting Intelligence must simultaneously provide several interfaces respectively operating modes for recommendation query/delivery. As targeted advertising in a converged scenario is basically a combination of the use case scenarios in the Web, IPTV, and mobile domains analyzed in the previous sections, the delivery of targeted ads over the different channels can be initiated through different triggers. This can also be seen in the above illustration and the depicted flows. As was described in section 4.1.3 the targeted advertising process in the Web requires that the targeting recommendation is written into a recommendation cookie on the user's PC. Ad requests are embedded into the HTML code of delivered Web pages and refer directly to the Campaign Management. Therefore, the target group recommendation must previously have been made and written into the recommendation cookie. In contrast, the implementation of direct messaging rather requires a direct dialogue between the Campaign Management and the Targeting Intelligence. This has been examined in section 4.3.4.2 in the context of location-based couponing, but the principle in this case is the same. The Campaign Management periodically requests the Targeting Intelligence for recommendations about users that should be provided with an SMS ad for the mobile TV offering. Therefore, the Campaign Management sends a profile of the target group addressed by this campaign to the Targeting Intelligence. Upon this trigger the Targeting Intelligence queries the Profiling Engine for profiles of users with mobile phones. This information should be stored as one attribute in the profile database in the course of the tracking process. Based on the result of the profile query and the target group information from the Campaign Management, the Targeting Intelligence derives the best matching subscribers. Appropriate recommendations are sent back triggering the Campaign Management for ad delivery. In order to initiate the actual messaging process, the Ad Server must be provided with the MSISDN of the user who shall receive the

message. Therefore, the Campaign Management resolves the virtual identity by requesting the IdM system.

4.4.2 Dynamic Ad Replacement in Pre-Recorded Content

While the previous use case description primarily examined how to manage different device identities in converged scenarios in order to leverage user data for targeted advertising across multiple channels, this case focuses on media convergence the user rather actively experiences. Roughly speaking the flow is that the user schedules the recording of an arbitrary IPTV show, which is interrupted by typical TV ad breaks, intending to later watch the recorded program on her mobile phone, whereas the original ad spots will be replaced by targeted advertising. In order to realize this scenario several problems have to be solved. Initially the video content must be transcoded to a mobile video format and somehow made available to the mobile device. Next, and more interesting in the context of targeted advertising, it has to be discussed how the system can detect ads already included in the content stream and in the following, which possibilities exist to replace these ad spots by targeted advertising especially in a changing online/offline environment and under consideration of a varying user context (e.g. location, traveling speed,...). This eventually requires a targeted advertising solution supporting network-based ad replacement as well as ad replacement within the mobile device depending on the user context. Due to the complexity of this scenario, the following analysis starts with a more detailed introduction than in previously discussed use cases, before the actual use case model will be examined.

Three Ways of Making TV Recordings Available to the Mobile Device

As was described in the introduction to this use case in section 3.4.2 the initial situation is that a user is about to go on a business trip and wants to schedule the recording of her favorite TV show. As a special benefit the IPTV operator she is subscribed to offers the service to access the recorded content from her mobile phone and watch it on the go.

There are basically three different approaches of making the recorded content available to the mobile device. In the first case, the TV recording is effectuated using a home DVR meaning that the recorded content data is held locally. In order to make the content available for consumption on the mobile device after the recording has been finished, the data is transferred to a central Web storage provided by the operator. In a next step, the video data must be transcoded to a mobile compliant format. This usually includes the conversion of high resolution and bit rate MPEG-2, MPEG-4 AVC/H.264, or proprietary (e.g. Microsoft's WMV9) encoded data as transmitted over IPTV to low resolution and bit rate versions that are more suitable for the mobile environment due to smaller screen sizes and limited bandwidth as well as storage capacities. In the following, the actual ad replacement process can take place, which will be the subject of discussion below. Afterwards the content is available for download to the mobile device via cellular or wireless local networks. While in this first variant it is assumed that transcoding of the content and provisioning of the mobile compliant version are realized network-based, as a second possibility it is also imaginable to perform the necessary processes within the home PVR, store the transcoded data locally, insert targeted ads and allow the user to directly access the home DVR through the local network or remotely. As a third option and in contrast to the previously described two home DVR based solutions, the operator may also offer network PVR (nPVR) functionality to his customers meaning that recording of the original content, transcoding, ad replacement, and provisioning are realized centrally at the operator's site.

A general recommendation for one of these three approaches to make TV recordings available to a mobile device cannot be given. Basically, a choice has to be made whether to follow a local or a network-based concept respectively whether to use a home PVR or an nPVR to store and manage the recordings. The first option mentioned above is effectively a hybrid of both concepts. Home DVR solutions are easy to deploy, as the concept in principle only requires having a hard disk installed in the IPTV STB and an adapted client middleware capable of managing the user's recordings. However, it is questionable if the computing power of an STB is sufficient for the transcoding and dynamic ad insertion tasks. In addition, different STB hardware configurations or versions may cause compatibility problems and limited functionality. Compared to home PVR solutions network-based recording offers better flexibility to the user as the recorded content is easily accessible and manageable not only at home via the STB but also via Web and mobile phones, moreover allowing direct streams and downloads right from the cloud to the mobile phone. These functionalities can in fact also be realized in home PVR environments. However, streaming from the home PVR to the mobile phone is limited by the upstream capabilities of the user's IPTV line and in addition is dependent on a working connection of the home DVR to the network. From the operator's point of view, nPVRs imply higher financial efforts compared to home DVRs due to the provision of central storage space and associated maintenance and service costs.

Attention should be paid to the fact that centralized PVR concepts can potentially rearrange the original video recording paradigm as in principle one central copy of a TV show is sufficient to satisfy the needs of every user who wants to watch it. This means that the whole system could rather work as a big centralized media center holding copies of all programs aired in e.g. the last four weeks than as an actual video recorder. In this case the operator could by default offer mobile compliant versions of the programs that can be downloaded or streamed on demand to mobile devices. This approach requires a huge amount of storage space in order to store copies of all programs in every single channel available in IPTV. The problem certainly increases if additional mobile versions shall be provided. Whether such a media center-like realization can be profitable or not is though the matter of a business case calculation.

Generally, network-based PVR solutions promise to better meet the flexibility and performance requirements of dynamic ad replacement in pre-recorded content. In practice, the choice between home or network-based solutions for making TV recordings available to the mobile device of a consumer will be affected by the present recording concept (home PVR or nPVR) already realized in the IPTV network as the operator will certainly try to leverage the existing infrastructure. Since it is reasonable to assume that most IPTV operators already have rolled out STBs with home PVR functionality as part of the subscription, they will probably go for an arrangement as described above where the customer uses her home PVR to record TV programs but transcoding and ad insertion tasks are performed in the network using a network storage to provide the transcoded TV recordings.

Ad Detection and Replacement Opportunities
Once the TV recording scheduled by the user has been effectuated and the content has been transcoded to a format suitable for consumption on mobile devices, the next step in the use case process is to perform the detection and replacement of the original ad spot included in the content file. Potential opportunities to perform these tasks strongly depend on the availability of information about start and end points of advertising breaks within the recorded content.

The simplest solution would be to effectuate the ad insertion based on a time schedule in a similar manner as for example described in the context of the banner ad insertion described in section 4.2.3.1. The start and end time of the recording are determined through the scheduling of the user. Therefore, the Campaign Management of the targeted advertising system in principle only needs to know the exact scheduling of ad breaks in order to be able to initiate the ad replacement process. Though, as mentioned during the analysis of linear TV ad insertion in section 4.2.4.1 such a time-based method does not meet the requirements of seamless splicing necessary to avoid inacceptable interruptions in the content stream. Moreover, the operator would need to somehow obtain the ad break schedules belonging to each TV channel. As the TV stations will probably not give away such information without getting their share of the targeted advertising revenues, it seems reasonable to take a similar concept as was discussed in the context of linear TV ad insertion into consideration. The idea of this approach was that TV broadcasters insert cue tones into the content stream signaling avails for potential ad replacements. In exchange, the broadcaster participates in the revenues generated through ad spots inserted by the targeted advertising system of the operator. The complete ad replacement process could then be performed according to the analysis in section 4.2.4.1. Especially in the U.S., where cue tone triggered ad insertion is already wide spread, this approach promises synergy effects by leveraging potentially existing cooperations and ad splicing infrastructure.

In Europe, where ad marking of content streams by broadcasters is not yet common and thus no metadata about the time schedule of ad breaks in a channel is available, the targeted advertising system must implement a method allowing to analyze the content of the TV recording in order to detect ad spots. This process may be performed as part of the transcoding process or as an additional stage. Some research work on the opportunities to automatically detect commercials within TV broadcasts has already been done. Traditionally, there have been two main reasons for these efforts. On the one hand advertisers seek to identify and track when specific commercials are broadcasted. On the other hand there is the group of consumers who want to detect commercials for the purpose of eliminating them from their recordings. Interestingly, the goals of both groups are generally opposed to each other, but the underlying methods are the same and may be adopted for this application. Commercial segments within TV broadcasts have certain characteristics based on which detection algorithms can be developed [180]. Most early approaches aimed at leveraging the fact that ad breaks within TV programs can be recognized by a series of black video frames simultaneously accompanied by an audio silence that typically occur before and after each individual ad [13]. The analysis can be performed in either compressed [176] or uncompressed [118] domains. Another audio clue to the presence of commercials is the tendency of broadcasters to increase the volume level of the audio track during commercials. Also, some methods try to leverage the fact that video shots tend to have a shorter duration within commercials. To better capture viewer's attention commercials are typified by a high number of cuts between frames [180].

The most prevalent approach to detecting commercial parts in the broadcast leverages the fact that TV stations usually display a channel logo overlay in the corner of the screen during regular programming and then remove it in ad breaks. Logo detection implementations are typically based on the static character of the logo region in contrast to regions where typical program content appears. Hence, the most obvious approach for logo detection is to exploit pixel-wise differences between frames in order to extract stable pixels [158]. One possible implementation is to simply calculate the amount each pixel varies over the duration of recording. Another similar method is to calculate the maximum and minimum values for all pixels during the duration of the clip. Since pixels in the video will vary greatly, there will be a large distance between the maximum and minimum values. In both variants the pixels that lay in the logo may vary a little due to noise but will largely remain stable over time allowing to distinguish regular content from commercials [81]. Such approaches that are based on pixel comparison work well for opaque logos but are limited in case of transparent and animated logos. Therefore, another class of algorithms assumes that a logo exists if it is possible to find an area in the image with stable contours. The idea is to use time averaged frame tracking in order to emphasize the logos while blurring out the background. The emerging stable contours or edges are morphologically operated and converted to binary logo masks that have to meet certain predetermined criteria (e.g. the area of the binary mask must be over some threshold) in order to make sure that the detection process has concluded. As this approach focuses on the area containing the contours and not the contours themselves, it also applies to the case of animated and transparent logos [13, 177, 158].

While the above-mentioned detection approaches focus on general characteristics of ad spots (feature-based recognition), other methods attempt to identify individual commercials in the broadcast by matching them against spots the system already knows (recognition-based detection). However, this proceeding is very complex and expensive since it requires the maintenance of a video database of known commercials. As this use case does not focus on identifying single ad spots, recognition-based detection methods can be discarded [180]. Attention should be paid to the fact that no matter which of the introduced ad detection approaches is realized, there remains a risk that ad parts in the content stream are not detected correctly or with a time offset resulting in non-seamless splicing. Albeit some sources claim to achieve recognition rates of almost 100% [13, 177], solutions where the broadcaster inserts cue tones for later ad insertion are thus preferable.

Eventually, it has to be settled whether ad detection and replacement shall be realized as one logical step or not. This depends amongst others on the location where the ad detection is effectuated and on possibly intended further ad replacements later in time. If the process shall be performed within the home PVR and only once at the time the recording is transcoded, it is reasonable to detect and directly replace obsolete commercials by targeted ad spots. If transcoding and ad detection are realized network-based (through an nPVR or at least a network storage for uploads from the home PVR), it can make more sense for the operator himself to insert cue tones into the files at time points where advertising is detected in order to later replace the standard ads when the recording is downloaded to the mobile device. This provides a better flexibility in terms of continuous ad updates, especially if ad replacement shall be repeated in offline mode when the

TV recording has already found its way to the mobile device. Complementary online/offline ad replacement opportunities will be discussed below in more detail. Finally, it should be noted that the separation of ad detection and replacement not only guarantees most recent advertising. In contrast for example to linear TV ad insertion, where ad replacement is performed live and on the fly, the sequence of advertising and content parts is not ultimately fixed. This means that the inserted ad spots do not necessarily have to be of the same length as the original spot. In order to better adapt the recording to typical mobile consumption behavior, it is even imaginable to completely delete the original ad spots and instead frame the recorded content by targeted pre- and post-roll ads.

The Use Case Model
Until now the opportunities to make recorded TV content available on mobile devices and the different aspects concerning the detection and replacement of commercial spots originally included in the recording have been discussed on a more theoretical level. In the following, a use case model will be introduced in order to analyze the above-described options exemplarily. The recording and further processing of the TV content and the modalities of online/offline ad replacement will be analyzed in more detail subsequently to the use case description.

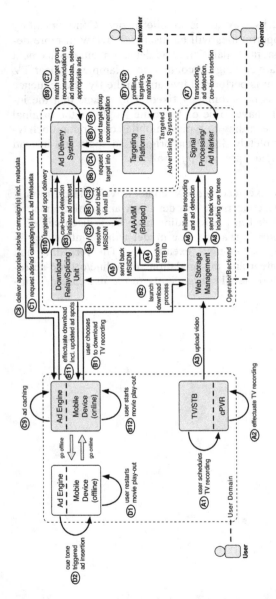

Figure 59: Overview dynamic ad replacement in pre-recorded content (source: own illustration)

Actors/Pre-Conditions/Post-Conditions

See basic definitions at the beginning of the IPTV, Web, and mobile use case sections and descriptions in previous use cases, especially sections 4.2.4.1 (Linear TV Ad Insertion) and 4.4.1 (Triple-Play scenario). Additional or modified functionalities of use case elements are defined as follows.

Additional Actor Description

TV/STB: incorporates home PVR (cPVR) capabilities for live TV recordings. STB provides EPG functionality allowing to browse TV programming and directly select shows for recording on the integrated cPVR. While scheduling the recording the user may activate an option to make the recorded content available to her mobile device.

Web Storage Management: organizes upload of recorded TV content that shall be made available for mobile consumption. This includes management of the transcoding to a mobile compliant format and of the ad detection process. The Web Storage Management possesses an interface to the AAA/IdM in order to resolve the ID of the STB the upload originates from into the corresponding MSISDN, which is used as identifier for the transcoded and ad marked videos in the Web Storage.

Signal Processing/Ad Marker: performs transcoding of the recorded IPTV content to a format with less resolution and bit rate, which is more suitable for the mobile environment. The ad marking functionality comprises a channel logo-based ad detection analysis. As a result the transcoded files include an in-stream trigger separating ad blocks from regular content.

AAA/IdM: bridged authentication and identity management systems. Besides enabling tracking of user actions across several converged ICT channels as described in the previous use case scenario, in this use case the identity tree of the IdM system is particularly used to resolve STB IDs, MSISDN and virtual IDs in order to link a user's STB to her Mobile Device.

Download Relay/Splicing Unit: intercepts the download stream from Web storage to Mobile Device in order to replace the original ad parts. Ad insertion functionality is similar to the Splicing Unit in the linear TV ad insertion case. When detecting splicing points in the video file, the unit requests targeted ads from the Ad Delivery System that are then spliced into the transcoded recording.

Targeting Platform: consists of Profiling Engine and Targeting Intelligence incorporating same tracking, profiling and matching functionalities across different ICT channels as described in the previous use case. For simplicity reasons the two units are aggregated and the tracking process is not depicted explicitly, albeit respective actions are certainly performed.

Ad Delivery System: combines functionalities of Campaign Management and Ad Server as described in the previous use case including an interface to the AAA/IdM. In addition, the Ad Delivery System provides an interface to the Ad Engine on the mobile device enabling the delivery of ads and ad campaigns including ad metadata for future ad replacement directly within the Mobile Device. In return, ad metrics generated from user interaction with ads are collected for updating user profiles and for reporting/billing purposes.

Mobile Device: provides a client application allowing to connect to the operator's Web storage in order to download and watch the transcoded TV recording including targeted ads that have been inserted during the download. In order to keep the ads within the recording updated, the client application features splicing capabilities allowing to detect cue-tones and to insert updated ads. Therefore, the Mobile Device incorporates an Ad Engine, which is connected to the Ad Delivery System and, either periodically or upon explicit request, downloads new, targeted ad spots or even ad campaigns including respective metadata and policies. The Ad Engine further incorporates ad selection capabilities allowing to choose matching ads from the local cache.

Additional Pre-Conditions
STB: IPTV middleware must support upload of local recordings to Web storage and provide a respective check box option when the user schedules a TV recording.

Ad Delivery System: must provide interface for communication with the Ad Engine installed on the Mobile Device.

Mobile Device: Mobile video application used for connection to Web storage has to implement interface to Ad Engine and must possess ad splicing functionality.

Additional Post-Conditions
Download Relay/Splicing Unit: has intercepted download stream for ad splicing purposes in order to update commercials originally included in the TV recording by targeted spots.

Mobile Device: Transcoded TV recording has been played directly after the download including targeted ad spots inserted in the network. When video was replayed later in time, the client software has performed local ad substitution based on local ad selection realized by the Ad Engine. Ad metrics concerning user's ad interaction have been reported to the Ad Delivery System for further analysis.

Use Case Flow
The use case flow is split up into activities belonging to the different phases of the scenario: TV recording and processing = A, ad replacement and download to

mobile = B, ad delivery to mobile and caching = C, on-mobile ad replacement = D. For reasons of simplicity less relevant parts of the flows are shortened.

TV Recording and Processing (A Numbers)

A1. User browses EPG and selects desired TV program for recording. As she will be away for two weeks she activates the "make available to my mobile device" check box.

A2. Home PVR integrated in the STB records TV program according to the schedule.

A3. As soon as the recording is finished the file upload to the Web storage in the operator's backend is initiated.

A4. – A5. Web Storage Management resolves the ID of the uploading STB into the corresponding MSISDN of the user's mobile phone, which is used as identifier to store the recording.

A6. Web Storage Management initiates transcoding of the TV recording to a less resource intensive format and the ad detection process.

A7. Signal Processing/Ad Marker unit effectuates transcoding to a mobile compliant format with less resolution and lower bit rate. In a next step, the unit performs channel logo-based ad detection and inserts cue-tones serving as an in-stream trigger for ad notification.

A8. The transcoded and ad marked video file is sent back to the Web storage and archived for mobile access by the user.

Ad Replacement and Download to Mobile Device (B Numbers)

B1. Following the use case plot, the user is now away from home for a week, while meanwhile the TV recording has been effectuated and the transcoded and ad marked file is ready for download. The user opens a client application on her Mobile Device allowing to connect to the Web storage. She initiates the file download.

B2. Web Storage Management recognizes the user's MSISDN transmitted with client request and launches download process.

B3. Download Relay/Splicing Unit intercepts download stream and analyzes video file for in-stream cue tones signaling commercials. When a cue-tone is detected the Download Relay/Splicing Unit triggers the ad replacement process by requesting the Ad Delivery System.

B4. – B5. Ad Delivery System resolves MSISDN of user into corresponding virtual identity by requesting the AAA/IdM unit. This is necessary as the Targeting Platform only uses the virtual identity.

B6. Ad Delivery System requests target group information from Targeting Platform.

B7. Targeting Platform analyzes user profile and matches appropriate target group attributes.

B8. Target group recommendations are sent back to the Ad Delivery System.

B9. Ad Delivery System matches target group recommendation, content and context information to ad metadata and campaign policies, and selects appropriate ad spot.

B10. Targeted ad spot is delivered to Download Relay/Splicing Unit, which inserts it into the video file replacing the original TV commercial.

B11. Video file including targeted ads is finally downloaded to Mobile Device.

B12. User starts watching video in the client software.

Ad Delivery to Mobile and Caching (C Numbers)

C1. In order to be able to perform ad replacement in the local content or when no online connection is available, the Ad Engine acquires a series of targeted ads for local caching. Therefore, it periodically or explicitly upon the request of a mobile app directs a request for ads/ad campaign(s) and corresponding metadata towards the Ad Delivery System when the device is online. At the same time, ad metrics generated from user interaction with ads are reported to the Ad Delivery System.

C2. – C7. See steps B4. – B9.

C8. – C9. Targeted ads or ad campaign(s) including corresponding ad metadata and campaign policies are delivered to the Ad Engine for local caching.

On-Mobile Ad Replacement (D Numbers)

D1. According to the use case scenario the user replays the video after a while. In order to provide the user with most recent advertising, the current ad spots integrated in the video file must be replaced.

D2. Ad insertion in local content is better performed locally as this implies that the process is independent of an online connection and network bottlenecks. The video client detects splicing points/cue-tones in the video stream and initiates the local ad replacement. The Ad Engine takes over the functionality of the Ad Delivery System and selects ads from its cache. Possibly existing local personalization and context information is used to find the most appropriate ads for insertion (see below for a more detailed description of the Ad Engine concept).

Detailed View on Recording and Further Processing of TV Content

As has already been described, it is reasonable to assume that most of today's IPTV line-ups include STBs with home PVR, which is why the use case model follows the approach to store user's TV recordings locally. Once recorded, programs can however be automatically uploaded to a Web Storage in order to enable mobile consumption. When scheduling the TV recording, the user thus has the option to make the recording available for viewing on her mobile phone, e.g. by checking a respective box. Transcoding to a mobile compliant video format is realized using the more powerful infrastructure residing in the operator's backend. It should though be noted that transcoding in the network implies the upload of recorded content in original size thus consuming a lot of bandwidth. Therefore, the operator might consider implementing a transcoding algorithm into the STB client software. As it cannot be assumed that the recorded content already comprises cue tones inserted by the operator, the ad detection process is performed based on a channel logo detection approach by a Signal Processing unit in the network. The algorithm shall be able to separate ad blocks from regular content and mark the ad parts e.g. by inserting SCTE 35 compliant cue tones (compare section 4.2.4.1). These cue tones are supposed to serve as an in-stream trigger for the ad replacement, first when the transcoded recording is downloaded to the Mobile Device, and later every time the content is watched (see below). The following illustration depicts a more detailed view on the respective processes. As the annotations are largely self-explaining a detailed flow description is considered dispensable at this point.

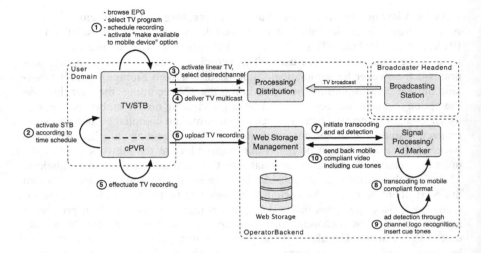

Figure 60: Detailed view on recording/transcoding/ad detection part (source: own illustration)

Detailed View on Modalities of Online/Offline Ad Replacement

As mentioned above the use case scenario comprises two different situations where ads must be inserted into the TV recording. The first replacement takes place when the user decides to download the transcoded file from the Web Storage. In principle, ads could also be replaced for the first time directly after the upload. However, as the user will actually not watch the transcoded video until it has been downloaded to the Mobile Device, it makes more sense to perform the replacement at that time. From a technical point of view, this ad insertion process is similar to the proceeding in the linear TV ad insertion use case described in section 4.2.4.1 for which reason it can be basically referred to the respective analysis. As a difference in this case, the transcoded file is not watched as a live stream but rather downloaded completely before consuming. This is due to the assumption that the user shall also be able to watch the TV show, when the Mobile Device has no permanent online connection making the scenario adaptable for classic iPod-like use cases. However, this does not change anything in the way the splicing is performed technically and a streaming functionality could be added supplementary. As already described above the splicing unit could though also be configured to cut off the entire original ad block and instead insert pre-roll and post-roll ads in order to better suit typical mobile consumption patterns. In this case the technical realization would be a combination of the splicing technology presented in the linear TV ad insertion scenario, used to detect and completely remove original commercials, and the playlist approach described in the context of VoD ad insertion in section 4.2.4.2. A detailed discussion of such modifications is out of scope. In the following, it is assumed that the file is downloaded completely before watching.

To keep the advertising the user consumes up-to-date the use case scenario also includes the approach to replace ads locally on the Mobile Device. Such functionality makes sense for two main reasons. First, it enables ad replacement on devices even if they are not permanently connected to the Internet. Second, video streaming requires a lot of bandwidth and due to the fact that mobile connections are inherently unreliable especially if the user is moving, the live streaming of inserted ads may result in undesirable interruptions during the video consumption. Therefore, the use case implements a local Ad Engine, which resides within the Mobile Device and interacts on the one hand with the client application requesting ad delivery and on the other hand with the Ad Delivery System in the network in order to keep the local ad cache updated and report ad metrics. The Ad Engine concept has already been introduced in the context of on-device advertising in section 4.3.5 and can be realized based on the OMA Mobile Advertising (MobAd) enabler architecture [151]. The goal of this approach is to provide a standardized software function allowing multiple mobile applications installed on the Mobile Device to request ad delivery, track user actions, and report ad interaction. The implementation of a MobAd compliant mobile advertising solution thus would enable a holistic mobile advertising approach providing targeted advertising features beyond the walled garden of the use case specific video client application.

Implementation of the MobAd Enabler Architecture
The objective of the MobAd enabler architecture is to define network-side and device-side MobAd enabler components, the interfaces between them, and the interfaces exposed by those components to some entities that rely on MobAd enabler including device-side Ad Apps as well as network-side Service Provider (SP) Apps [151]. This means that the MobAd concept not only standardizes device-side elements of a targeted advertising infrastructure, but also takes into account components residing in the network. As will become obvious, the MobAd architecture coincides with already described considerations concerning network-based targeted advertising. The following illustration depicts the MobAd architecture enhanced with external Contextualization and Personalization Resources (C&PR) that are though not part of the actual MobAd definition. Basic functional elements and interfaces are described below, whereas the information is largely aggregated from the Mobile Advertising Architecture [151] and Mobile Advertising Requirements [152] documents.

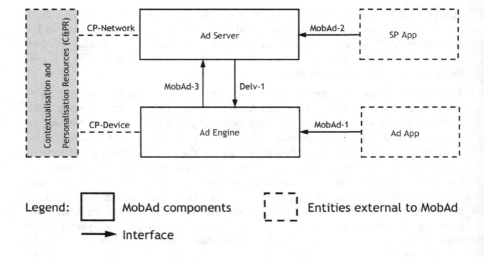

Figure 61: MobAd architecture diagram enhanced with C&PR (source: [151])

The MobAd enabler addresses two general targeted advertising models:

- Ad App/Ad Engine/Ad Server model (device-based ad insertion)
- SP App/Ad Server model (network-based ad insertion)

The Ad Server component resides in the network (outside the device) and performs ad selection, ad delivery, ad metrics data handling, and user/service data management functions. Ad selection comprises the selection of the most appropriate ads/ad campaigns using contextualization and personalization, ad metadata, and applicable MobAd rules (service provider's rules related to e.g. ad prefetching and caching policies). The ad delivery function delivers ads/ad campaigns or references (e.g. via Uniform Resource Locator, URL) including ad metadata to the Ad Engine and SP Apps. Ad metrics data handling includes the collection of ad impressions and user actions with ads from the SP App and the Ad Engine. These ad metrics data are then processed for billing the advertiser and enhancing user profiles for improving future ad selection. Finally, the user/service data management function handles data delivered from C&P Resources and manages MobAd rules as well as ads and ad metadata.

The Ad Engine resides on the device and performs ad acquisition and delivery, ad selection, ad metrics data handling, and user/service/device data handling functions. As is obvious the Ad Engine thus covers similar tasks as the Ad Server but effectuates its work within the Mobile Device. Therefore, the ad acquisition and delivery function consists of receiving ad requests from Ad Apps, obtaining ads/ad campaigns including ad metadata from the Ad Server, caching ads received from the Ad Server, updating/deleting ads previously received from the Ad Server, and delivering the selected ads to Ad Apps. Ad acquisition from the Ad Server can be effectuated in pull, push, or broadcast mode. Ad selection basically comprises the same functions as described in the context of the Ad Server. The Ad Engine's cache is the primary source of the ads, whereas under certain conditions, the Ad Engine can request additional ads directly from the Ad Server. Ad metrics data are received from Ad Apps, merged with other metrics-related information collected by the Ad Engine, and forwarded to the Ad Server for further reporting. The user/service data handling function as described above is enhanced by the capability to process static and dynamic device-related information as e.g. the device resource threshold.

The above illustration further depicts two entities that are actually external to the MobAd enabler. The SP App is an ad enabled network application executed in the service provider environment. This can be an SMSC, a Web portal or as in this use case the Splicing Unit. It interacts with the MobAd enabler, requests ads/ad campaigns from the Ad Server, and embeds them into the content that is provided to the user. In addition, it records ad metrics data and reports them to the Ad Server. In contrast, the Ad App resides on the Mobile Device and requests and receives ads from the Ad Engine in order to present them to the user. Moreover, it reports ad metrics data back to the Ad Engine. Examples for an Ad App include gaming apps, Web browsers, or as in this use case the mobile video client software.

In order to enable communication between the above-described four components, the MobAd enabler architecture includes four interfaces MobAd-1, MobAd-2, MobAd-3, and Delv-1. MobAd-1 is an interface exposed by the Ad Engine to the Ad App for requesting and obtaining ads and reporting ad metrics data. Correspondingly, the MobAd-2 interface connects the Ad Server to the SP App enabling similar communication opportunities but on the network-side. The MobAd-3 interface is used by the Ad Engine to request ads/ad campaigns and ad metadata from the Ad Server for local caching on the Mobile Device. In return, the Ad Server may communicate ad deletion information and MobAd rules to the Ad Engine. The Delv-1 interface is optional and can be implemented to enable push/broadcast delivery scenarios.

As mentioned the MobAd enabler exposes reference points to C&P Resources, which are necessary to realize targeting and improve the ad selection process. As described in section 2.1.2 user information can be considered as formed by two sets of data: static user profile information and the dynamic user context. User profile information are basically user preferences such as demographics and interests aggregated in profiles and tracked from user actions as described in all above use cases. User context data describe the current general status/the environment of the user and include for example location and presence information. C&P Resources may reside either in the service provider domain or on the device and can be accessed by both the Ad Server and the Ad Engine. The above illustration of the MobAd architecture comprises CP-Network as a reference point between the Ad Server and all external C&P Resources that may be accessed by an Ad Server implementation. Correspondingly, CP-Device refers to all C&P Resources accessible by an Ad Engine implementation. In this use case, the Targeting Platform can be considered to be an external Personalization Resource, which is accessed by the Ad Server through a CP-Network reference point. Examples for Contextualization Resources include location data stemming from the HLR of a GSM network respectively a location server as described in section 4.3.4.2 made available through the CP-Network reference point, or also on-device GPS functionality that may be accessed via the CP-Device reference point. The OMA has defined some enablers that may serve as Contextualization Resources as for example SIMPLE (presence status, type of place, activity, mood), MLS and SUPL (current location), UAProf (device capabilities, see section 4.3.3), DPE (device capabilities, phone profile) [152, 151]. However, the C&P reference points are not specified in the MobAd enabler standard and thus the use of OMA C&P enablers is not mandatory. The targeting opportunities that emerge from contextualization are tremendous. One possible use case example would be to exploit a user's GPS data not only for providing advertising targeted on her location but also take into account her current traveling speed. This might result in presenting the user with an advertisement e.g. for a railway ticket, after she has traveled at high speed on a highway and suddenly finds herself in a traffic jam (compare also section 5.3.5 on context-aware recommender systems).

As the MobAd enabler standard has only been released in 2009 there are not yet any reference implementations available. However, the ETSI working group Telecoms & Internet converged Services & Protocols for Advanced Networks (TISPAN) has already integrated the specification into their draft on IMS-based IPTV architecture showing up possible implementation opportunities for targeted advertising within mobile TV services [69]. As mentioned above, the MobAd architecture coincides with the targeted advertising concepts developed in this book. The following illustration depicts a subsumption of architectural elements introduced in the above use case model under the MobAd enabler concept.

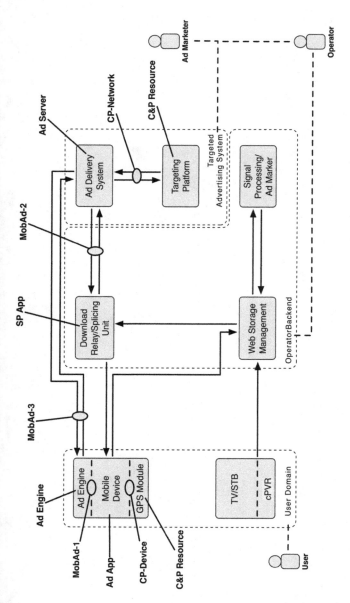

Figure 62: Use case model and corresponding MobAd functions (bold)/interfaces (circles) (source: own illustration)

5 Analysis of Key Building Blocks in Targeted Advertising Technologies

The analysis of the different use case scenarios in the Web, in IPTV, and in the mobile environment has revealed that the actual targeted advertising process relies on some typical core functionalities that can be found in almost each case. This includes the Profiling Unit and the Targeting and Recommendation Units that are merged to the Targeting Intelligence in the above cases, as well as the Campaign Management and the Ad Server.

In the following section the tasks of these key elements will be examined closer in order to give a good understanding of the involved logical units, their interconnection, and the interaction within the framework. As has become obvious in the technical descriptions above, the user identity management is a critical factor because user identification is needed to realize targeting and will thus be discussed in the subsequent section. Finally, the analysis of key building blocks in targeted advertising closes with an introduction to common and state-of-the-art recommendation technologies.

5.1 Generic Description of a Targeted Advertising Platform

Targeted advertising technologies in the Web are very sophisticated and comprehensive information about architecture and processes are available. Therefore, the following analysis will be based on the underlying technologies of the T-Online Web scenario i.e. the Wunderloop targeting platform[39]. However, the description will abstract from the Web as far as possible in order to develop a more generic targeted advertising framework. The goal is to provide a general overview of major logical units and processes inside a targeted advertising platform that can be applied in various scenarios in the ICT space. Major input for this section is taken from [225] and [208].

---

[39] As already mentioned in section 4.3.4.2 Wunderloop was acquired by AudienceScience and Wunderloop's targeting technology was integrated into AudienceScience's targeting solution [220]. Deutsche Telekom is now cooporating with AudienceScience [17]. The research for this work was based on the Wunderloop system and thus the following analyses will refer to the Wunderloop targeting solution.

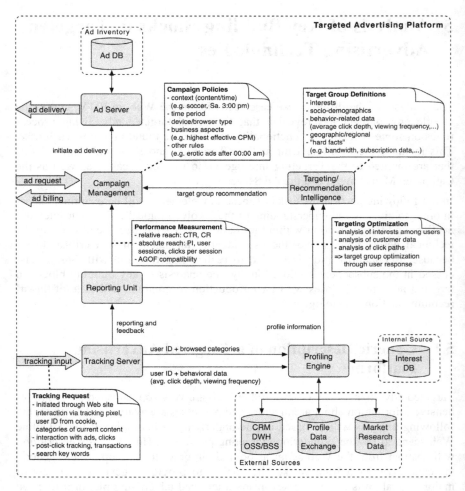

Figure 63: Generic targeted advertising platform (source: own illustration)

5.1.1 Content Categorization and Tracking

Before user behavior can be tracked a way must be found that allows categorizing the content a user consumes. This step is necessary to enable the targeting system of recognizing the user's interests. In the case of Web advertising, this means that every single page of a Web presence has to be classified according to predefined categories. These categories can for example include sports, traveling, computer,... The categorization process is usually completed automatically and uses special keywords belonging to the categories and which appear within a Web page. In browser-based IPTV and mobile scenarios, a content categorization can be realized similar to the Web. It is e.g. imaginable to use EPG metadata to describe the content of EPG pages a user is interested in. In scenarios like ad splicing the TV consumption behavior is determined according to the viewed content again represented by EPG metadata. The point is that tracking of user behavior requires predefined categories content can belong to, in order to generate consistent user information.

The actual targeting process begins with the tracking of user interests by a Tracking Server. Initiated by user interactions the server must record the content categories of browsed websites and collect behavioral data. Correspondingly, the user's mobile browsing or TV watching behavior has to be tracked. Therefore, the user device must be able to launch a request towards the Tracking Server. In the Web case the request is launched via a tracking pixel (= Web bug, Web beacon) [192] that is integrated in the code of the current website. This pixel is a 1x1 image whose address links to the Tracking Server and thus initiates tracking. In other scenarios the tracking request may be triggered directly by user actions like channel switching events in linear TV. In each case, the request must include a user ID e.g. stored in a cookie and information about the actual event. Further tracking requests can be initiated due to ad interaction or even transactions.

5.1.2 Profile Generation and Enrichment

Once the Tracking Server receives a tracking request, the user ID and the categories of the browsed websites, respectively meta information about consumed media content, are forwarded to the Profiling Engine. According to these classifications the Profiling Engine assigns interest characteristics to the user and stores the information in the interest database. The user interest profile is further improved by behavioral data like the click depth and viewing frequency. This information can be used to evaluate and weigh the significance of the user's current consumption behavior comparing it to historical data. In the Wunderloop system this feature is called "relevancy weighting". In IPTV the system could measure and evaluate the time a user watches a special movie or TV show, in order to derive the relevancy of its content and include this information into the profile.

In order to improve quality, the interest profile can be enriched by specific pseudonymized CRM data from the operator's subscriber database. Profile data can also be exchanged within a partner network as long as the data is anonymized (see section 6.2.2). In addition, market research data is used to predict missing information and fill gaps in the user profile. These secondary data sources help to improve the profile quality by incorporating additional user information like "hard facts" about operator products used by the customer (DSL connection type, bandwidth,...) and sociodemographic characteristics (gender, age, region,...). The type and availability of such secondary data sources depend on the current use case scenario. In IPTV, the Profiling Engine may for example be connected to OSS/BSS systems in order to integrate user subscription data or even information about VoD usage.

5.1.3 Targeting and Recommendation

The actual recommendation process requires user profiles on the one hand and items or elements, which are compared to the user profiles on the other. These recommendation items can be the single ads themselves. But usually they are represented by target groups that are created based on selected user attributes and serve as a basis for the ad selection. These target groups may include the users' interests, sociodemographics, or behavior-related data that can be linked together in order to generate trait combinations. The target group definitions can be simple (e.g. target group 1: "mystery movies = true OR sci-fi movies = true") or more complex (e.g. target group 2: "male = true AND age 18-24 = true AND lifestyle affinity = true").

The system matches the user profile to the interest and behavioral pattern of the target groups and computes a recommendation that is provided to the Campaign Management. In common Web scenarios, this is realized using a recommendation cookie stored in the user device that can be accessed by the Campaign Management. In other cases where cookies are not supported, the Campaign Management may directly request the recommendation information when a targeted advertisement is about to be selected.

The underlying technology of this recommendation process is based on Content-Based (CB) filtering methods using content metadata for matchmaking.[40] In addition, feedback about user reactions towards special advertisements can also be used to integrate Collaborative Filtering (CF) techniques into the recommendation process. Such information about user preferences can be collected and stored as ratings of the target group that yielded the delivery of the ad the user was interested in. Hence, some kind of hybrid recommender algorithm may be applied to recommend a target group to a user not only based on her interests (CB approach), but also on the ratings/preferences of similar users (CF approach).

---

[40] For an overview on recommendation technologies please see section 5.3.

5.1.4 Campaign Management and Ad Selection

It has to be realized that in the generic case described here, recommendation and actual ad selection are two subsequent steps that are realized by two distinct logical units. In practice, these processes may be implemented in one ore two systems. However, the important thing to notice at this point is the fact that besides the targeting of user interests and behavior realized by the Targeting and Recommendation Intelligence, several additional rules must be incorporated into the final ad selection. Here, this is the task of the Campaign Management.

The actual ad delivery is initiated by an ad request that is received by the Campaign Management. In the Web scenario this process is triggered by an ad link integrated in the Web page. In other cases other triggering events signaling an ad opportunity are possible. The Campaign Management may even have its own time schedule according to which the ad delivery is launched.

In either case the Campaign Management selects appropriate ads according to the target group recommendations as well as to the policies of the campaigns that are managed by the system. First of all, this includes the classic content or context targeting meaning that an ad agency or advertiser has booked ad space in the context of special topics, e.g. ads that shall be displayed on lifestyle associated websites. In addition, the time context is being considered. This means that a sports article advertiser may choose to have his ads delivered only in the context of the soccer sports pages on Saturdays during the Bundesliga games. The Campaign Management can also consider technical information about the device type, e.g. PC or mobile, or browser type. This feature is especially interesting for all mobile scenarios as mobile devices are very divergent. Finally, the Campaign Management includes business and legal rules into its ad selection. If two ads from different advertisers both fit equally concerning other criteria, the system will choose the ad that delivers the highest possible effective Cost Per Mille (CPM) value. An example for a legally induced rule would be that ads with adult focus must not be delivered before 12:00 am.

Once the Campaign Management has selected the ads that have to be delivered, it initiates the actual delivery process through the Ad Server.

5.1.5 Reporting and Feedback

According to the general personalization process depicted in section 2.1.1, targeted advertising can be understood as a circle of tracking, profiling, matching and ad delivery that is being closed by user interaction with the advertising media. User reactions are then tracked again and the circle restarts.

User interaction data that is recorded by the Tracking Server is not only used to update user profiles. An important additional step is to measure and analyze data about user feedback for reporting purposes. This includes a performance measurement to evaluate the efficiency of ad campaigns as well as an optimization of the actual targeting process.

The purpose of performance measurement is to determine the success of distinct ad campaigns. This comprises the absolute and relative reach of advertising messages. Absolute performance measures are e.g. in the Web case Page Impressions (PI), click rates, the number of user sessions, and the average rate of clicks per session. Indexes that represent the relative performance are the Click-Through-Rate (CTR, share of clicks on an ad banner in relation to the number of displays) or the Conversion Rate (CR, share of users buying a product after clicking on an ad banner, monitored through so-called "post-click tracking"). In other use case scenarios, similar measures must be defined that allow drawing conclusions about ad efficiency. These results are used to report the success of distinct campaigns to the advertising customer and to initiate the billing process. For each campaign the generated revenues are calculated. Finally, ad campaigns are optimized to further improve their success.

Feedback data about user interaction can also be used to control and optimize the targeting process. As the targeting platform can track the interests and behavior of all users consuming the offered services, it is possible to aggregate the information and create a general overview about user preferences. Additional information like customer data from CRM systems and typical click paths of website visitors can be integrated for further improvement. An analysis of these insights can be used to optimize the targeting and recommendation process. Target groups may be adapted to recent developments and new groups can be defined if the monitored data reveals new tendencies about content preferences. An example would be to redefine a target group according to recent browsing behavior of users that in the past typically have received recommendations for this group. The targeting system thus learns from the interests and behavior of each single user.

5.1.6 General Implications for Targeted Advertising Implementations

The targeted advertising framework introduced above describes the logical steps and units that typically occur in targeted advertising systems. Albeit the concept is derived from the Web environment, the basic ideas of the architecture are applicable in IPTV and mobile scenarios. Essentially, the single steps of the personalization process illustrated in section 2.1.1 are mapped on logical subsystems whose tasks have been discussed in detail.

Concerning the subdivision into these units and their concrete functionality, there are generally different realization possibilities. In each case, it is important to notice that targeted advertising does not only comprise the personalization according to user interests and behavior. The ad selection process includes additional rules that have to be considered when talking about targeting, e.g. additional targeting methods (time, device,...) and business considerations that are needed for the actual ad selection.

Depending on the respective allocation of these tasks, the logical units involved in the targeted advertising process may be part of integrated systems. In the Wunderloop based Web scenario, the Tracking Server and the Profiling Unit are for example integrated with the Targeting Intelligence, while the Ad Server is part of the system that realizes the Campaign Management. Reporting functionality is typically needed in several points in the system. Therefore, it makes sense to have one central statistics unit that provides reporting and feedback functionality to all systems that need this information.

The breakdown of the different steps in the targeting process into several units usually correlates with the recommendation methodology applied by the targeting solution. This means that the recommendation technologies, which shall be implemented in the targeting system, are reflected by the system layout. The concept of matching a user interest profile to a target group specification based on metadata about the content of the recommendation item stems from CB filtering and is realized by the Targeting and Recommendation intelligence. The here-described generic architecture follows a hybrid recommendation approach. Hence, the Targeting and Recommendation Intelligence also integrates CF technology into the recommendation process treating the users' reactions to ads like ratings that represent their preferences. Both technologies can be combined in different ways (see section 5.3.4). Depending on whether the applied hybrid approach uses CB and CF methods simultaneously or in a sequence, the realization may comprise one integrated unit as illustrated above or two different systems. The actual ad selection and application of further targeting rules (e.g. time, device,...) into the targeting process takes place in the Campaign Management. This method can be understood as a kind of contextual post-filtering as described in section 5.3.5 and is applied in a sequence after the main recommendation methods.

Instead of this sequential processing, an integrated targeting approach realizing the whole process in one unit may be considered. Such a system can potentially achieve a better targeting quality as it incorporates several aspects all at once. On the other hand, the modular approach of the here-described framework allows combining different solutions that can be customized according to specific needs (see section 5.3.5 for more information on context-aware recommender systems).

5.2 Identity Management Issues

As became obvious in the use case discussions, one of the crucial points in targeted advertising is Identity Management (IdM). Especially the analysis of converged advertising has shown that a multi-channel operator who wants to realize a targeted advertising platform serving Web, IPTV, and mobile environments simultaneously faces the challenge of integrating multiple user identities and profile databases.

IdM is thus an enabler technology for targeted advertising in converged scenarios and needed to manage and analyze real-time dynamic data of individual customers. In this context IdM can be defined as the capability to resolve and map unidentified customer data to an existing customer record using unique identification information [46]. However, enabling targeted advertising is certainly only one possible scenario for IdM systems. Besides this potential application IdM plays an important role in so-called Single-Sign On (SSO) scenarios in the Web environment, where a user logs in once and is seamlessly authenticated when navigating to another site, respectively accessing other resources and services across multiple identity domains supporting the same IdM technology [119, 80]. IdM thus facilitates the exchange of data between 3rd parties. As will be shown this context opens up additional business opportunities for Telco operators, as they can leverage their carrier unique assets (e.g. subscriber data, presence, location information) by positioning themselves as identity provider across multiple channels. However, such scenarios are controversial due to regulatory and privacy concerns.

Historically, IdM systems are closely related to directory services that store, organize, and provide a centralized access to all kinds of network related data. Different network resources like users, devices, and services are considered objects on a directory server thus providing a unified view of the different network components and their relations. Important standards in this field are the X.500 and the Lightweight Directory Access Protocol (LDAP) specifications, whereas the latter is the most common method for querying directories as it is based on the TCP/IP protocol stack. Today's IdM systems are usually realized as metadirectory services that aggregate data from different directory sources and databases and synchronize the information into one or more LDAP-based directory servers in order to enable user provisioning for different applications. IdM systems are often connected to the so-called access management that authorizes service access resulting in integrated Identity and Access Management (IAM) solutions, which are needed for example for enabling SSO scenarios (for an overview on basic IdM architecture compare [79]).

Eventually, it should be noted that there exist many different formal definitions and concepts of IdM differing according to the application context [82]. In order to provide a better understanding of the terms identity and IdM a short general introduction to these topics will be given in the next subsections. This is followed by an examination of what IdM means for Telco operators and which application scenarios exist. Finally, the role of IdM in the context of targeted advertising will be analyzed closer.

5.2.1 Identity and Related Concepts

Before analyzing how to manage and use identity in the context of computer systems or telecommunication networks, it makes sense to consider what identity is and how it can be used. In addition, some further identity related terminology will be explained in the following.

Identity is a unique representation of a real world entity (user/subscriber, user device, group, organization, service provider) within a specific application domain respectively a specific context. The context might be local (within a department), corporate (within an enterprise), national, or global. A single identity can usually not be associated with more than one entity. However, shared identities may exist, for example in the case of a family identity that corresponds to several people in a family unit. From the service provider's perspective this means dealing with one real world entity (the family or e.g. in IPTV the household) and not with multiple individuals. A person may have multiple identities in a given context. As an example, an employee often has different identities for payroll systems, email systems, and other legacy line-of-business applications [191, 106].

An identity consists of a set of characteristics and attributes that can have various properties. Some of these associations might be formal, mostly permanent relationships or informal, changing affiliations, self-selected or issued by an authority, suitable for human interpretation or only by computers. This depends on the type of real world entity being identified. Examples include age, presence status, and location. An attribute that uniquely identifies the identity within a defined scope is called identifier. Possible examples are MSISDN, email address, account number. A name space of unique identifiers builds an identity domain allowing one-to-one relationships between identities and identifiers. In common language the terms identity and identifier are often used synonymously. It should be noted that a pseudonym might be used as unique identifier where only the party that assigned the pseudonym knows the real world identity. Such an approach could be interesting in a targeted advertising scenario that includes an external service provider for ad delivery [191, 105, 106]. The relationship between entities, identities, and attributes is depicted below.

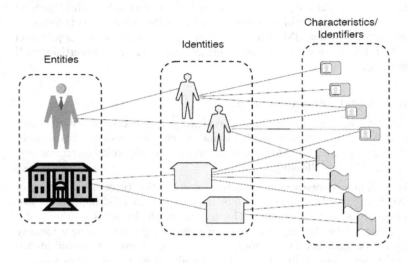

Figure 64: Relationship of entities, identities, and attributes (source: [105])

As mentioned there is currently no international agreement on the definition of the terms identity and IdM, which is due to the evolving application scenarios of IdM systems. Attempting to find the least common denominator one can define digital identity as information about an entity, which results from the digital codification of characteristics and attributes in a way that is suitable for processing by computer systems and that is sufficient to identify that entity in a particular context. IdM thus is the combination of technologies and practices for representing and recognizing entities as digital identities, allowing to provide identity-based access control to systems and resources in accordance with established policies [106, 82].

5.2.2 Description of Identity Management Models

After having defined the basic IdM terminology and concepts in the previous subsection, now the most important IdM models will be introduced in order to provide an overview of classic and emerging IdM architectures. The description includes the silo model that is implemented in most legacy systems, the SSO driven centralized and decentralized models, and finally the recently emerging user-centric IdM concept. The diagrams and explanations represent a high abstraction level in the sense that actual communication protocols are omitted. However, the depiction shows the most important aspects covering the management of identifiers and authentication tokens, indicating Identity Providers (IdPs), authentication providers, and places where authentication takes place [106].

5.2.2.1 Isolated Silo Identity Management Model

In most legacy IdM implementations the Service Provider (SP) acts himself as IdP meaning that he manages the name space and authentication tokens for all his users. Users are authenticated based on their identifier token pairs during service access. Each user is provided with separate identifiers and credentials (e.g. passwords) from each SP she transacts with. SPs may be actors within the organizational structure of one company or 3rd party providers. The advantage of this model is that it is easy to deploy, as an integration of IdM infrastructure in the respective service domains does not take place. However, the implementation of an isolated IdM in each service has the disadvantage that an increasing number of services leads to an identity overload and a decreasing usability, as the user has to memorize passwords for each service [106]. The silo model can be transferred to typical non-convergent Telco scenarios where operators provide services in different channels that are operated separately.

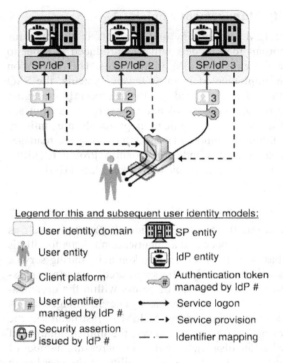

Figure 65: Silo IdM model and legend (also applies for following illustrations) (source: [106])

5.2.2.2   Centralized Identity Management Model

In a centralized identity model a single authority manages the name space, issues authentication tokens, and authenticates users during service access. This central authority then sends a security assertion to the SP, either directly or indirectly via the client machine, in order to perform an automated authentication enabling a classic SSO experience. Centralized IdM solutions provide a good usability and work especially well in closed networks where multiple SPs are managed by the same organization such as in large companies where the IdP and the SPs are governed by the same authority under a single policy. The disadvantage of a centralized IdM approach is that it is hardly applicable in open environments where SPs are not governed by a common policy and authority. Centralized IdM is for example implemented in Kerberos[41]-based authentication networks like the Microsoft Active Directory Services (ADS). As an example for a centralized IdM in the Internet Microsoft's Passport[42] authentication service was introduced in 1999 that has meanwhile been renamed to Windows Live ID. However, the market reaction was negative, as SPs did not accept Microsoft as the sole IdP on the Internet and users were very hesitant in entrusting Microsoft to centrally hold their personal information such as credit card numbers that should be made available to collaborating SPs [106].

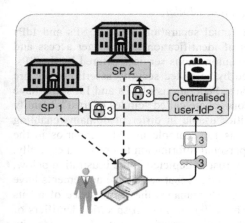

Figure 66: Centralized user identity model (source: [106])

As a reaction to the failure of the Passport service and in order to leverage the existing Windows Live ID Microsoft introduced the Windows CardSpace[43] (formerly codenamed InfoCard) as part of a new interoperable architecture called Identity Metasystem [45]. The Windows CardSpace Identity Selector is integrated with the Windows environment. Other implementations of the Identity Metasystem architecture are for example DigitalMe[44] and the Higgins Project[45]. The idea

[41] http://web.mit.edu/kerberos/
[42] http://www.passport.net/
[43] http://www.microsoft.com/windows/products/winfamily/cardspace/
[44] http://code.bandit-project.org/trac/wiki/DigitalMe/
[45] http://eclipse.org/higgins/

of the Identity Metasystem is to provide a storage repository for different identities called Information Cards and which might be used in different situations. Each Information Card points to a centralized IdP (e.g. the Windows Live ID SSO service) who stores user credentials and is involved in the communication with the SPs, but there is no direct communication between IdP and SP [106]. Due to the local Information Card repository, the Windows CardSpace concept is more a user-centric IdM approach (see below section 5.2.2.4) than a pure centralized solution.

5.2.2.3   Federated Identity Management Model

Identity federation is based on a conceptual separation between SPs and IdPs allowing entities to use the same sets of identification data, to get access and authorization to the different otherwise autonomous services offered by the SPs. Cross-domain authentication is realized by so-called security assertions that are made by IdPs towards the respective SPs. Federations of SPs and IdPs that have operational agreements based on this concept are called "circles of trust". Identity federation aims to make digital identities usable in different domains enabling entities to seamlessly access services, as for example in SSO scenarios in the Web, but without requiring the user's personal information to be stored centrally. SSO is supported both within a circle of trust as depicted in the illustration below, but also across different circles of trust provided that respective agreements have been made [119, 117]. In practice, each SP manages the name space of all its users like in the silo identity model. The different domain specific identifiers of each user are mapped defining an "abstraction layer" over the legacy identity environments of these domains [80]. The federated model is thus compatible with the traditional silo model so that SPs can keep existing name spaces and even authentication systems. A main advantage besides the downward compatibility is that it does not depend on a central authority and hence is predestined for open environments. However, federated IdM creates technical and legal complexity. The mapping between identifiers allows IdPs and SPs to correlate information about users within a federation domain. On the one hand this opens up great opportunities in terms of personalization and may be exploited for targeted advertising. On the other hand users might be afraid of privacy violations. Therefore, IdPs/SPs that want to leverage the opportunities of aggregated user profiles based on virtually unified identities will have to assure their customers that they adhere to a strict privacy policy. This can for example be realized by using anonymized or pseudonymized identities within a specific silo domain meaning that only the "home" SP actually knows the real world identity of a user [106].

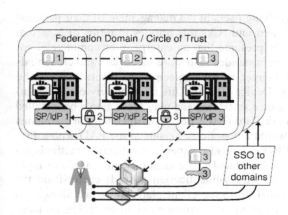

Figure 67: Federated user identity model (source: [106])

Important standardization efforts in the field of federated IdM include the Liberty Identity Federation Framework (ID-FF) released by the Liberty Alliance[46] and the Security Assertion Markup Language (SAML) developed by the Organization for the Advancement of Structured Information Standards (OASIS) whose recent versions ID-FF 1.2 [120] and SAML 2.0 [146] are interoperable. Both frameworks specify protocols and interfaces for exchanging authentication and authorization data between identity domains.

5.2.2.4   User-Centric Identity Management Model

The above described IdM approaches have more or less disadvantages in terms of user privacy and usability. The larger the number of parties to which a user discloses personal information, the higher is the risk of privacy violations. A low usability is due to the lack in scalability when users must manage an increasing number of passwords. Although especially the federated model has been motivated by the need to simplify the user experience, it is still inconceivable that only one single federation domain will exist in future. In order to give the user more control over personal data and at the same time achieve a better usability the user-centric IdM paradigm has emerged [106].

---

[46] Please note that the work of the Liberty Alliance has been contributed to the Kantara Initiative founded in 2010. See http://kantarainitiative.org/.

User-centric IdM focuses on involving users in the management of their personal information, with all the advantages and risks this implies in terms of how that information is used, rather than to presume that an enterprise or commercial entity holds all the power [121]. The basic idea is to store identifiers and credentials from different SPs in a single tamper resistant piece of hardware that can be called a Personal Authentication Device (PAD). This functionality could be implemented as a "cardlet" running on a smartcard and may for example be installed on the Universal Integrated Circuit Card (UICC) of a mobile phone that contains the SIM application. The user would authenticate herself to the PAD with a Personal Identification Number (PIN), albeit also other authentication methods including biometric verification are imaginable. The customer only needs to login once and the mobile phone realizes the authentication towards each SP on the user's behalf as long as it is connected to the client platform, hence allowing a kind of virtual SSO. As the mobile phone is a typical single-user device, no identifier is needed. However, in very critical applications (e.g. banking) the mobile phone would also allow advanced authentication methods through a secondary channel as for example SMS authentication. This might be necessary as there is no guarantee that the entity, which originally established the service session, is continuously present at the same access point during the whole session [106].

The user-centric approach can be integrated with any of the above described traditional IdM models where the below figure illustrates the combination with silo user identity domains.

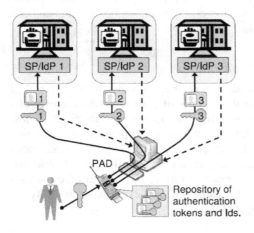

Figure 68: User-centric identity model with silo domains (source: [106])

As mentioned above the Microsoft CardSpace solution is actually an example for a user-centric centralized approach. Recent developments tend to integrate user-centricity into federated identity domains [200]. An example is the Deutsche Telekom "Netzausweis"[47] SSO solution that is based on Liberty technology but implements user-centric protocols like CardSpace and OpenID[48] in a prototype thus linking different IdM approaches in order to achieve a consistent IdM user experience [124]. Hence, it should be noted that the user-centric approach and federation are not competing models. However, issues about where user-centric begins, where federation begins, and where user centric and federation converge are being controversially debated [122]. A comprehensive overview on recent trends and developments in the IdM space is provided by [133].

5.2.3 Identity Management in the Telco Domain

As mentioned in the introduction to this section, IdM can open up new business opportunities for Telcos as they could aim to position themselves as IdPs, which must be seen in the context of the emerging two-sided telecoms market introduced in section 2.1.3.1. In the Telco 2.0 world there is no longer a one-to-one relationship between services and access technologies. The increasing availability of broadband access in the fixed and mobile environment and the development towards an all-IP infrastructure open up the value chain to so-called "Webcos" like Google and Ebay offering communication applications as part of their service portfolio and attracting customers away from traditional Telcos. Services developed outside the Telco domain are thus driving fundamental changes in the industry such as Web services that are emerging as the paradigm for communication between applications. IdM can potentially become a major element in the future structure of converging communications and IT sectors made up of operators, content providers and service providers [122].

As was shown in the previous subsection standards for managing identities have already begun establishing in the Internet and Web technologies making services easier to access and involved business parties more trustworthy by concepts like the federated identity. However, operators traditionally regard IdM in the context of authentication of subscribers into the network and authorization of their access to services essentially realized by so-called Authentication, Authorization, and Accounting (AAA) systems [227, 86].

---

[47] http://www.t-online.de/service/microsite/netzausweis/index.html
[48] http://openid.net/

5.2.3.1   Identity Management Enabled AAA Services

The term identity is perceived differently in the Web and the Telco domain. In the Internet environment, identities are usually associated with usernames, while in the Telco domain an identity is an access customer or subscriber. As already described in the context of IPTV services this induces for example that family members using the same fixed line cannot be provided with personal services since they simply cannot be differentiated. On the other hand, users of classic Telco services like voice or SMS do not need to handle and maintain passwords, since they are authenticated by the network. As they have grown separately, both the Internet and the Telco world have evolved their own identity solutions and protocols [125].

As described in the previous subsections IdM is a broad administrative area dealing with identifying individuals in computer networks and controlling their access to resources within that system by associating user rights and restrictions with the established identity. Driven by Internet and especially Web services developments IdM covers concepts and mechanisms on the service layer, while AAA systems operate on the network layer. They basically provide a framework for controlling access to computer or network resources, enforcing policies, controlling usage, and collecting information necessary to bill services. Authentication means the validation of a user's identity by having her entering a valid user name and password or through subscriber line verification. The AAA server compares the user's credentials with the credential information stored in a database and grants access to the network in case of a match. The authentication dialogue between the user and the AAA server is typically based on the Remote Authentication Dial In User Service (RADIUS) protocol or its successor Diameter. A Network Access Server (NAS) may act as a relay device between the subscriber and the AAA server. Authentication is followed by an authorization process necessary for accessing the network service and determining what types or qualities of activities, resources, or services a user is permitted to. Accounting mechanisms measure the consumed resources during a session as for example the volume of data a user has sent and/or received. The AAA server collects the transaction data that is then used for billing and other business, or technical purposes like e.g. capacity planning [227].

While most Telcos operate sophisticated AAA mechanisms, the deployment of IdM infrastructure is still in an early stage. However, both AAA and IdM cover key enabling technologies needed for future converged Telco services. The convergence of heterogeneous access technologies requires IdM solutions that enable seamless network access, which is basically close to Telcos' core business. Though, existing authentication systems must be enhanced by the capability to manage interworking between different administrative domains. Operators must aim at bringing the AAA and the IdM world together in order to keep step with Webcos in the upcoming business of Web-based services. The well developed network access infrastructure and the possibility to exploit the current customer base give operators a competitive advantage for deploying unified and federated IdM enabled AAA approaches across all their services as well as towards 3rd party service providers. In order to leverage this potential, a key strategy must be to realize an IdM/AAA bridging integrating AAA and IdM infrastructures in telecommunication services and wrapping them into enabling services [227].

As an example for an integrated IdM/AAA solution the Deutsche Telekom "Net-zausweis" implements Liberty IdM based SSO functionality in combination with automated "zero login" through fixed line authentication [124]. Standardization specifications in the IdM field have been mostly Web-focused. However, in January 2009 the Liberty Alliance established the Liberty Alliance Project Telecom-munications Special Interest Group (LAP Telco SIG) [126], which later merged into the Telecommunications Identity Work Group (TelcoID WG) [107] of the Kantara Initiative and is occupied with developing best practices for managing identity information and identity-enabled transactions and services in the global telecom sector. Besides that the 3GPP provides a specification on Interworking of the Liberty Alliance Identity Federation Framework (ID-FF) with the IMS Ge-neric Authentication Architecture (GAA) [2]. The works of both organizations will be examined more closely in the following.

5.2.3.2   IdM/AAA Bridging in Next Generation Networks

As described in the previous subsection digital identity has grown separately in the Telco and Internet domains. While Telco authentication systems basically enable "walled garden" services, the IdM in the Internet is focused on openness and 3rd party integration. Although specifications like Liberty/SAML provide identity federation and SSO standards, they don't specify how the authentication is implemented. Hence, an interworking of underlying technologies in both do-mains is needed for future Telco business. With the transition from Plain Old Telephony System (POTS) infrastructure to Next Generation Networks (NGN), standardization efforts in the Telco community have led to the definition of the IP Multimedia Subsystem (IMS) framework, which describes the implementation of IP-based Telco services and has been shortly introduced in section 2.3.1. Origi-nally aimed at future mobile network services, the 3GPP IMS architecture is becoming a key enabler for both mobile and fixed network operators to provide the NGN architecture allowing to integrate across network and Web protocols and technologies that have been traditionally deployed in silos. The IMS stan-dards include advanced identity mechanisms that though still specify a separated and rather closed world requiring additional efforts for interoperability with the Internet [1, 125].

With their widely deployed and strong authentication systems Telcos own the basic technical requirements to become authentication and identity providers. Especially mobile operators possess excellent authentication mechanisms inherent with the SIM/UICC cards in GSM or UMTS networks that could be leveraged to address complex IdM use cases. With the Generic Bootstrapping Architecture (GBA) [6] the 3GPP provides a framework for the reuse of IMS authentication, which brings the assets of networks into the service layer following a convergent approach. This allows for example that a mobile network subscriber may use the credentials stored in her 3G device typically used to sign-on to mobile telephony services in order to register with Web-based services. By integrating 3GPP GBA backend functions with frontend Internet IdM standards and technologies as for example Liberty/SAML [2] or even CardSpace and OpenID, Telcos can implement a standards-based and unified IdM/AAA architecture leveraging 3GPP network security standards. Such an architecture positions for example a mobile handset not only as an Internet access device, but also as an IP-connected authentication token securing both fixed and mobile Internet applications. It should be noted that while the GBA itself is based upon the use of 3G authentication mechanisms, a 2G version of the GBA is available in order to leverage the existing populations of 2G SIM cards [1, 125].

Overview of GBA and Liberty/SAML Interworking
As described GBA is a method for using existing Telco authentication mechanisms for IdM purposes on the service layer. In the following the combination of GBA and the Liberty/SAML framework will be analyzed shortly in order to provide an overview of how AAA/IdM bridging can be realized in IMS-based NGN networks. For a more detailed technical examination and possible integrations with other frontend Internet IdM technologies like CardSpace and OpenID see [125] and [1].

The GBA essentially defines two new functional entities: the Bootstrapping Server Function (BSF) and the Network Application Function (NAF). The NAF is a server owned by the operator or a 3rd party provider that constitutes an HTPP- or HTTPS-based service requiring network-based authentication. The BSF resides at the operator's core network and is the authenticator for the User Equipment (UE) that needs to be authenticated. The BSF acts as an interface to the Home Subscriber Server (HSS) or HLR where the user's USIM/SIM are stored, actually enabling the NAF to verify whether a UE was correctly authenticated. The below illustration describes a solution where the GBA components are located within the user's home network. The NAF is co-located with the Liberty/SAML based IdP. It should though be noted that other options especially the co-location of the IdP and the BSF are possible [123, 125].

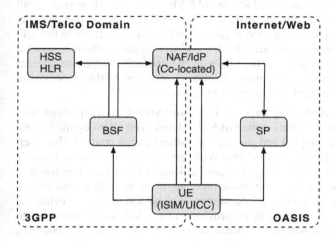

Figure 69: AAA/IdM bridging in IMS based NGN networks (source: own illustration based on [125])

In order to better understand how GBA enabled AAA/IdM bridging works, the authentication process in a simple use case taken from [125] shall be analyzed. A user wants to access a Web application with her 3G mobile device. Instead of entering a password, user identification shall be realized by seamlessly exposed IMS authentication. In a first step, the UE contacts an internal or 3rd party SP within the same circle of trust to gain access to the desired service. The header of this HTTP request contains an authentication indication (*user-agent: 3ggb-gba*) signaling GBA support. The request is redirected to the Liberty/SAML based IdP. As the UE is not yet authenticated with the IdP the combined NAF/IdP unit switches to NAF function and sends an HTTP response (*401 Unauthorized*) back to the UE. The UE recognizes that it has to supply NAF-specific keys and initiates the authentication by sending a request to the BSF, which includes its IMS Private Identity (IMPI) and is based on the 3GPP Authentication and Key Agreement (AKA) security protocol. In response, the BSF fetches a set of authentication information for that IMPI from the HSS and sends back an MD5 (Message-Digest algorithm 5) encrypted challenge. The IP Multimedia SIM (ISIM)/UICC within the UE calculates the corresponding response that is sent to the BSF. In case of a match, the BSF derives a session key (Ks-NAF) and assigns a BSF-Transaction Identifier (B-TID). The B-TID and a key lifetime parameter are sent back to the UE. In the next step, the UE forwards the B-TID as a username and the Ks-NAF as a password to the NAF/IdP unit. The IdP answers with a redirect URL containing a SAML artifact. Using this URL the UE contacts the SP, which then sends an authentication request with the SAML artifact to the IdP. Finally, the IdP can construct and send back a SAML assertion, which is verified by the SP and causes it to provide the UE with the originally requested content respectively to grant access. For a more detailed description of this process and further GBA/SAML interworking use cases please consult [125].

Authentication Context Sharing between GBA and Web Client Applications
In the previously described solution the GBA client and Web client on the UE are considered to be tightly coupled and sharing the authentication context. However, this will usually not be the case for existing Web browsing environments. In order to allow Web applications to leverage the possibilities of GBA based authentication, there must be found a way to provide these applications with a kind of session token. Therefore, some cookie information may be activated conveying the authentication context, which has to be provided to the IdP when redirected to retrieve the authentication assertion. Such a concept is also needed for enabling targeted advertising scenarios using GBA/IdM authentication to identify user devices. One realization option is to let the GBA client directly pass the cookie information to the Web application. As not all browsers allow offline cookie injection, it might be necessary to provide the Web browser with a temporal Uniform Resource Identifier (URI) under the IdP domain allowing to retrieve the cookie information through the network [125].

In their prototype implementation of an IdM enabled IMS-based IPTV scenario, [223] use cookie based authentication context sharing to allow cross-service transactions through targeted advertisements. They describe a use case scenario based on the collaboration between the IPTV provider and an online DVD shop selling DVDs on the Internet. The user starts to watch a VoD movie via IPTV. At some point during the movie she is provided with a targeted ad containing a link to a Web-based 3rd party SP selling the movie the user is currently watching on DVD. If the user selects the link, the IPTV client's browser is activated and directs the viewer to the SP's Web shop where she is authenticated automatically. The underlying architecture used to combine the STB login with authentication at the IdP is similar to the solution described in the previous subsection. After a successful IMS authentication the NAF notifies the IdP about the user authentication. The IdP creates a new authentication context and sends it back to the NAF, which forwards it to the STB. The STB stores the session token as a cookie for the integrated Web browser. This cookie can then be used by the trusted 3rd party SP to request a SAML assertion from the IdP [144, 223].

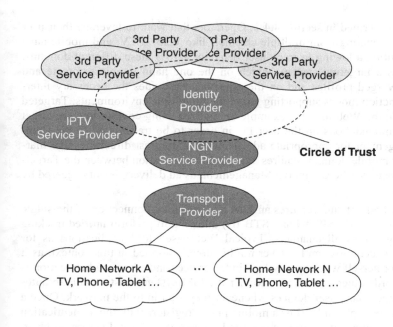

Figure 70: Circle of trust in an IPTV environment (source: own illustration based on [144])

Special attention should be paid to the fact that in this implementation the user is transferred to the Internet DVD shop anonymously meaning that at this point the DVD shop has no information except a pseudonym and the selected movie. If the user decides to buy a product, the shop requests the required shipping address and billing details to complete the transaction from the IdP. Before the requested information is passed along to the SP the IdP asks the user to agree. Liberty/SAML compliant IdPs are able to manage multiple accounts for a user providing signed assertions to federated services. In order to keep user privacy ensured each service can be allotted a (pseudonymized) unique identifier, thus preventing SPs from tracking user's activity [144, 223].

5.2.4 Identity Management in the Context of Targeted Advertising

In addition to the application scenarios analyzed in the previous subsections, IdM is needed to realize targeted advertising in converged Telco use cases such as in the scenario described in section 4.4.1. Operators that want to leverage their user data assets originating from multiple channels like Web, IPTV, and mobile have to find a solution allowing to track user behavior across these different domains. This requires a targeting system, which on the one hand is able to create and manage converged profiles and on the other hand provides the necessary interfaces and function modes supporting targeting in multiple environments. Targeted advertising in the Web may for example be realized using cookies to store target groups recommendations on the user PC in order to be transmitted to the Campaign Management for appropriate ad selection. In contrast direct message marketing in the mobile domain requires a direct communication between the Targeting Intelligence and the Campaign Management, as ad delivery is not triggered by user actions.

Multi-channel advertising requires an IdM that realizes a connection of the single identities (e.g. IMSI/MSISDN and STB ID) allowing to perform unified tracking and targeting across all channels. Typical Web-based IdM applications as for example SSO scenarios can however not be directly applied in this context, as it is not the user herself who actively logs in to services and whose authentication is asserted towards other trusted SPs. Rather the IdM system must be able to automatically authenticate user devices whenever they sign in to the network. Once a device as for example an STB or a mobile phone registers with the authentication system in its network it should be assigned a token that is valid across all channels. This requires the implementation of two key functionalities. First, operators should deploy an IdM system capable of managing multiple kinds of identifiers that must be organized in a hierarchical tree structure providing several abstraction layers for device and user identities with a kind of virtual master identity at the top [178]. This enables a collective IdM allowing to represent undifferentiated users in one household [161]. The identity tree can also include pseudonymized identities that may be used in case of privacy concerns. Second, some bridging between the AAA systems of each Telco channel and the IdM system as described above in the context of GBA/SAML interworking must be realized in order to notify the IdM system when a user device registers in the network.

Implications for the Implementation of IdM Enabled Targeted Advertising
In the analysis of the triple-play use case in section 4.4.1 some basic considerations about the implementation of IdM enabled targeted advertising have already been made. Incorporating the knowledge about IdM in the Telco scenarios elaborated on in the previous subsections, two possible implementation alternatives concerning the mapping of identities emerge. Basic assumptions that hold true in each case include that the Profiling Engine of the targeting system should store user data using a virtual identity as key in the interest profile database and that the

IdM must be bridged to the AAA systems of different operator channels and manage an identity tree for each user entity.

As a first option, user activity could be tracked by the Profiling Engine using the original device identifier (e.g. MSISDN, STB ID). In this constellation the mapping of these identities on the virtual identity is realized within the Profiling Engine requesting the IdP for the corresponding virtual identity each time a tracking request is initiated. This approach coincides with the description in the triple-play scenario and is still a valid realization opportunity especially in cases where legacy infrastructure is used towards which the whole identity virtualization process must be kept transparent. However, in NGN networks allowing to deploy a GBA/SAML based solution for IdM, the targeting process could also work as follows. As soon as a device connects to the network, the respective AAA system requests a session token including the virtual and maybe pseudonymized user identity from the IdP. This token is forwarded to the user device and stored as cookie or in some other format that can be read out by other services. The targeted advertising system can basically be considered as an SP as described in the previous subsections. User actions are tracked by the Profiling Engine within the targeting system upon respective tracking requests sent by the user device using the session token as identifier. In order to handle these requests the Profiling Engine verifies the submitted tokens by requesting an assertion and the virtual identity from the IdP. Profiling data is then stored using the virtual identity as identifier and includes information about the different devices belonging to a virtual identity.

The further process of computing target group recommendations and performing the actual ad selection strongly depends on the channel in which shall be advertised. Representatively, it can be referred to section 4.4.1 where further issues in direct mobile message and Web advertising in a converged context are analyzed. The differences of the two above described identity mapping approaches should however have become clear without going through the whole process step by step.

Finally, it should be noted that in a GBA/SAML based solution the exposure of system resources as for example presence or location information, and also the exchange and sharing of attribute/profile data with other SPs can be effectuated using secure SAML based communication [125]. Potential SPs include for example OSS/BSS/CRM systems or even 3rd party SPs within the same circle of trust. The 3GPP also provides a specification for standards based user profile management called Generic User Profile (GUP) [4]. The intent of GUP is to enable the creation of a virtual common profile capturing the location of data from multiple resources based on a federated model [87]. Hence, upcoming standards for IdM in

NGN networks promise to provide excellent conditions for future targeted advertising solutions.

5.3 Recommendation Technologies

The following section will give an introduction to recommender systems in order to provide the reader with a basic understanding of common recommendation technologies, especially in the context of targeted advertising. After having started with some remarks on the terminology and possible business scenarios, the next part of this section will deal with prevalent recommendation methods. This is followed by a deeper analysis of modern hybrid recommendation technologies and an outlook on future context-aware systems.

5.3.1 Terminology and Business Scenarios

Literature concerning recommender systems especially in popular science can to some extent be confusing. Sometimes, the term personalization is used as a synonym for recommendation even though personalization is more extensive [113]. As mentioned in the definitions chapter, personalization comprises the three disciplines targeted advertising, content targeting, and product recommendation. Recommendation is one of the steps in the personalization process.

In targeted advertising systems, a recommender system is the unit that analyzes a user profile received from the profiling system in order to find out which type of advertisements fits best the user's preferences. In most cases the output of the recommender system is a target group recommendation that is used to assign certain advertisements according to campaign policies.

However, recommender systems are not always hidden somewhere deep inside the technology process. They may also be directly available to the customer in form of product recommendation services. Probably the most famous example for this application is the Amazon.com book recommendation service [127].

One has to understand that the two cases targeted advertising and product recommendation are two different business scenarios, at least to the customer. She wants to know in which situation she finds herself: advertising or unbiased recommendation. Albeit the underlying recommendation technology can be used either to provide neutral product recommendations or to enable the selection of appropriate advertisements, it is important to make and communicate a clear decision in order to maintain credibility. Otherwise the clientele will be skeptical against the service [166].

5.3.2 Overview and Definition of Recommender Systems

Recommender systems can be applied in versatile scenarios. The need to identify contextual useful data is probably as old as the ability to archive information. The larger the amount of data grows, the more difficult is the task to find more relevant data and select the information with the highest degree of usefulness. This is even more valid for the World Wide Web (WWW) with its more than 880 million Internet hosts by January 2012 that has become the primary source of information [100]. Mostly, Web search engines are used to address the issue of finding Web pages, news, or products. However, it is difficult to specify explicit queries for information that is unknown beforehand and the retrieved information is typically not personalized to individual users or their prevailing context. This is the point where recommender systems come into play [217, 164, 113].

Definition
Recommender systems attempt to find relevant information based on data about past user behavior or statistical models. They help making choices among recommendations from all kinds of sources without the users needing to have sufficient personal experience of all these alternatives. A recommendation is a reference to an item that is directed to a user looking for information. Thus, the main tasks of recommender systems are to aggregate information and match the recommendations with appropriate recipients [166, 217, 164].

More formally, a recommender system can be defined as a system that, in a given context, actively recommends a subset of useful items from a given entity set [113]. The usefulness of items is a subjective measure that is hard to evaluate. If the user base is large enough it can be derived using empiric methods. Otherwise, the usefulness of items is often defined by their similarity within the context.

Formal Description
The *Context C* consists of a *User Profile P*, the *Entity Set M*, and the *Situation S*. The Profile P includes explicit (gender, age, interest,...) and implicit (frequency of website visits, consumed ads, bought products,...) information. The Entity Set M is part of the context because a change of M (new items) leads to a change in the recommendation even without profile modifications. The items of M are called recommendation items. In targeted advertising these recommendation items would be the possible target groups a user can belong to or the available ads themselves. The Situation S consists of a framework of parameters of the real world (date, time, geographical information, device, currently displayed ad,...). The *Recommended Items T* (subset of M) shall maximize the utility of the *User U* in a given Context C. In targeted advertising these are the matched target groups or ads. The described relation can be formulated as follows [113]:

$$\max\big(utility(U,C,T)\big) \text{ with } C = (P,M,S)$$

The importance of the definition of the utility function is obvious. The quality of the recommender system depends strongly on the selection methods that determine how useful items are to a customer. Roughly speaking, the utility function can be seen as an umbrella for the recommendation algorithms of a recommender system provider that are typically protected as a corporate secret. Nevertheless, a classification according to underlying technological design principles is possible.

5.3.3 Basic Types of Recommender Systems

To date, a large number of recommendation techniques have been developed. However, they are mainly based on Content-Based (CB) and Collaborative Filtering (CF) [217, 164, 61, 113]. Newer hybrid filtering techniques combine characteristics of both methods aforementioned and will be the subject of a deeper analysis in the next section.

5.3.3.1 Content-Based Filtering

CB filtering methods stem from the field of information filtering and retrieval. Items are generated and set up by features, metadata, or attributes. The recommendations are based on the similarity between new items and items that a user has liked before (user-to-item). This means that user profiles and item profiles are matched directly looking for best matches [164, 61].

Property Analysis
CB filtering techniques are based on the properties of recommendation items. Particularly, the behavior of other users does not influence the recommendation process at all. Usually, characteristic item properties are shaped out in a property analysis (also called feature selection). The result should be a set of properties that allows an algorithmic comparison. In order to reduce runtime complexity, an appropriate relation between the amount of item properties and the discriminatory impact regarding the recommendation items must be maintained. [113] gives an overview of approaches for the property analysis of text documents. The goal in this case is to extract relevant properties out of an unstructured text. The same principles can be applied on music or pictures.

In the case of targeted advertising, target groups or advertisements are the recommendation items. Here, it does not make sense to analyze the items for their properties. The ad marketer will rather explicitly tag the advertisements with target group information according to the target group information predefined by the advertiser or ad agency.

Representation of Item Properties

Properties of recommendation items are usually stored as vectors being part of a multidimensional vector space. The item properties are represented as distinct dimensions. Assuming e.g. that the result of the property analysis is a Boolean style vector in six dimensions, representing six different properties, the vectors of two recommendations items could look like this:

$$\text{Item 1}: v = (v_1, \quad v_2, \quad v_3, \quad v_4, \quad v_5, \quad v_6) = (1, \quad 1, \quad 0, \quad 0, \quad 1, \quad 0)$$
$$\text{Item 2}: w = (w_1, \quad w_2, \quad w_3, \quad w_4, \quad w_5, \quad w_6) = (1, \quad 0, \quad 0, \quad 0, \quad 1, \quad 0)$$

In this example, the two items only differ concerning the second component/property of the vector.

Similarity as a Selection Criterion

As mentioned in the definition of recommender systems, the purpose of a recommender system is to provide the user with useful recommendations. The utility of a recommendation for a user strongly depends on the context that can influence recommendations that are exclusively based on the similarity of single properties. Nevertheless, similarity plays an important role in the environment of recommender systems. As will be shown later, similarity measures are not only used to compare item properties in CB filtering methods, they are also needed as selection criteria in CF. A good overview on common similarity measuring methods can be found in [113].

Distance measures are the "classic" way to mathematically compute similarity. Properties of recommendation items or user profiles are first transformed to vectors before they can be matched using a distance measure. As shown above, the vectors can be binary with each component/dimension representing the existence or not-existence of a property. It is also possible to define real numbers as components representing the characteristics of a property. These can be ratings of recommendation items or even weights like the number of occurrences of a word within a text.

Pros and Cons of Content-Based Filtering Methods

As CB filtering matches user profiles and item profiles directly, it is very sensitive to user and item profile definitions. The generation of an exact user profile is prerequisite for valid recommendations and can therefore be the bottleneck of CB filtering methods. However, provided that the profile is specified, CB filtering methods can easily provide valid recommendations to new users, even if they have never used the system before. In addition, they are not reliant on user ratings for items. Hence, they are able to provide recommendations for new items that were never rated before based on the item description. This makes them useful for environments where new items are constantly added [170].

One weakness of CB filtering methods is that they cannot take into account the subjective perception of users. While a user's selection is often based on the subjective perception of item attributes, the filtering system is based on objective information about the items. This makes it impossible to compute the relevance of items with a non-machine-parsable format. A second weakness is that CB filtering techniques are not able to generate serendipitous finds. Therefore, they tend to recommend more items that resemble the ones the user already knows [217].

5.3.3.2   Collaborative Filtering

The idea of Collaborative Filtering (CF) is to emulate the advice from a friend. CF recommender systems derive their recommendations on the basis of content ratings from people with similar interests (either user-to-user or item-to-item) [164, 61].

CF is based on the similarity of user profiles instead of the similarity between items. This means that CF systems compute the similarity of user's interests in contrast to CB filtering systems that compute the similarity of items based on a machine analysis of content. In turn, subjective data about items, that is personal tastes, are incorporated into recommendations [217, 113].

The user profiles represent the usage behavior in form of recommendation items resulting in a user-item matrix with $U_1,...,U_n$ as user and $I_1,...,I_m$ as recommendation items:

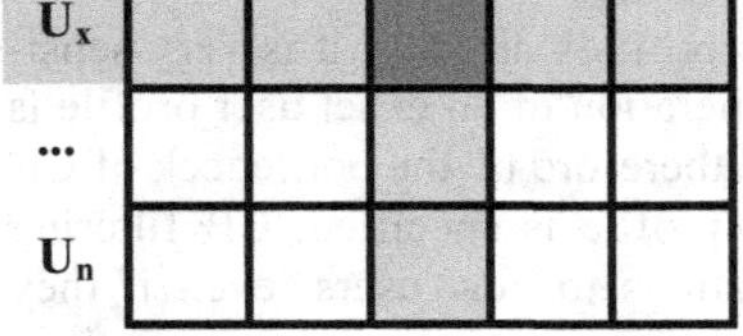

Figure 71: Collaborative Filtering matrix of user-recommendation item relations (source: own illustration based on [113])

One cell $[U_x, I_y]$ of the matrix represents an implicit or explicit rating of recommendation item I_y by user U_x. The rating can be realized in Boolean ("good"/"bad") style or on a discrete scale. Recommendations are now derived from the behavior of users with a similar profile. CF algorithms can be divided up into the two main categories user-based and item-based algorithms. A fundamental difference between the two methods is that in case of user-based CF the similarity is computed along the rows (= users) of the matrix. In case of item-based CF the similarity is computed along the columns (= items) [179, 113].

User-Based Collaborative Filtering
Determining the most interesting recommendation items for a user based on a user-based CF method basically works as follows [179, 113].

According to the preceding description, a matrix $R = (r_{ij})$ with $i = 1,...,n$ and $j = 1,...,m$ where n is the number of users and m the number of recommendation items is created. r_{ij} represents the rating of item j by user i. The task is now to evaluate the relevance $R(U_x, I_y)$ of a recommendation item I_y for a user U_x, who does not have any information about the item.

The solution is to compute the relevance $R(U_x, I_y)$ of every single recommendation for user U_x based on the ratings of similar users. The similarity of the users is being determined using similarity or distance measures. The most often used method is a combination of the Nearest-Neighbor approach [50] and the Pearson Correlation Coefficient [23]. Finally, the recommendation items with the highest relevancies are selected.

Simplified Process Flow Example
Based on the ratings of user U_x (step 1) similar users are searched (step 2). The items rated good by most of the users (step 3) are recommended to user U_x (step 4). The example is illustrated in the figure below.

Item-Based Collaborative Filtering
In order to determine whether a recommendation item fits the user's interests, item-based CF methods work basically as follows [179, 113].

Another matrix $R = (r_{ij})$ with $i = 1,...,n$ and $j = 1,...,m$, n being the number of users and m the number of recommendation items, is created. Again, the task is to evaluate the relevance $R(U_x, I_y)$ of a potential recommendation item I_y for a user U_x, who does not have any information about the item.

For this purpose, based on the objects $I_1,...,I_u$ that are already rated by user U_x the similarities S with I_y are computed as follows. For each pair of recommendation items $(I_y, I_1),...,(I_y, I_u)$ [= $(I_y, I_{1...u})$] a vector based on the item ratings from other users is created using similarity or distance measures. The highest possible similarity is reached when all users have rated I_y and the respective other item identically. Eventually, the relevance $R(U_x, I_y)$ must be determined, e.g. using the weighted average of the user's ratings of the most similar recommendation items. The more similar an item I_j is compared to I_y (the higher thus is $S(I_y, I_j)$), the more influencing is the rating of this object by the user:

$$R(U_x, I_y) = \frac{\sum_{j=1...u} S(I_y, I_j) \cdot R(U_x, I_j)}{\sum_{j=1...u} S(I_y, I_j)}$$

$I_{j=1...u}$ are the recommendation items already rated by user U_x.

Simplified Process Flow Example

Based on the recommendation item rated good by user U_x (step 1), all pairs of items that contain one of these items are selected (step 2). The best rated other items in the pairs (step 3) are recommended to user U_x (step 4).

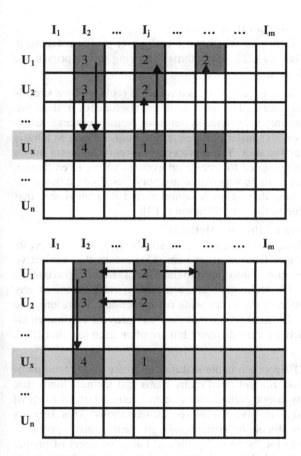

Figure 72: Collaborative Filtering: (1) user-based concept, (2) item-based concept
(source: own illustration based on [113])

Model and Memory-Based Collaborative Filtering

CF can also be classified depending on whether the entire user profile database is used to compute recommendations [32]. Algorithms following this approach are called memory-based CF methods.

In case of model-based methods the CF matrix as a whole is replaced by a simplified model, e.g. a user-cluster matrix. The most common approaches in this area are Bayesian Networks, clustering, rule-based systems, or neural networks. Clustering means that user groups with similar preferences are built, serving as a basis of recommendations for the active user. The preference values of the users inside the active user's cluster are aggregated to receive an average value. Even though the model-based approach seems to be superior to memory-based CF, it has to be noticed that the addition of new data is more complex and it is inevitable that relevant information is lost due to the simplification [113].

Pros and Cons of Collaborative Filtering Methods

As mentioned above CF techniques are based on the similarity of users' interests and thus independent of the specification of an item. This means that subjective data about items can be incorporated into recommendations facilitating serendipitous new finds. In addition, CF techniques are completely independent of any machine-readable representation of the items being recommended. Therefore, one of the biggest advantages of CF methods is that they can provide recommendations for complex items, which are very different but are often used together [217, 170].

The main drawback of the CF approach is the inability to create good recommendations for new users that have not yet rated many items and for new items that have not been rated by many users. Hence, the system needs a critical mass of user actions before being able to give useful recommendations. This issue is known as the "cold-start" problem, or correspondingly "early-rater" problem. Another shortcoming is due to the "sparsity" problem. Large numbers of people must participate to increase the likelihood that other users with similar interests can be found. Otherwise, the quality of recommendations is dropping drastically. Finally, popular items can cause the so-called "lemming"-effect. This means that items that are often recommended tend to increase further, especially if they are implicitly rated through mere impression. This results in new objects having no chance to climb up in the recommendation order [217, 170, 113].

Applying the item-based approach instead of a user-based method can reduce some of these shortcomings of CF. Item-based algorithms first explore the relationships between items and then compute recommendations by finding items that are similar to other items the user has liked before. This helps to reduce the effects of sparsity, and at the same time increases scalability by avoiding the bottleneck that appears in user-based algorithms when searching for neighbors among a large user population of potential neighbors [179].

5.3.3.3   Other Recommendation Methods and Further Reading

Some sources distinguish additional methods besides CB and CF. Amongst these is e.g. rules-based filtering that is based on simple "if-then" rules that are applied to the customer profile. The applied rule is predefined by experts. Another approach is demographic filtering that uses descriptions of people to learn the relationship between a single item and the type of people who like it. [78, 132, 217] provide an overview of these and further recommendation methods. The learning algorithms and prediction methods used by today's recommender systems are strictly tailored to the service for which the system was designed. [53] and [113] provide good surveys of concrete implementations of recommender systems. A classification of recommender systems based on the technical design as well as on the domain space of the service application can be found in the often cited [166].

5.3.4 Hybrid Recommender Systems

The idea of hybrid recommender systems is to combine CB and CF approaches in order to reduce the disadvantages of the individual methods. In principle, the following approaches to combine the methods into one hybrid recommender system are imaginable [8]:

1. *Implementing collaborative and content-based methods separately and combining their predictions.* Either the outputs obtained from individual recommender systems can be combined into one final recommendation, or alternatively, the individual recommender whose recommendation is "better" than others is chosen based on some recommendation "quality" metric. This could e.g. include switching from the content-based to the collaborative method once the cold-start phase is over.

2. *Incorporating some content-based characteristics into a collaborative approach.* One approach is to use a traditional collaborative technique but also maintain the content-based profiles for each user that are then, instead of the commonly rated items, used to calculate the similarity between two users (also called community-based filtering).

3. *Incorporating some collaborative characteristics into a content-based approach.* The most popular approach in this category is to apply some dimensionality reduction technique on a group of content-based profiles. Collaborative approaches are used to group a collection of user profiles resulting in a performance improvement.

4. *Constructing a general unifying model that incorporates both content-based and collaborative characteristics.* One modern approach in this field is the stereotype-based recommender system that is based on the idea of combining content clusters with affinity vectors. This solution will be the subject oft the below discussion.

[7, 8] provide a good survey on various hybrid recommender system approaches including an overview of implementations.

5.3.4.1 A Stereotype-Based Hybrid Recommender System

The stereotype-based recommendation approach was developed in the context of an innovation project on media content recommendations within Deutsche Telekom Laboratories (T-Labs)[49] [189, 61]. It integrates CB and CF techniques into one algorithm rather than combining the results of the individual methods.

The Stereotype Model
Stereotypes are known as a generalization of a user. They can also be described as an abstract user identity that is used for a general description of a set of similar users. The idea of the approach is to have a limited set of abstract stereotypes that act as a mediator between a huge number of media items and each individual user [189].

While in CF systems stereotypes are described by a set of ratings over items, in CB filtering systems stereotypes are a set of preferences over item attributes. In both cases, users can belong to a single stereotype or to multiple stereotypes. The stereotype model of the algorithm discussed here follows the CB approach by defining an ontology over media items. The media item profiles are instantiations of this ontology, and a stereotype profile assigns relevance values for various attribute values of the ontology. The user is modeled by an affinity list of stereotypes. Eventually, each media item and each user are assigned an individual profile [189].

Stereotype and Media Item Profile Creation
Before the stereotype approach can be applied the following steps have to be taken [61]:

Step 1: A set of stereotypes is defined using the Simulated Annealing method, a probabilistic meta-algorithm for local optimization problems [28]. Here, it is used for searching and optimizing a limited set of stereotypes (the optimal number lies between 25 and 40). Parameters of media items can be content-related (e.g.

---

[49] See http://www.laboratories.telekom.com/ and http://tlabs.bgu.ac.il/.

source, genre, actors,...) or representation-related (e.g. duration, language, format,...).

Step 2: For each media item, the item profile, respectively the item profile vector, is generated. The coefficients of the vector represent the weights regarding each stereotype that belongs to each media item and are computed by a matching engine based on the relevance i.e. similarity of a media item to a stereotype. The item profile P_I is represented as a linear combination of the item profile vector i and the stereotypes s [61]:

$$P_I = \sum_{p=1}^{m} i_p \cdot s_p = i \cdot s = \begin{pmatrix} i_1 \\ \vdots \\ i_m \end{pmatrix} \cdot \begin{pmatrix} s_1 \\ \vdots \\ s_m \end{pmatrix}$$

P_I : profile of item I
i : item profile vector
s : stereotype vector
m : number of stereotypes

Step 3: Pre-calculated media item lists are generated and assigned to each stereotype. Since the number of stereotypes is not expected to be too high, these lists can be persistent in the database leading to a higher performance. As mentioned, media items can be attached to several stereotypes.

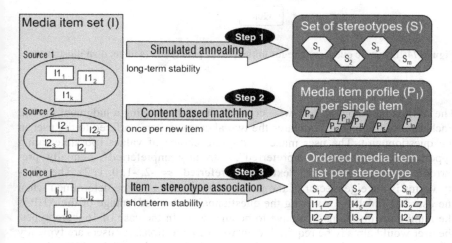

Figure 73: Stereotype and item profile creation (source: [61])

User Preference Elicitation

The initial stereotypes and media item profiles have been defined now. The next step is to generate a profile and the corresponding affinity vector that weights the different stereotypes for each user. The initial user profile is created by means of a dynamic questionnaire. The questionnaire comes as a sequence of questions, comparing two proposed media items per step [61]. This process is based on the Analytic Hierarchy Process (AHP) methodology, originally developed for solving multi-criteria decision problems [174, 175].

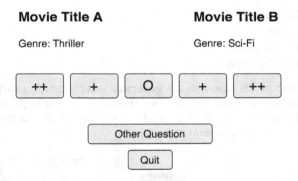

Please answer the following question by clicking on your favourite answer. You are shown two media items, which you can rate relative to each other. If you would like to skip to the next pair of items, click on the appropriate button. You may quit this process anytime you like by clicking on the 'Quit' button.

Figure 74: Dynamic questionnaire for initial profile generation (source: own illustration based on [61])

The AHP is based on the pair-wise comparison of items using a judgment matrix. Each item of the matrix compares the two alternative items offered to the user in the questionnaire. The user makes a discrete choice of values (possible rating opportunities: "extremely unpreferred", "strongly unpreferred", "equally preferred", "strongly preferred", "extremely preferred" $\Leftrightarrow$ -2, -1, 0, 1, 2). The affinity vector is the eigenvector of the judgment matrix and can be determined when the user has finished answering the questionnaire. A disadvantage of the AHP is the number of questions that have to be answered. In the case of 16 stereotypes, the user would already be required to answer 120 questions. As users are typically reluctant to answer long questionnaires a modified version of the AHP, the Incomplete Pair-wise Comparison algorithm (IPC) is used [170]. This approach guarantees at least some classification, even if the user stops answering questions [189, 170, 61].

After having solved the eigenvalue problem of the judgment matrix, each user profile P_U can be described as a linear combination of the affinity vector u (= eigenvector) and the stereotypes s [61]:

$$P_U = \sum_{p=1}^{m} u_p \cdot s_p = u \cdot s = \begin{pmatrix} u_1 \\ \vdots \\ u_m \end{pmatrix} \cdot \begin{pmatrix} s_1 \\ \vdots \\ s_m \end{pmatrix}$$

P_U : profile of user U
u : affinity vector
s : stereotype vector
m : number of stereotypes

The relation of the stereotype vector, the item profile association vector, and the user profile affinity vector is illustrated below. The user affinity vector and the item profile vector refer to the same stereotype vector.

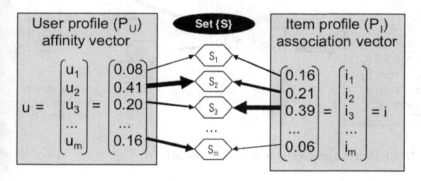

Figure 75: User profile and media item representation (source: [61])

Recommendations
After calculation of item profile vector i for each single media item and the user profile vector u, the system is now ready to compute media item recommendations for every profiled user. In order to optimize the performance the recommen-

dation R as a ranked list for each user is generated in advance to actual recommendation requests [61]:

$$R_U = f(P_U) = Ls < I_i >$$

R_U :   recommendation specific to the user U
P_U :   individual user profile of user U
$Ls < I_i >$:   ranked list including media items I_i

The whole process is much more efficient than matching each user with all items in the database as it would be the case in a CB recommender system. Thus, the system can scale up much better. A recommendation stays the same as long as the user profile and the set of media items remain stable resulting in very fast recommendation computing. It should though be noted that the introduction of new items is time consuming, as it requires the reinvention of all stereotype-related lists [189, 61].

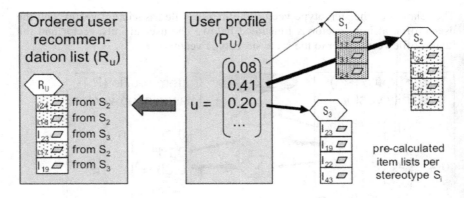

Figure 76: Creation of user recommendation lists (source: [61])

Feedback and Profile Updates
The stereotype-based recommender system supports two types of feedback (explicit/implicit) to update user profiles. In terms of explicit feedback, the user is given a chance to influence her personal profile by a rating (like/dislike) of recommended media items that is reflected in slight changes of the coefficients of the user's affinity vector. When a user is presented a list with five items and she chooses the third item, the system implicitly assumes that she does not like the first two items and her profile is updated. Another type of implicit feedback that

leads to profile updates is triggered by the media server that streams the recommended media items. The server is aware whether a user watched the item fully or stopped the play-out after some time. The ladder case would be interpreted as a negative rating that is forwarded to the recommender system. In addition to these feedback methods, the system incorporates community-based ("friend-of-a-friend principle") and collaborative influences (similar profiles) in the recommendation process that can lead to a re-ranking of items in the user recommendation list [189, 61].

5.3.4.2   Evaluation of the Stereotype-Based Approach

The stereotype-based recommender system is a hybrid approach that combines features of various recommendation methods. The initial user affinity vector construction is CB oriented because it identifies attributes of the media items that the users prefer. The anytime questionnaire approach, that allows a user classification even if the user stops answering the questions, helps handling the "cold-start problem". As the system creates media item lists that are associated to stereotypes right from the start, an "early-rater problem" will not appear. A "sparsity problem" cannot appear since the system does not depend on ratings from other users to recommend an item to a single user. A shortcoming of the system, known as the "long tail problem", is that media items, which have already a low rank regarding all stereotypes, are never recommended. To overcome this, selected items are randomly inserted into user recommendation lists. This also helps to avoid the "lemming effect". The common problem of CB systems, which can only recommend items to the user that are similar to the ones she has seen and liked before, does not exist here because users also receive CF-like recommendations based on data regarding preferences of similar users. Eventually, it should be noted that applying a hybrid recommendation approach can potentially solve many of the problems of CB and CF recommender systems, while at the same time increasing the performance through better scalability.

5.3.5 Context-Aware Recommender Systems

A was shown in the previous sections, traditional recommender systems can be differentiated according to various aspects. But they all focus on recommending the most relevant items to users or appropriate users to items. Hence, they abstract from the prevailing situation and do not include the contextual information of the user's decision scenario into the recommendation process. In some cases like e.g. location- and time-based services, it may not be sufficient to operate within a "2D" user x item space. The recommender system must rather include additional rating dimensions [9]. A simple example from the advertising world would be to send a mobile user an advertising SMS of a restaurant that is located within a radius of 500m of her current location. Such a scenario requires specific targeting and recommendation technologies to incorporate contextual information into the recommendation process.

Terminology and Motivation

There are several terms that can potentially be used to describe recommender systems taking advantage of contextual information. While some authors talk about "context dependent" or "contextual" recommender systems, most sources use the terminology "context-aware" recommender systems [9].

Context-aware recommendation means basically to add an additional dimension to the recommendation process. As mentioned earlier this can for example be the location the user finds herself in when receiving a recommendation. However, context-aware recommender systems must be able to map much more extensive scenarios beyond location-based services. A recommender system can for example consider the current season when a user wants to book a vacation. A movie recommendation may adapt to the scenario if the user decides to see it on Saturday night together with her boyfriend. It is even imaginable to recognize the user's mood (e.g. by analyzing the typing behavior on the keyboard) and incorporate this information into the recommendation process. The variety of possible scenarios is closely related to the channel in which the scenario takes place and the availability of contextual information. Especially the increase in mobile Internet usage enables a diversity of context-aware use cases due to the wide spectrum of input sources mobile devices provide to obtain contextual data (e.g. GPS, compass, camera,...). A fast traveling car driver may for example be recommended to buy anti stress pills but also to attend the next Formula 1 race at a racecourse nearby. An often-cited practical example for context-aware recommendations can be found on the Amazon bookstore [9, 76]. Amazon's recommender system differentiates between a user shopping according to her own interests or someone who looks for gifts. It is pretty obvious that it makes a huge difference whether a user buys books, music or DVDs for herself or someone else, as otherwise the shopping profile of a user will be completely distorted.

These examples show that it is often important to know not only what to recommend to whom, but also under what circumstances. Depending on the application, certain contextual information can be relevant for generating recommendations [9].

What is Context?

Before further discussing context-awareness in recommender systems it is crucial to understand the notion of "context". Depending on the discipline, there are many different approaches and views about what context actually is. First attempts to describe context in context-aware systems include for example definitions like "location of the user, identity of people and objects near the user" [181], "date, season, temperature" [37], or "physical and conceptual statuses of interest to a user" [173]. However, these definitions are obviously too specific. Context is rather about the whole situation relevant to an application and its users. It is impossible to predefine which aspects of all situations are important, as this will change depending on the situation. In order to cover a broad range of context-aware use cases, the definition needs to be more generic. Following a more holistic approach [57] define context as "any information that can be used to characterize the situation of an entity. An entity is a person, place, or object that is considered relevant to the interaction between a user and an application, including the user and applications themselves". In other words, if a piece of information can be used to characterize the situation of a participant in an interaction, then that information is context. This more open understanding of context is widely accepted and leaves enough space for application developers to define the context for their given application [9, 195, 76].

Potential methods of obtaining contextual data are determined by the use case scenario and its implementation. In general, contextual information can either be specified by the user herself or deduced by the system, whereas especially methods of deriving data from user behavior gain importance. However, the question of how to obtain contextual data is a separate problem beyond the scope of this analysis [9].

Context in Recommender Systems
As already mentioned, incorporating context into recommender systems means adding a new dimension to the recommendation process. Context in recommender systems is thus any additional information, besides information on users and items that is relevant to recommendations. By providing various types of constraints on recommendation outcomes, context allows identifying pertinent subsets of data. It can further enable building richer rating estimation models [9].

In practice, the actual meaning of context strongly depends on the goal of the respective application and the system processing contextual information. In consequence, the understanding of context-awareness in recommender systems is not unambiguous. As mentioned in section 2.1.2, it is reasonable to distinguish static from dynamic context information. Static context includes mostly unchanged "properties" like gender, age group, ZIP code,... that are stored in a user profile. A close look reveals that this type of contextual data can actually be processed like any other profile information. Hence, classic recommendation technologies as introduced in the previous sections can be applied in order to achieve the best match of user and item profiles. In contrast, dynamic user context comprises the current situation of a user that may change at any time like the speed someone travels in a car or current location information. This requires a very adaptive recommendation process being able to consider dynamically changing context information in addition to static profile data. Incorporating contextual data hence requires a complex recommendation framework.

Views of Context

Potential approaches to model context-aware recommender systems depend on how context is perceived. Basically, two views of context can be distinguished: the representational view and the interactional view. Both aiming at incorporating contextual information into the recommendation process, the two views represent different methodological approaches.

The representational view makes four key assumptions: Context is a form of information; it is delineable, stable and separable from activity. This means that context is information that can be described using an explicit set of static attributes (i.e. it is "extensional"). These attributes do not change and are predefined on the characteristics of the domain and environment (e.g. time, date, location, mood, device). This implies that contextual variables must be identified at the design stage and contextual information has to be acquired as part of data collection before actual recommendations are made. The attributes are clearly distinguishable from features describing the underlying activity undertaken by the user within the context. In contrast, the interactional view suggests that contextuality is a relational property meaning that some information may or may not be relevant to some activity. The scope of contextual features is defined dynamically, and is rather occasional than static. This implies a cyclical relationship between context and activity. Rather than assuming that context predefines a static situation an activity occurs in, the activity can itself change the context hence creating a new situation giving rise to an activity and so on. Thus, context can cause behavior that is observable, though context itself may not be observable (i.e. it is "intensional") [14, 76].

The main distinction between both approaches is that while the representational view is concerned with what context is and how it can be represented within an application, the interactional view is focused on a mutual understanding of the context for user and system actions and does not care about how the context is actually defined. A detailed elaboration on characteristics and potential drawbacks of the two approaches can be found in [59] and also in [14, 76] who especially focus on the interactional view including the development of a concrete interactional model and possible implementations.

Architectural Models for Context-Aware Recommender Systems

Originally introduced based on the representational view, three architectural models for using context in recommendations can be differentiated. However, these approaches are generally also applicable in the interactional view and variants as well as combinations of these are possible [76]. The architecture of context-aware recommender systems can be classified along the lines of contextual integration and algorithmic deployment. According to [9] contextual information can be tightly integrated into the recommendation process, or used independently from the traditional recommendation methods and complement them by being separately applied to improve recommendations. Further, they conclude that from the algorithmic perspective, contextual information can be used before the main recommendation methods are launched (contextual pre-filtering), as a part of the preprocessing step, simultaneously with recommendation methods (contextual modeling), or after the main recommendation methods (contextual post-filtering).

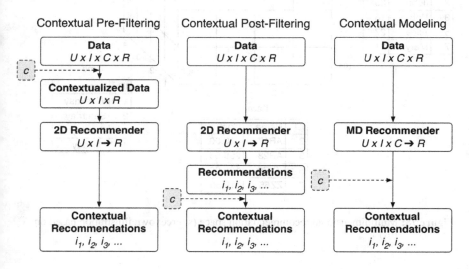

Figure 77: Architectural models for context-aware recommender systems (source: own illustration based on [9])

In the case of contextual pre-filtering, contextual information is used to preselect the most relevant data for generating recommendations, in the case of post-filtering the contextual information is used to adjust ("contextualize") the resulting set of recommendations. Both approaches allow using traditional 2D recommender systems. They can thus be more easily realized than contextual modeling. Here, context and user preferences are coupled tight and contextual information is used directly in the modeling technique as a part of the rating estimation through a multidimensional recommender [9].

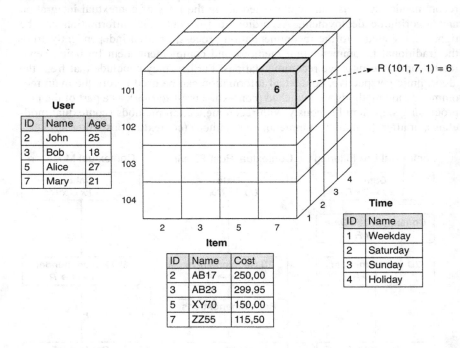

Figure 78: Multidimensional recommendation space (source: own illustration based on [9])

Further reading on architectural modeling of context-aware recommender systems is provided by [7] who introduce and elaborate on the multidimensional recommendation approach. [164] propose a generic framework that delivers contextual recommendations.

6 Business and Legal Aspects of Targeted Advertising

Being the primary focus of this book, the previous sections mainly dealt with technological aspects of targeted advertising in the ICT space. Though, the subject certainly can be approached from multifold directions especially including business and legal aspects. The basic business environment of targeted advertising has already been introduced in section 2.1.3. Various legal concerns of targeting technologies have emerged in the context of the use case analysis.

The purpose of this section is now to provide the reader with an introductory overview of business and legal aspects around targeted advertising, in order to give an idea of potential topics in these areas. More detailed analyses of issues in these regards are out of scope and are subject to respective specialized works.

6.1 Business Aspects of Targeted Advertising

One of the major business impacts of targeting is that it helps to tackle the problem of information overload in advertising.[50] With more and more media consumption opportunities that become available to the user, advertisers increasingly face the problem of choosing the right channel for reaching the desired audience. Targeted advertising can help to reduce the waste coverage thus making advertising more efficient, while at the same time providing consumers with more relevant information. Hence, targeted advertising can potentially generate significant new revenue, albeit the pre-conditions, the business environment and thus the business prospects, differ in the different ICT channels. Moreover, targeted advertising offers a big opportunity for telecom operators to gain a foothold in the TV and mobile advertising market enabled by their unique assets of subscriber information and multiple delivery channels. Aspects like these have partially been mentioned in the introduction at the beginning of this book and in some of the use case analyses. This section will now summarize the most important business concerns and opportunities in order to give a short overview beyond the technological aspects, which so far have been the focus of discussion.

---

[50] Estimates for the number of ads the average American is exposed to range between several hundred up to 3,000 ad messages a day [142].

6.1.1 Developments in Web Advertising

While first attempts of Web personalization around 1999/2000 basically failed due to small user numbers and a lack of capable technology, targeted advertising in the Web is meanwhile widespread. Classic Internet ad formats (see section 2.5.1) are well established and the user numbers are large enough to realize efficient targeted advertising. Web targeting solutions are today offered by numerous providers whose technologies have reached a sophisticated level. According to Deutsche Telekom [206], the demand for targeting solutions was further stimulated subsequent to the financial crisis of 2007/2008, as they promise to reduce the waste coverage and many advertisers carefully deliberate about investing in expensive ad campaigns.

Besides increasing ad efficiency on traditional portal sites targeted advertising emerges as the long-awaited business model promising to make Web 2.0 services like Facebook or Twitter profitable. However, users are full of skepticism concerning the handling of their private data facing the non-transparent implementation of targeting methods for example in Facebook and StudiVZ, or in the case of British Telecom (BT) and Phorm that were using Deep Packet Inspection (DPI) to analyze browsing behavior [221]. An introduction to these legal concerns of targeted advertising will be given below in section 6.2. From a business perspective transparency of data handling in the context of targeting is very important as otherwise users might register with incomplete or wrong profiles or decide to generally opt out of targeted advertising. As a consequence, neither advertisers will be able to leverage targeting and reduce waste coverage, nor the user will benefit from more relevant ad messages, eventually reducing the business potential of the whole targeted advertising approach.

6.1.2 IPTV Environment

TV is still by far the most important advertising channel with a global ad market share steadily rising from 39.8% of spend in 2010 up to an estimated share of 40.5% in 2013 equalling $ 207 Billion. However, Internet advertising is growing much faster than any other medium, from an ad market share of 14.4% in 2010 to 18.9% in 2013 meaning an average growth of 14.6% a year. Display is the fastest-growing segment in the online advertising market, growing by 17.2% a year, driven mainly by online video and social media with streaming video ads growing extremely quickly [226]. One of the reasons for the success of Internet advertising are the excellent audience measurement metrics, interaction possibilities e.g. compared to classic TV advertising, and the opportunity to reach individual users all enabled by the two-way communication of IP networks. Telco's big asset is that IPTV is inherently bidirectional providing many of the features of display advertising, and can tie together the strengths of Internet advertising with the richness of TV. IPTV operators hence are in a situation, where they can leverage and benefit from sophisticated ad formats and successful advertising models from the Internet [111, 40, 218].

A general asset of IPTV operators is that they own the whole delivery network from the headend to the STB having direct access to all potential ad insertion points. But according to Deutsche Telekom [203] and SeaChange [218], a key problem operators face in IPTV is that they are still predominantly seen as technical enablers and not as full service providers. Operators must tackle this issue and aim at becoming a new link in the advertising value chain, which will not be easy as programmers are certainly not interested in sharing advertising revenues with an additional stakeholder. Most of the TV stations have their own ad marketing subsidiaries (e. g. ProSiebenSat.1/SevenOne Media[51], RTL/IP Deutschland[52]) responsible for selling ad opportunities to advertisers. Thus, IPTV operators will have to convince TV stations that they can achieve enough additional revenue through the offered targeting capabilities. However, Sun [40] points out that TV advertising is a very conservative business with a "sit-and-wait" mentality complicating negotiations for potential revenue sharing deals.

As for advertising formats chances of success in the current market situation and state of technology are good for interactive advertising formats and VoD advertising. Supporting interactive advertising can already today generate some incremental revenue, even before IPTV has reached a substantial user base [111]. The capability of being able to offer VoD is generally a big advantage that IPTV operators have compared to one-way network operators (e.g. satellite TV). VoD can integrate the same advertising formats that are already being used on Web video pages. Another example for adopted Web advertising technology are targeted display ads as part of the EPG providing great revenue opportunities.

Significant business potential further lies in copying the U.S. model of local ad replacement. As mentioned in section 2.1.3.2 European broadcasters so far do not offer so-called "avails" for ad insertion to cable or IPTV operators. In future, this technology could be implemented in IPTV networks to realize targeted advertising maybe even on household level. However, linear addressable advertising creates significant bandwidth challenges, which must be considered when calculating the advertising business case. In the case of linear TV ad insertion, ad slots are often situated at about the same time across multiple channels. This means that, if each channel has e.g. four versions of an ad for insertion aimed at four

---

[51] http://www.sevenonemedia.de/
[52] http://www.ip-deutschland.de/

different demographic groups, and there are five channels doing this at the same time, the bandwidth required can increase exponentially. VoD streams, in contrast, are unicast, so there is no incremental bandwidth required for addressable advertising [111]. However, attention must be paid to the fact that the infrastructure required for realizing unicast streaming is increasingly complex and expensive the more parallel streams are transmitted. Generally, network-based ad insertion, be it in linear TV or on demand video, requires huge investments in network infrastructure not only in terms of bandwidth but also concerning high-performance insertion units and content management respectively storage requirements. Sun [40] says the decision whether to realize targeted advertising in IPTV or not is hence not least a business optimization problem. As SeaChange [218] puts it, the operator has to solve a "money per GHz" problem meaning that he must calculate if it is e.g. more profitable to sell more broadband Internet or to implement targeted advertising.

6.1.3 Mobile Environment

As was described in the previous subsection Internet advertising is growing rapidly. Since mobile access to websites and multimedia is likely to be tied directly to the Internet, this also implies a positive trend for mobile advertising with an estimated global mobile advertising market volume of $ 10 Billion in 2013 [112]. Hence, mobile advertising revenues grow significantly though not as rapidly as many anticipated. Like IPTV mobile advertising profits from the bidirectional network architecture allowing accurate usage tracking and delivering real metrics to advertisers, hence enabling better targeting and personalization opportunities. Mobile advertising is thus also driven by Internet advertising formats and models. As described in section 2.5.3 the MMA has released several guidelines aimed at standardizing mobile ad formats. After all, standardization efforts in mobile advertising are yet not sophisticated enough. Access and pricing models as well as measurement metrics are not yet sufficiently standardized respectively accepted enough to support a dramatic increase in revenue. Hence, mobile advertising systems are still very much in a state of evolution with a very high degree of unpredictability. Central buying, consistent measurement, and technology standardization like the OMA Mobile Ad (MobAd) enabler introduced in section 4.4.2 are however key to driving advertiser interest. Carrier collaboration and support of initiatives from industry groups such as the MMA, the OMA, and also the GSM Association (GSMA) will be the primary driver of mobile advertising. The evolution of services would benefit greatly from a well-developed advertising model giving both content owners and mobile carriers greater financial flexibility by enabling new pricing models [112].

According to Sun [40] and NSN [129], a shift in usage of mobile Internet services stimulated by the increasing availability of 3G networks and through the advent of the iPhone and its followers is a major driver for the current spread of mobile advertising technologies in general and also for mobile targeted advertising. These new technologies allow leveraging the large mobile subscriber base for advertising purposes. Generally, mobile advertising offers carriers a great opportunity to insert themselves into the advertising value chain. In contrast to IPTV, in mobile advertising carriers have been involved from the start such that their position is more powerful as they are gatekeepers for the delivery of mobile advertising. In addition, the versatility of modern device technology and service offerings allows for multimedia campaigns integrating alternative media formats across multiple advertising channels (e.g. interaction via bar codes displayed on billboards) [112].

The biggest business asset of mobile advertising, NSN [129] says, originates from the fact that mobile phones are very personal devices users carry always with them. Operators can potentially track which services a customer uses on her phone and at which location. In addition, and in contrast to IPTV, they can be pretty sure that it is the user herself who is using the phone and not some other member of the household she lives in. Operators may either exploit these assets for usage on their own mobile Web portals or offer integrated targeted advertising solutions in cooperation with technology vendors. So far carriers have been able to leverage their position as gatekeepers to gain the majority of their mobile advertising revenues through on-portal advertising. However, as users become more comfortable with the mobile Web beyond the operator's desk, the importance of the carrier will decline and walled garden approaches will not succeed anymore. This results in a decline in the carrier's share. But since the overall advertising revenue will grow through increasing usage of mobile content, apps, and services, carriers can profit as well, especially when collaborating with advertising networks beyond their own portals [112].

Another excellent business opportunity for mobile operators is SMS advertising. They can either provide network-based text ad insertion capabilities or enable direct message marketing based on subscriber and location information as described above in section 4.3.4. In this context, completely new business models emerge like for example offering free talking time or free SMS subsidized through push message advertising (e.g. Blyk, E-Plus Gettings). With a share of almost 90% SMS advertising generates by far the majority of today's global mobile advertising revenues [112] and has also the greatest reach of all formats. Hence, SMS advertising is perhaps not the most innovative mobile advertising format, though it guarantees to reach a divergent set of users, as it may be the only format available at low-income levels [112].

6.1.4 Converged Scenarios

According to Sun [40], in the long-term good business opportunities for targeted advertising will emerge in converged ICT scenarios that combine several operator services presenting the user with an integrated user experience. This can e.g. be a case where a user starts watching a movie on her mobile TV device while she is on her way home, and then continues watching on a large screen in the living room resulting in tremendous targeting opportunities. The major operator asset in converged scenarios is that he can aggregate information about a user's interests and behavior collected in the context of different channels and use these data for personalized services including targeted advertising. Telcos typically have massive subscriber bases across wireline and wireless services, allowing to create integrated multi-platform advertising solutions. Creative campaign ideas leveraging mobile and broadband will offer additional value to advertisers [111, 112].

However, as described in the use case analyses in section 4.4 converged scenarios cause a lot of specific challenges as for example in the context of user identification, identity management, and profile management that have to be tackled. In addition, it should be noted that what was mentioned as a problem in the context of IPTV is even more true in the context of converged scenarios. As Sun [40] and Deutsche Telekom [203] point out, operators will face significant challenges when it comes to buying advertisements respectively advertising campaigns across all channels, since specific advertising value chains and respective rules must be considered when planning multimedia campaigns.

6.2   Legal Aspects of Targeted Advertising

The public reception of technology developments in the context of targeted advertising is always strongly affected by a privacy discourse. As already mentioned efforts of BT and Phorm to implement Deep Packet Inspection (DPI) technology in order to profile browsing behavior have triggered a public outcry, since the users who participated in the trials were not made aware of the profiling [215, 221]. Another unfortunate example is the introduction of targeted advertising on Facebook. In 2007, Facebook launched the "Beacon" service that automatically made personal data available to cooperating 3rd party websites without prompting the users for permission [199]. Experiences like these have caused a great mistrust among consumers making efforts to establish personalized services very difficult. It is thus of crucial significance to focus on transparency and inform users about what happens to their data and how they can profit from personalized services. Transparency is moreover a legal requirement that has to be considered when implementing targeted advertising.

In the previous sections the privacy issue has already been shortly addressed for example in the context of mobile Web advertising, as it was pointed out that user profiling must be effectuated without keeping any references to personal data. This section will take a closer look at the legal requirements for the collection, processing, and use of personal data using the example of Germany. The analysis will especially examine under which preconditions opt-in or opt-out opportunities must be given, and when pseudonymization and anonymization is legally required. The section will close with an analysis concerning the legal aspects of ad insertion as for example proposed in the context of zone-based advertising. Potential problems arise from the fact that in this case the operator necessarily manipulates the content stream delivered from broadcasters, which may violate property rights.

6.2.1 General Principles of the Legal Framework

The German data protection law is regulated in the Federal Data Protection Act (Bundesdatenschutzgesetz, BDSG)[53], the Data Protection Acts of the German states, and regulations in specific fields of law. The Data Protection Acts of the German states are applicable if the controller is a public body of the respective state. The Federal Data Protection Act is applicable if the controller is a public body of the Federation or a private body. The controller is a natural or legal person, public authority, agency or any other body, which alone or jointly with others determines the purposes and means of the processing of personal data. As the potential players in the context of this book are private bodies, the German state laws are not relevant [51, 55].

Generally, Sec. 3a of the Federal Data Protection Act requires data processing systems to be "designed and selected in accordance with the aim of collecting, processing or using no personal data or as little personal data as possible". Furthermore, the collection and processing of personal data requires a statutory basis or the consent of the data subject to be legal. According to Sec. 3 Par. 1 BDSG personal data are "any information concerning the personal or material circumstances of an identified or identifiable individual (the data subject)". The Federal Data Protection Act provides general rules on the collection, processing and use of personal data. It is ruled out if a specific law is in place regulating the respective field, but supplements the specific laws if they do not conclusively cover a case [51]. The following figure gives an overview of the general relation of provisions covering the use of personal data in German law.

---

[53] http://www.gesetze-im-internet.de/bdsg_1990/

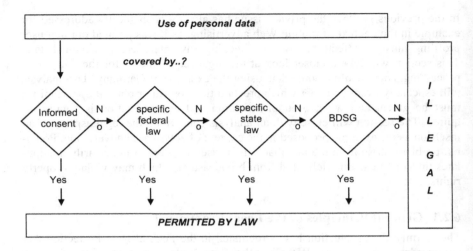

Figure 79: Order of application of legal regulations (source: [51])

Specific laws that may be applicable in the context of targeted advertising include the Telemedia Act (Telemediengesetz, TMG)[54], the Telecommunications Act (Telekommunikationsgesetz, TKG)[55], and the Interstate Treaty On Broadcasting (Rundfunkstaatsvertrag, RStV)[56]. The Telemedia Act contains a negative definition, which defines telemedia services as all electronic information or communication services, which are neither telecommunication services according to Sec. 3 Lit. 24, 25 TDG nor broadcasting services according to Sec. 2 RStV. It should be noted that the Telemedia Act transposes the EU Directive 2002/58/EC[57] on privacy and communications, which is sometimes called "ePrivacy" Directive. In practice, it is sometimes hard to differentiate which of these regulations is appropriate (see e.g. [88] on the application of the TMG in comparison to the TKG and the RStV). While the Telecommunications Act mainly covers the actual transmission of signals using telecommunication networks (transport level), the Telemedia Act is aimed at the transported content (applica-

---

[54] http://www.gesetze-im-internet.de/tmg/
[55] http://www.gesetze-im-internet.de/tkg_2004/
[56] http://www.die-medienanstalten.de/fileadmin/Download/Rechtsgrundlagen/Gesetze_aktuell/13._RStV_01.04.2010_01.pdf
[57] http://europa.eu/legislation_summaries/internal_market/single_market_services/l24120_en.htm

tion level). In the case of LBS for example, privacy issues during the collection of location data by the telecommunication service provider (e.g. via cell ID) and the transmission of location data from the telecommunication service provider to the content provider are covered by the Telecommunications Act, while a potential abuse of personal data through the content provider when using location data to provide content would be a concern of the Telemedia Act (compare [51] and [33] for more detailed analyses of the legal framework of LBS). In contrast, IPTV services are considered broadcasting services addressed by Sec. 2 Par. 1 RStV thus falling under the jurisdiction of the Interstate Treaty On Broadcasting [89]. As a discussion of each use case in terms of potential privacy issues would be far out of scope, the following subsection will effectuate an analysis of privacy concerns in the case of targeted advertising in the Web. Although the consequences of the regulations in the above specific laws are quite similar in terms of privacy matters, it should be noted that in practice the differentiation between the appropriate laws might be significant. As an example the Telemedia Act allows the creation of user profiles without user's consent if a pseudonym is used (see below section 6.2.2.2), while the Telecommunications Act explicitly requires the user's explicit consent and also anonymization of personal data. However, the exemplary discussion of the application of the Telemedia Act in the case of targeted Web advertising can provide a good introduction to the subject. For a comprehensive overview of the applicability of the different specific laws it can be referred to [60].

6.2.2 Privacy Aspects of Targeted Web Advertising

As a necessary condition any kind of targeted advertising or personalized services requires the collection of data, the aggregation of data into user profiles, and the usage of these data and user profiles to be legal. In the Internet the legitimacy of data collection and usage is covered by the Telemedia Act, especially Sec. 11 et sqq. TMG. The legitimacy of user profile creation and usage in the Internet is regulated by Sec. 15 TMG. In cases where the TMG is inapplicable it is supplemented by the regulations of the BDSG [25].

6.2.2.1 Legitimacy of Personal Data Collection and Usage

The TMG defines two kinds of personal data that must be distinguished in order to discuss the legitimacy of collecting and using personal data for targeted advertising. Customer data in the sense of Sec. 14 Par. 1 TMG are data like the name, the email address, or the date of birth that have to be entered when registering and therefore for the purpose of concluding a contract. Usage data in the sense of Sec. 15 Par. 1 TMG are data concerning the service provision as for example the usage time, page impressions, the number of downloads, or the visited subsites, and also the user name and the password that are though at the same time customer data. Usage data are typically necessary for billing purposes [25].

According to Sec. 14 Par. 1 TMG customer data may only be collected if they are necessary for the creation, implementation or modification of the contractual relationship between the user and the service provider. Pursuant to Sec. 15 Par. 1 TMG usage data may only be collected as far as required in order to allow and bill the telemedia service. This means that neither Sec. 14 Par. 1 TMG nor Sec. 15 Par. 1 TMG explicitly legitimate the usage of personal data for targeted advertising purposes. According to Sec. 12 Par. 1 and 2 TMG the collected customer and usage data may thus only be used for targeted advertising with the user's consent. The conditions that must be observed for obtaining the user's consent are regulated in Sec. 13 TMG. In particular, the transparency requirement of Sec. 13 Par. 1 TMG commits the service provider to inform the user about the manner, extent and purpose of data collection and usage for example through a link to "privacy policies". The consent must thus be a so-called informed consent [51].

It should be noted that the service provider might follow an opt-out approach only giving a user access, if she agrees with the terms of usage including privacy policies. However, the service provider must provide and point out the opportunity to opt out of usage of her personal data afterwards (Sec. 13 Par. 3, Par. 4 Lit. 4 TMG) [25]. StudiVZ for example requires the user to agree with their terms of usage that contain targeted advertising based on personal data, in order to gain access to their service. Though, after having registered with StudiVZ, the user may deactivate the targeted advertising option[58].

6.2.2.2   Legitimacy of User Profile Creation and Usage

The above subsection focused on explicitly entered customer data and usage data collected in order to enable and bill a service, and under which circumstances these data can be used for targeted advertising. However, in addition the creation and usage of user profiles is especially interesting for targeted advertising purposes. The term "user profile" is not explicitly defined in German law, though it can be considered as the systematic aggregation of usage data in the sense of Sec. 15 Par. 1 TMG. In the Web context this particularly includes tracking of users' browsing behavior in order to derive their interests. Customer data as defined by Sec. 14 Par. 1 TMG may not be stored in the user profile [25].

---

[58] See http://www.studivz.net/l/policy/declaration/ paragraph 5 and http://www.studivz.net/ Terms/Options option 3 (login required).

Legitimacy without User's Consent (Opt-Out Approach)

Sec. 15 Par. 3 TMG allows the creation of user profiles for the purpose of advertising without the user's consent provided that a pseudonym is used. According to Sec. 3 Par. 6a BDSG pseudonymization is the "replacement of the name and other identifying characteristics by a code in order to prevent identification of the person in question or to make this significantly more difficult". The user must be granted the right to contradict the profiling (i.e. to opt out) and he must be made aware of this right. Attention should be paid to the fact that pseudonymized profiles must however not be combined with data related to the bearer of the pseudonym. This requirement was already emphasized in the above use cases on Web and mobile Web advertising and has a direct impact on the implementation of profiling systems. Sec. 13 Par. 4 Lit. 6 TMG commits the service provider to make technical and organizational provisions in order to prevent the opportunity to combine customer data with user profiles [25, 60]. In the mobile Web environment in section 4.3.3 the separation of pseudonymized user profiles and personal data was realized using a mediating ad broker.

The legal situation is though different again, if the service provider technically realizes a completely anonymized profiling. This requires that profiling data have to be anonymized already during data collection. Pursuant to Sec. 3 Par. 6 BDSG anonymization means "the modification of personal data so that the information concerning personal or material circumstances can no longer or only with a disproportionate amount of time, expense and labor be attributed to an identified or identifiable individual". Anonymized analyses of usage information generally do not have to comply with any privacy regulations, as personal references cannot be made [60]. A service provider who realizes anonymized usage profiling is thus not required to offer opt-out opportunities, although this may be advisable for reasons of credibility and reputation. In addition, anonymized user profiles may also be shared and used across legal entities both within a corporate group and also in the context of a partnership e.g. an advertising network, which otherwise would only be allowed with the user's consent (compare the Facebook "Beacon" service mentioned in the introduction to this section that meanwhile was modified and now asks users for permission before using their profiles for advertising purposes). As an example implementing anonymized usage profiling, the privacy aspects of the Wunderloop targeting platform will be described in the next subsection.

Legitimacy with User's Consent (Opt-In Approach)

The above described regulations of Sec. 15 Par. 3 TMG only concern the creation and usage of pseudonymized user profiles without the user's consent. In cases where the user explicitly agrees with profiling activities (i.e. she opts in), it is legal to create user profiles without pseudonymization and even to combine the profiles with personal data for example for targeting purposes. The legitimacy is only limited by the extent of the informed consent. Pursuant to Sec. 13 Par. 1 TMG the service provider must precisely inform the user about the fact that usage profiles are created, that they may be combined with existing customer data of the user, and that these data will be analyzed in order to enable targeted advertising. According to Sec. 13 Par. 2 Lit. 4 TMG the user must be granted the opportunity to completely or partially withdraw her consent at any time. Correspondingly to the legal situation of personal data collection and usage described in the previous subsection, the service provider may deny access to the service if the user does not give her consent for the usage of customer and profile data for targeted advertising [25].

Table 7: Legal consequences of Web usage profiling (source: table based on [156])

Profiling Method	Requirements
Personal Data	· Targeting requires informed consent (opt-in) · Users must explicitly agree with user profile creation and a possible combination with customer data and targeting
Pseudonymized Data	· Targeting without user's consent but with right of objection (opt-out) · Users must be informed about user profile creation, targeting purposes and the right to object, e.g. through a highlighted link to privacy policies · Profiling data must not be combined with data about the bearer of the pseudonym
Anonymized Data	· Privacy laws not applicable, no legal requirements · Information and opt-out opportunity recommended by the BVDW OVK

6.2.3 Privacy Matters in the Wunderloop Targeting Platform

In the following, the implementation of the above described privacy requirements in Web advertising shall be described shortly using the example of the Wunderloop[59] targeting platform, which already served as a basis for the development of the generic targeting system introduced in section 5.1. Wunderloop enables targeted advertising based on user interests derived from browsing behavior. Users are not addressed by their name, but by using non-personal cookies generated from a random number and the current date meaning that no reference to the user can be made. As was already described, these cookies are used for identifying the user in the tracking process. For technical reasons, the cookie and the IP address are transmitted in conjunction. As the IP address can be considered personal data, these information are not sent directly to Wunderloop, but rather to a legally and economically independent 3rd party company who acts as an anonymizer separating the cookie from the IP address. Hence, the IP address belonging to the user only reaches the 3rd party anonymizer and will not be forwarded to Wunderloop. In a separate process the IP address is translated into country or region information, then added to the other information transmitted by the cookie, and finally sent to the Wunderloop system. In the same transaction recommendation information for the user is requested from the Wunderloop targeting system and then written back to the user's PC in form of a recommendation cookie. As was described in section 5.1.3 this cookie contains a target group recommendation that can be read out by an ad server for targeted ad delivery. Eventually, the IP address is irreversibly deleted making re-personalization of a particular user technically impossible. Thus, Wunderloop thus does not receive and not process any personal data; it only deals with anonymous data [41, 208].

In previous sections it was mentioned that existing user data available at the service provider, e.g. through a CRM system, may be used to enrich the user profile created from user behavior. As an ID is needed to merge data from user tracking with CRM data, the above described anonymization process cannot be kept the same way. However, in order to still legally perform targeting without user consent, Sec. 15 Par. 3 TMG requires the usage of a pseudonym. Hence, the respective data extracted from the customer database must be pseudonymized before it can be made available to the targeting system. The identification cookie then contains the pseudonymized user ID. The exact process can be realized similar to the pseudonymization method described in the mobile Web advertising use case in section 4.3.3.

---

[59] Due to the acquisition of Wunderloop by AudienceScience [220], the respective privacy policy can be found at http://www.audiencescience.com/de/privacy.

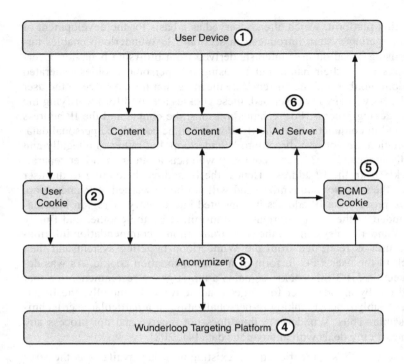

Figure 80: Data flow in the Wunderloop targeting platform (source: own illustration based on [208])

Users (1) are identified by User Cookies (2); the IP address belonging to the users only reaches the 3rd party Anonymizer (3) and will not be given to the Wunderloop system(4). It is generally impossible for Wunderloop to link users and IP address data. All tracking enquiries are initiated by a 1×1 counting pixel; the target segment information is transferred to the Ad Server (6) by a recommendation cookie (RCMD Cookie) (5).

6.2.4 Limitations for Stream Manipulation through Targeted Advertising in IPTV

Another legal problem area besides privacy matters concerns potential copyright issues arising from manipulations in the content stream, which are necessary for targeted ad insertion in IPTV. The German copyright law is regulated in the

Copyright Act (Gesetz über Urheberrecht und verwandte Schutzrechte, UrhG)[60]. In German law the copyright is generally not transferrable unless in execution of a testamentary disposition (Sec. 29 UrhG). Pursuant to Sec. 31 UrhG the author may however grant a right to another to use the work in a particular manner or in any manner (exploitation right). These exploitations rights are often called licenses. According to Sec. 88 et sqq. UrhG exploitation rights for films are owned by the producer. This includes the exclusive right to reproduce and distribute a video recording and especially the right of broadcasting (Sec. 20 UrhG) and making available to the public (Sec. 19a UrhG). The right of broadcasting is the right to make a work accessible to the public by broadcasting such as radio or television transmission, or by wire, or by other similar technical devices. The right of making available to the public is the right to make a work wiredly or wirelessly accessible to the public in a manner such that it can be accessed by members of the public from any location and at any time of their choice. The decision criterion between both is thus whether the streaming video is sent in a fixed sequence or not. Hence, linear TV is broadcasting in the sense of Sec. 20 UrhG, while video on demand is covered by Sec. 19a UrhG, i.e. the right of making available to the public [38, 214]. This differentiation is important as it influences the modalities of contract conclusion an operator willing to realize targeted advertising must consider.

Broadcasting Linear IPTV Content (Sec. 20 UrhG)

As mentioned above authors respectively film producers own the right of broadcasting a film or video recording. In practice, this right is usually granted to broadcasting organizations. According to Sec. 20b and Sec. 87 UrhG broadcasters further own the right to retransmit the once transmitted work by a cable or microwave system (cable retransmission). Hence, an IPTV operator, who wants to broadcast content over his network must acquire the right of retransmission from the broadcasting organization. Generally, broadcasting organization and operator are free to conclude a contract ad libitum. However, Sec. 87 Par. 5 UrhG specifies an obligation to contract for simultaneous, unaltered and unabridged cable retransmissions. This obligation further requires broadcasting organizations and operators to conclude the cable retransmission contract under reasonable conditions. Pursuant to Sec. 20b UrhG the acquisition of the retransmission right can though only be exercised by a mediating collecting society as for example the Gesellschaft für musikalische Aufführungs- und mechanische Vervielfältigungsrechte (GEMA, representing the public TV stations) or the Gesellschaft zur Verwertung der Urheber- und Leistungsschutzrechte von Medienunternehmen (VG Media, representing private TV stations as e.g. ProSiebenSat.1 and RTL).

---

[60] http://www.gesetze-im-internet.de/urhg/

This actually means that the freedom of contract is limited in terms of the subject matter and the conclusion of the contract [219, 160].

On the one hand, these regulations guarantee that the operator will receive a re-transmission right for broadcasting content and also that the broadcaster cannot drive him out due to exaggerated terms. On the other hand, the regulations contain the requirement to retransmit unaltered content. In how far the requirement to retransmit programs unaltered includes the prohibition of technical measures necessary for targeted advertising is a matter of interpretation and will have to be clarified with broadcasting organizations and respective collecting societies before implementing targeted advertising technologies. The GEMA tariff agreements [75] for cable retransmission at least include the annotation that "the requirement of unaltered retransmission implies that, if no other arrangements are made, the display of programs must be effectuated in full screen mode and without any modifications in terms of program content (no advertisements, no overlays,…) as well as in terms of program signals". The VG Media tariff agreements [211] do not contain respective annotations.

Making VoD Content Available to the Public (Sec. 19a UrhG)

Besides the right of broadcasting, film producers also own the right of making their work available to the public, which they may grant to media agencies, e.g. in order to promote a recent movie for on demand viewing. In contrast to linear TV where the right of retransmission and the obligation of contract between broadcasting organizations and operators may cause legal concerns regarding stream manipulations in the context of targeted advertising, there is no legal limit regarding the freedom of contract in this case. The operator must individually acquire the exploitation right of making available to the public from the media agency holding the respective license. There is neither a need for a mediating collecting society nor any legal requirements concerning unaltered retransmission [214]. Whether and, if yes, which kinds of technical measures regarding content stream manipulation in the context of targeted advertising are allowed, is only a question of the terms of the contract both parties can agree on. This may also include qualitative regulations regarding the allowed topics in the context of the movie (e.g. no advertisements for alcoholic drinks in the context of a Disney movie).

7 Conclusion and Outlook

The Information and Communication Technology (ICT) world is currently experiencing disruptive changes. "Webcos" like Google are making more and more money with Internet-based services thereby degrading Telcos to "bit pipes". In addition, Webcos are increasingly pushing into traditional Telco businesses. One example in this area is the "Telco as a service" provider Ribbit[61], who offers VoIP soft switching capabilities allowing to create voice apps in a familiar Web application development environment that can easily be linked to other Web applications. Telcos must hence develop beyond pure technical enabling and start providing integrated services on top of their network infrastructure, in order to generate new revenue opportunities. This is a first step towards "Telco 2.0", meaning the idea of a two-sided telecom market providing platforms through which 3rd parties can interact with the Telco user base. Targeted advertising is one of these advanced platform services allowing Telcos to leverage their core assets namely their hold on customers and the ability to reach them through many different ICT channels.

Today targeting technology is already very common on Web portals presenting their users with personalized advertisements and all kinds of product recommendations. These business models are highly accepted and the underlying technologies are very sophisticated. The most promising target areas for targeted advertising services in the Telco domain include Internet Protocol Television (IPTV), the mobile environment and especially converged scenarios. However, in all of these areas targeted advertising use cases are far from being established. The IPTV world is still a very nascent domain currently gaining momentum but still remaining at low user numbers. Advertisers and ad marketers are not yet recognizing targeted advertising in IPTV as a valuable business opportunity in large scale, since the small user base does not allow defining and addressing attractive target groups. However, broadband networks are currently being heavily expanded delivering a solid groundwork for more evolved services beyond pure linear television. Therefore, Telcos start considering first pilot implementations, at the same time being scared about heavy investments into the network infrastructure that might not pay off. There are though several scenarios that can be realized without high investments into costly network components and which promise to generate incremental revenues even at a lower subscriber base. These first stage use cases include advanced Electronic Program Guide (EPG) portals based on Web tech-

---

[61] http://www.ribbit.com/

nology allowing to leverage frameworks approved in the Internet. A crucial point can emerge if the Set-Top-Box (STB) does not allow using cookies for user identification as is common in the Web. However, in IPTV usually the unique identity provided by the middleware of the STB can be used as an identifier. Besides portal services Telcos should evaluate other STB-based approaches extending the middleware, in order to locally insert Web-like banner ads over the linear TV stream. Certainly, displaying of ads over the actual TV content cannot be performed without collaboration of programmers and advertisers, which can potentially be a showstopper. However, Telcos should try to attract them by showing up the high potential of interactive features that may be implemented extending the same technology. In times where user generated content and participation is all around, this represents a significant added value enabled through the inherent bidirectionality of IPTV networks. Interactive advertising in IPTV provides the opportunity of smooth integration with the Web, hence opening up a tremendous advertising potential. STB-based ad insertion approaches are hence a good starting point for targeting considerations in IPTV. Due to the limited processing power of these devices, they are however not capable of handling complex multimedia advertising. Especially when it comes to in-stream ad insertion limits are reached soon. Such scenarios can only be realized using cutting-edge network-based ad insertion components adopted from the cable environment allowing to insert ads into the compressed stream and even in encrypted content. Since the multicast nature of linear IPTV requires insertion infrastructure to be installed in the access network in order to enable fine-granular targeting, network-based ad insertion causes huge investment costs. Therefore, these approaches should only be considered after having reached a critical mass of users and having established first successful collaborations with programmers and advertisers. As for Video on Demand (VoD) ad insertion, the situation is different from linear TV since in this case targeted advertising can be implemented based on existing network components, simply playing out ads using the VoD management and server infrastructure, hence predestining VoD advertising as part of the first stage of an operator's IPTV advertising strategy. However, a general problem IPTV operators are facing is that initially only STBs can be addressed, which is not necessarily equivalent to single users. As in most households there is a changing auditorium ranging from children to parents, viewing habits are different and profiling of viewing preferences may lead to inconsistent user profiles. In consequence, targeting must focus on content and geographical information unless a distinct identification of single users is made possible through single user login. Though, customers are usually very reluctant to login before starting to watch TV requiring to attract them to login voluntarily by additional services like for example a personalized portal including mail services and instant messaging. A very different approach to tackle this challenge is taken by the personal TV channel concept. Here, profiles are not generated on a user basis but rather for distinct channels. The idea behind is that every family member can create its own very special topic channels making the mapping of adequate advertising a lot easier.

In the mobile environment the initial position for targeted advertising deployment is somewhat different than in IPTV for several reasons. First of all, the market penetration has already been extremely high for a while, therefore principally making this environment very attractive for advertisers as the basis for personalized services is broad. The technological limitations in terms of device and network capabilities have though constrained more advanced advertising concepts including targeting in the past. However, the recent emergence of high-performing Web enabled smartphones and the increasing availability of broadband wireless technologies are now laying the foundations for sophisticated mobile targeted advertising services. In addition, the individuality of mobile devices, and the opportunity to easily leverage user context information based on location data act as additional drivers of mobile targeted advertising. Most of today's mobile phones are meanwhile capable of browsing regular websites hence bringing existing Web targeting to the mobile world. However, mobile operator portals are today quite common as an entry point for mobile Web consumption, therefore representing an optimal starting point for Telcos' targeted advertising efforts as they can leverage their subscriber data for targeting purposes. Like in IPTV, the issue of user identification arises if cookie-storage is not supported. Then, another identifier i.e. the Mobile Subscriber Integrated Services Digital Network Number (MSISDN) or the International Mobile Equipment Identity (IMEI) must be made available to the targeting system. This information can usually not be accessed by an arbitrary website the user visits and is only available to the operator, hence potentially allowing mobile carriers to position themselves as targeting provider for off-portal advertising. Besides mobile Web advertising scenarios first targeted advertising implementations in mobile messaging have gone commercial. Currently accounting for almost 90 percent of all revenues in mobile advertising, mobile messaging is an absolute hot spot for targeting. Mobile messaging can extremely benefit from the availability of user location data made available through the Home Location Register (HLR) of the mobile network or even the Global Positioning System (GPS) receiver of modern smartphones. This location awareness allows for very interesting advertising models as for example direct message marketing in form of couponing triggered by the user's proximity to advertising relevant locations. Another very promising area for targeted advertising are subsidized messaging business models providing the user with targeted ads in exchange for free talking time or messaging. If based on the direct messaging approach they can be quite easily implemented based on adapted targeting platforms from the Web as is being demonstrated by the collaboration of E-Plus and Wunderloop in the Gettings service. As for in-message advertising the attractiveness for mobile carriers strongly depends on possible re-routing capabilities of the existing Short Message Service Centers (SMSCs) necessary for efficient ad insertion. Otherwise, unacceptable delays in message delivery can result being a showstopper for this approach. Except for mobile TV and video, where technology development and rollout of commercial services are still at an early stage, it can be stated that targeted mobile advertising is currently taking off. This is also due to the fact that in contrast to IPTV, the business background is by far more convenient as mobile operators are already involved in an existing advertising value chain and do not have to struggle as hard as in IPTV to reach a place in the sun.

The future of targeted advertising belongs to converged scenarios. Most multi-platform operators start offering integrated products and services across multiple ICT channels (triple play or even quadruple play), in order to provide a comprehensive user experience to the customer. These environments provide excellent targeting opportunities as the operator can aggregate user data across several channels and hence derive more exact profiles, potentially increasing the ad efficiency. The integration of business lines and underlying platforms and technologies causes multiple challenges, which is even more valid for advertising in these environments. Converged scenarios can though become arbitrarily complex including for example requirements for content transcoding capabilities or concerning the ability to perform ad insertion in changing online/offline modes as described in the analyses of the converged use cases. The most crucial point is the identification of devices across different channels belonging to one customer, in order to collect and integrate respective profiling data. This requires an Identity Management (IdM) system realizing a tree-like connection of the single identities (e.g. MSISDN and STB ID) under a virtual master identity. Traditionally, operators regard IdM only in the context of authentication of subscribers into the network and authorization of their access to services realized by Authentication, Authorization, and Accounting (AAA) systems. Hence, the implementation of a unified IdM system that is bridged to the AAA systems of each ICT channel is a necessary step operators must take in order to provide converged advertising services.

Another key technology in the context of targeted advertising are recommender systems. In targeting platforms they are part of the targeting intelligence and analyze user profiles in order to derive target group recommendations for ad selection. Current recommendation technology is mostly based on Content-Based (CB) and Collaborative Filtering (CF) approaches, making recommendations based on the similarity of user and item profiles respectively similarities of user profiles. State-of-the-art recommender systems as for example the stereotype-based recommendation solution analyzed in section 5.3.4.2 use hybrid approaches combining both methods, but are still abstracting from the current user situation. However, mobile and especially complex converged targeting scenarios require a recommendation technology, which includes dynamic contextual information regarding the actual situation of a user into the ad selection process. In order to realize location- and time-sensitive targeted advertising scenarios as for example the classic couponing use case, Telco's advertising platform must be able to incorporate this additional "dimension".

Eventually, the future success of targeted advertising strategies in the ICT environment will strongly depend on the operators' ability to leverage their massive user base across PC, TV, and mobile devices. Therefore, on the one hand operators must adopt an iterative learn-and-adapt approach to handle constantly changing customer behavior, technology standards and business models. As customers often do not have a clear idea of what targeted advertising actually means, operators can only gain a hold in the advertising value network by actively engaging, educating, and creating awareness of the benefits of targeted advertising. On the other hand, Telcos will have to consolidate existing targeting platforms in different channels, in order to enable seamlessly converged advertising scenarios. Besides the above-mentioned key technologies, Telcos must aim at unifying targeted advertising processes and implementing a cross-channel targeting platform. The reason for this is not only internal cost reduction and optimization aspects. Telcos will only be able to sell multi-channel ad campaigns to ad marketers if they present one face to the customer, which will not be possible when operating separate platforms by several different business units responsible for each ICT channel. Therefore, an integrated targeting platform must be developed. As this work has shown, the underlying technology always relies on some typical core functionalities, which are basically the profiling unit, a targeting intelligence consisting of targeting and recommendation units, and in addition the campaign management with an attached ad server. Depending on the use case scenario additional ad insertion units may be connected to these systems. Based on these insights a first approach towards the development of a generic targeted advertising framework has been taken. A next step would be to further develop this proposition in order to finally implement a reference system with interfaces towards several ICT channels. Further starting points for future research work could emerge from the current lack of standardized targeting solutions in IPTV as well as in the mobile environment. One future task could for example be to research on the Open Mobile Alliance (OMA) MobAd enabler standard, trying to implement a test system following the analysis in section 4.4.2.

Bibliography

[1]   3G Americas. *Identity Management: Overview of Standards and Technologies for Mobile and Fixed Internet*. White Paper, 2009. Retrieved 2012/04/30, from http://4gamericas.org/documents/3GAmericas_Unified_Identity_Management_Jan2009.pdf.

[2]   3GPP (3rd Generation Partnership Project), TSG SA WG3. *3GPP TR 33.980 v. 10.0.0. Liberty Alliance and 3GPP security interworking; Interworking of Liberty Alliance Identity Federation Framework (ID-FF), Identity Web Services Framework (ID-WSF) and Generic Authentication Architecture (GAA)*. Standards Specification, 2011. Retrieved 2012/04/30, from http://www.3gpp.org/ftp/Specs/html-info/33980.htm.

[3]   3GPP (3rd Generation Partnership Project), TSG SA WG1. *3GPP TS 22.146 v. 10.1.0. Multimedia Broadcast/Multicast Service (MBMS); Stage 1*. Standards Specification, 2011. Retrieved 2012/04/30, from http://www.3gpp.org/ftp/Specs/html-info/22146.htm.

[4]   3GPP (3rd Generation Partnership Project), TSG SA WG2. *3GPP TS 23.240 v. 10.0.0. 3GPP Generic User Profile (GUP) requirements; Architecture (Stage 2)*. Standards Specification, 2011. Retrieved 2012/04/30, from http://www.3gpp.org/ftp/Specs/html-info/23240.htm.

[5]   3GPP (3rd Generation Partnership Project). *3GPP - IMS*, 2012. Retrieved 2012/04/30, from http://www.3gpp.org/article/ims/.

[6]   3GPP (3rd Generation Partnership Project), TSG SA WG3. *3GPP TR 33.220 v. 11.2.0. Generic Authentication Architecture (GAA); Generic bootstrapping architecture*. Standards Specification, 2012. Retrieved 2012/04/30, from http://www.3gpp.org/ftp/Specs/html-info/33220.htm

[7]   G. Adomavicius, R. Sankaranarayanan, et al. Incorporating contextual information in recommender systems using a multidimensional approach. *ACM Trans. Inf. Syst.*, 23(1): 103-145, 2005.

[8]   G. Adomavicius and A. Tuzhilin. Towards the Next Generation of Recommender Systems: A Survey of the State-of-the-Art and Possible Extensions. *IEEE Trans. on Knowl. and Data Eng.*, 17(6): 734-749, 2005.

[9]   G. Adomavicius and A. Tuzhilin. Context-aware recommender systems. *Proceedings of the 2008 ACM conference on Recommender systems*, Lausanne, Switzerland, ACM, 2008.

[10]   AfterDawn. *Glossary of technology terms*, 2012. Retrieved 2012/04/30, from http://www.afterdawn.com/glossary/.

[11]   A. Al-Hezmi, T. Magedanz, et al. Evolving the convergence of telecommunication and TV services over NGN. *International journal of digital multimedia broadcasting*, 2008.

[12]   S. Albers and B. Skiera. *Marketing mit interaktiven Medien : Strategien zum Markterfolg*. F.A.Z.-Institut, Frankfurt, 3rd edition, 2001.

[13]   A. Albiol, M. J. C. Fullà, et al. Detection of TV Commercials. *Proceedings of the International Conference on Acoustics, Speech and Signal Processing (IEEE ICASS)*, Montreal, Canada, 2004.

[14]   S. S. Anand and B. Mobasher. *Contextual Recommendation*. From Web to Social Web: Discovering and Deploying User and Content Profiles. B. Berendt, A. Hotho, D. Mladenic and G. Semeraro. Springer-Verlag: 142-160, 2007.

[15]   ARD/ZDF. *ARD/ZDF-Onlinestudie 2009*, 2009. Retrieved 2012/04/30, from http://www.ard-zdf-onlinestudie.de/.

[16]   K. Asp, F. Badiee, et al. Advertising Solutions. *Ericsson Review*, (2): 4-9, 2009.

[17]   AudienceScience. *Deutsche Telekom Selects AudienceScience for Digital Marketing Solution and Data Management Partner*, 2012. Retrieved 2012/04/30, from http://www.audiencescience.com/press-room/press-releases/2012/deutsche-telekom-selects-audiencescience-digital-marketing-solution-a.

[18] Axel Springer AG. *Axel Springer Digital TV Guide acquires APRICO recommendation technology from Philips*, 2012. Retrieved 2012/04/30, from http://www.axelspringer.de/en/presse/Axel-Springer-Digital-TV-Guide-acquires-APRICO-recommendation-technology-from-Philips_5822886.html.

[19] C. Bachelet, Analysys Mason. *Monetising pay-TV services: content strategies, business models and pricing*. Research Report, 2009.

[20] M. Bakhuizen and U. Horn. Mobile broadcast/multicast in mobile networks. *Ericsson Review*, 82(1): 8, 2005.

[21] H. Balzert. *Lehrbuch der Software-Technik - Software-Entwicklung*. Spektrum Akademischer Verlag, Heidelberg, 1996.

[22] S. J. Barbeau, M. A. Labrador, et al. Location API 2.0 for J2ME - A new standard in location for Java-enabled mobile phones. *Computer Communications*, 31(6): 1091-1103, 2008.

[23] J. Basilico and T. Hofmann. Unifying collaborative and content-based filtering. *Proceedings of the twenty-first international conference on Machine learning*, Banff, Alberta, Canada, ACM, 2004.

[24] B. Bates. *Electronic Programming Guides for IPTV*, 2006. Retrieved 2012/04/30, from http://www.althos.com/IPTVArticles/IPTVMagazine_2006_09_electronic_programming.htm.

[25] S. Bauer. Personalisierte Werbung auf Social Community-Websites. *Multimedia und Recht*, (7): 435-438, 2008.

[26] BBC Interactive. *BBC – FAQs – TV – Red Button*, 2012. Retrieved 2012/04/30, from http://faq.external.bbc.co.uk/questions/television/red_button/.

[27] H. Benoît. *Digital television: Satellite, cable, terrestrial, IPTV, mobile TV in the DVB framework*. Elsevier/Focal Press, Amsterdam, 3rd edition, 2008.

[28] C. M. Bishop. *Pattern recognition and machine learning*. Springer, New York, 2007.

[29]   BITKOM. *Mehr als 100 Millionen Mobilfunkanschlüsse in Deutschland*
        (2008) - *BITKOM*, 2008. Retrieved 2012/04/30, from
        http://www.bitkom.org/de/presse/56204_51915.aspx.

[30]   BITKOM. *Jeder vierte Mobilfunktnutzer plant Kauf eines neuen Handys*
        (2009) - *BITKOM*, 2009. Retrieved 2012/04/30, from
        http://www.bitkom.org/de/presse/8477_61548.aspx.

[31]   C. Borrman. *Mobile App Stores & On-Device Portals*, 2012. Retrieved
        2012/04/30, from http://www.on-deviceportal.com/.

[32]   J. Breese, D. Heckerman, et al. *Empirical Analysis of Predictive*
        Algorithms for Collaborative Filtering, 1998. Retrieved 2012/04/30, from
        http://research.microsoft.com/pubs/69656/tr-98-12.pdf.

[33]   D. Bremer. Möglichkeiten und Grenzen des Mobile Commerce. *Computer*
        Und Recht (CR): 12-17, 2009.

[34]   Broadband TV News. *MFD hands back German T-DMB licence*, 2008.
        Retrieved 2012/04/30, from http://www.broadbandtvnews.com/2008/05/
        01/mfd-hands-back-german-t-dmb-license/.

[35]   Broadcast Engineering. *Orange, T-Mobile UK plan MBMS-based mobile*
        TV trial in the U.K., 2008. Retrieved 2012/04/30, from
        http://broadcastengineering.com/RF/orange_tmobile_plan_mbms_0219/.

[36]   D. Broto. *GPRS Network Architecture*, 2008. Retrieved 2012/04/30, from
        http://www.denmasbroto.com/index.php?pilih=news&mod=yes&aksi=liha
        t&id=5.

[37]   P. J. Brown, J. D. Bovey, et al. Context-Aware Applications: from the
        Laboratory to the Marketplace. *IEEE Personal Communications*, 4(5): 58-
        64, 1997.

[38]   W. Büchner. Wie kommt der Ball ins Netz? Fußball im IPTV und Mobile-
        TV. *Computer Und Recht (CR)*: 473-480, 2007.

[39]   T. Bugir. *The New Economics of Customer Reach: Advanced Advertising.*
        White Paper, 2009. Retrieved 2012/04/30, from http://www.scribd.com/
        doc/49854813/AdvAdvertising-media-economics.

[40] T. Bugir, Sun Microsystems, Inc. *Targeted Advertising.* Guided Interview (see Appendix), Phone Call, 2009.

[41] BVDW (Bundesverband Digitale Wirtschaft). *Meine Cookies - Rechtliche Aspekte*, 2009. Retrieved 2012/04/30, from http://www.meine-cookies.org/ alles_ueber_cookies/rechtliche_aspekte.html.

[42] BVDW (Bundesverband Digitale Wirtschaft), Fachgruppe Mobile. *Mobile Advertising Guide*, 2009. Retrieved 2012/04/30, from http://www.bvdw.org/medien/mobile-advertising-guide?media=1257.

[43] CableLabs. *Open Cable - Enhanced Television (ETV)*, 2012. Retrieved 2012/04/30, from http://www.cablelabs.com/advancedadvertising/etv/.

[44] G. Camarillo and M. A. García-Martín. *The 3G IP multimedia subsystem (IMS) : merging the Internet and the cellular worlds.* Wiley, Chichester, 3rd edition, 2008.

[45] K. Cameron, R. Posch, et al. *Proposal for a Common Identity Framework: A User-Centric Identity Metasystem*, 2008. Retrieved 2012/04/30, from http://www.identityblog.com/wp-content/images/2009/06/UserCentric IdentityMetasystem.pdf.

[46] Capgemini, Telecom & Media Technology Insights. *Targeted Advertising. Unleashing the value of next generation customer intelligence*, 2008.

[47] A. Cockburn. *Use cases, ten years later*, 2002. Retrieved 2012/04/30, from http://alistair.cockburn.us/Use+cases%2c+ten+years+later.

[48] A. Cockburn. *Writing effective use cases.* Addison-Wesley, Boston, 13th edition, 2005.

[49] Computerwoche. *Mobile 3.0. DVB-H-Konsortium in Deutschland gescheitert*, 2008. Retrieved 2012/04/30, from http://www.computerwoche.de/netzwerke/mobile-wireless/1875212/ index.html.

[50] T. Cover and P. Hart. Nearest neighbor pattern classification. *IEEE Transactions on Information Theory*, 13(1): 21-27, 1967.

[51]   C. Cuijpers, A. Roosendaal, et al., FIDIS (Future of Identity in the
        Information Society), FIDIS Deliverables. *D11.5: The legal framework for
        location-based services in Europe*, 2007. Retrieved 2012/04/30, from
        http://www.fidis.net/fileadmin/fidis/deliverables/fidis-WP11-del11.5-
        legal_framework_for_LBS.pdf.

[52]   F. Dawson. New IPTV Advertising Platforms Could Put Telcos at Cutting
        Edge. *ScreenPlays - Strategic Information For The Broadband
        Marketplace*, 2009.

[53]   D. DeRoure, W. Hall, et al. MEMOIR - an open framework for enhanced
        navigation of distributed information. *Inf. Process. Manage.*, 37(1): 53-74,
        2001.

[54]   Design and Marketing Dictionary. *Design and Marketing Dictionary*,
        2009. Retrieved 2012/04/30, from http://design-marketing-dictionary.
        blogspot.com/.

[55]   A. Deuker, FIDIS (Future of Identity in the Information Society), FIDIS
        Deliverables. *D11.12: Mobile Marketing in the Perspective of Identity,
        Privacy and Transparency* 2009. Retrieved 2012/04/30, from
        http://www.fidis.net/fileadmin/fidis/deliverables/new_deliverables3/fidis-
        wp11-del11.12_mobile_marketing_in_the_perspective_of_identity_
        privacy_and_transparency.pdf.

[56]   Developer's Home. *Tutorial about Detecting User Agent Types and Client
        Device Capabilities*, 2011. Retrieved 2012/04/30, from
        http://www.developershome.com/wap/detection/.

[57]   A. K. Dey. Understanding and Using Context. *Personal and Ubiquitous
        Computing*, 5(1): 4-7, 2001.

[58]   digitalfernsehen.de. *Italien: Weltpremiere für DVB-H. Pünktlich zur
        Fußball-WM ging das digitale Handy-Fernsehen DVB-H in Italien auf
        Sendung.*, 2006. Retrieved 2012/04/30, from
        http://www.digitalfernsehen.de/news_92221.html.

[59]   P. Dourish. What we talk about when we talk about context. *Personal
        Ubiquitous Computing*, 8(1): 19-30, 2004.

[60]   J. Eckhardt. *Datenschutz - Was ist beim Online-Marketing zu beachten?*
       Leitfaden Online-Marketing : [Das kompakte Wissen der Branche]. T.
       Schwarz. Marketing-Börse, Waghäusel, 2nd edition: 755-771, 2008.

[61]   G. Eichler and K.-H. Lüke. A personalized recommendation community
       framework for user self-controlled edutainment. *International technology,*
       Education and Development Conference, INTED 2009, 2009.

[62]   Elektronik-Kompendium. *DMB - Digital Multimedia Broadcast*, 2012.
       Retrieved   2012/04/30,   from   http://www.elektronik-kompendium.de/
       sites/kom/1207031.htm.

[63]   Elektronik-Kompendium. *DVB-H - Digital Video Broadcast for Handheld*,
       2012. Retrieved 2012/04/30, from http://www.elektronik-kompendium.de/
       sites/kom/1207021.htm.

[64]   ETSI (European Telecommunications Standards Institute). *Digital Video*
       Broadcasting (DVB); Transmission System for Handheld Terminals (DVB-
       H).   *DVB-H   System*,   2004.   Retrieved   2012/04/30,   from
       http://webapp.etsi.org/WorkProgram/Report_WorkItem.asp?WKI_ID=198
       98.

[65]   ETSI (European Telecommunications Standards Institute). *Digital Audio*
       Broadcasting (DAB); DMB video service; User Application Specification.
       DMB   video   service,   2005.   Retrieved   2012/04/30,   from
       http://webapp.etsi.org/WorkProgram/Report_WorkItem.asp?WKI_ID=222
       23.

[66]   ETSI (European Telecommunications Standards Institute). *Digital Audio*
       Broadcasting (DAB); DMB video service; User application specification.
       DMB   video   service,   2009.   Retrieved   2012/04/30,   from
       http://webapp.etsi.org/WorkProgram/Report_WorkItem.asp?WKI_ID=304
       38.

[67]   ETSI (European Telecommunications Standards Institute). *Digital Video*
       Broadcasting (DVB); Transport of MPEG-2 TS Based DVB Services over
       IP Based Networks. DVB over IP-based Networks (DVB-IPI), 2009.
       Retrieved 2012/04/30, from http://webapp.etsi.org/workProgram/Report_
       WorkItem.asp?wki_id=29338.

[68] ETSI (European Telecommunications Standards Institute). *GSM*, 2011. Retrieved 2012/04/30, from http://www.etsi.org/WebSite/Technologies/gsm.aspx.

[69] ETSI (European Telecommunications Standards Institute). *Telecommunications and Internet converged Services and Protocols for Advanced Networking (TISPAN); IPTV Architecture; IPTV functions supported by the IMS subsystem. IPTV stage 2 (IMS-based)*, 2011. Retrieved 2012/04/30, from http://webapp.etsi.org/WorkProgram/Report_WorkItem.asp?WKI_ID=34209.

[70] European Commission. *Commission opens Europe's Single Market for Mobile TV services*, 2007. Retrieved 2012/04/30, from http://ec.europa.eu/information_society/newsroom/cf/itemlongdetail.cfm?item_id=3535.

[71] O. Fontana. *Windows CE 5.0 and Windows XP Embedded - Scalable Software Platforms for Building Flexible IP Set Top Boxes*, 2004. Retrieved 2012/04/30, from http://download.microsoft.com/download/6/c/1/6c1d7e1e-5582-41f1-8cd2-ef516220607a/IP_Set-top_Boxes_Whitepaper%20v2.doc.

[72] W. Fritz. *Internet-Marketing und Electronic Commerce : Grundlagen - Rahmenbedingungen - Instrumente ; mit Praxisbeispielen*. Gabler, Wiesbaden, 4th edition, 2007.

[73] D. Frosch-Wilke. *Marketing-Kommunikation im Internet : Theorie, Methoden und Praxisbeispiele vom One-to-One- bis zum Viral-Marketing*. Vieweg, Braunschweig, 1st edition, 2002.

[74] E. Gamma. *Design patterns : elements of reusable object-oriented software*. Addison-Wesley, Boston, 35th edition, 2007.

[75] GEMA (Gesellschaft für musikalische Aufführungs- und mechanische Vervielfältigungsrechte). *Gemeinsamer Tarif für die Weiterversendung von Hörfunk- und Fernsehprogrammen in Kabelnetzen (Kabelweitersendung)*, 2007. Retrieved 2012/04/30, from https://www.gema.de/fileadmin/user_upload/Musiknutzer/Tarife/Tarife_sonstige/tarif_kabelweitersendung.pdf.

[76] W. Geyer, J. Freyne, et al. 2nd Workshop on Recommender Systems and the Social Web. *Proceedings of the fourth ACM conference on Recommender systems*, Barcelona, Spain, ACM, 2010.

[77] Z. Ghadialy. *Tutorial: Multimedia Broadcast / Multicast Service (MBMS)*, 2007. Retrieved 2012/04/30, from http://www.3g4g.co.uk/Tutorial/ZG/Mbms/.

[78] S. Grabner-Kräuter and C. Lessiak. Web-Mining als Ansatzpunkt für personalisiertes Internet-Marketing. *der markt*, 40(4): 123-141, 2001.

[79] S. J. F. Graf. *Durchgängiges Identity Management und interoperable E-Portfolios zur Unterstützung lebenslangen Lernens*, Dissertation, TU München, 2009. Retrieved 2012/04/30, from http://mediatum2.ub.tum.de/doc/681362/document.pdf.

[80] GSMA (GSM Association). *White paper on Identity Management Requirements, Issues, and Directions for Mobile Industry*. White Paper, 2007. Retrieved 2012/04/30, from http://www.gsma.com/go/download/?file=se4710.pdf.

[81] T. Hargrove. *Logo Detection in Digital Video*, 2001. Retrieved 2012/04/30, from http://www-prima.inrialpes.fr/perso/Tran/Documents/Articles/Divers/logo-detection.ps.

[82] M. Harrop. Identity Management. *4th ETSI Security Workshop*, Sophia Antipolis, 2009.

[83] L. Harte. *Introduction to IP television (IPTV) : why and how companies are providing television through data networks*. Althos, Fuquay, NC, 2005.

[84] L. Harte. *IPTV dictionary : [the leading IP television information resource ; over 10,000 definitions, more than 4,000 IPTV terms]*. Althos, Fuquay-Varina, NC, 2006.

[85] G. Held. *Understanding IPTV (Informa Telecoms & Media)*. Auerbach Publications, Taylor & Francis Group, Boca Raton, FL, USA, 2007.

[86]   T. Hills. *Customer Focus Through Identity Management*, 2007. Retrieved
       2012/04/30, from http://www.lightreading.com/document.asp?doc_id=
       126782&page_number=1.

[87]   J. Hodges, Heavy Reading. *Subscriber Data Management & the Era of
       Analytics*, 2009.

[88]   T. Hoeren. Das Telemediengesetz. *Neue Juristische Wochenschrift (NJW)*,
       60(12): 801-806, 2007.

[89]   B. Holznagel and T. Ricke. *IPTV - Eine medienrechtliche Einordnung*.
       Informationelles Vertrauen für die Infomationsgesellschaft. D. Klumpp, H.
       Kubicek, A. Roßnagel and W. Schulz. Springer, Berlin, Heidelberg: 276-
       281, 2008.

[90]   IAB (Interactive Advertising Bureau). *Digital Video Ad Format
       Guidelines & Best Practices*, 2008. Retrieved 2012/04/30, from
       http://www.iab.net/guidelines/508676/digitalvideo/DV_Guidelines.

[91]   IAB (Interactive Advertising Bureau). *Ad Unit Guidelines*, 2012.
       Retrieved 2012/04/30, from http://www.iab.net/iab_products_and_
       industry_services/1421/1443/1452/.

[92]   J.-A. Ibanez, T. Lohmar, et al. Mobile TV over 3G networks – Service and
       enablers evolution. *Ericsson Review*, 85(1): 38-42, 2008.

[93]   IEC (The International Engineering Consortium), Web ProForum
       Tutorials. *Global System for Mobile Communication (GSM)*, 2007.
       Retrieved 2012/04/30, from http://ipv6.ppk.itb.ac.id/~dikshie/buku/
       tutorial/gsm.pdf.

[94]   IEC (The International Engineering Consortium), Web ProForum
       Tutorials. *Universal Mobile Telecommunications System (UMTS)
       Protocols and Protocol Testing*, 2007. Retrieved 2012/04/30, from
       http://ipv6.ppk.itb.ac.id/~dikshie/buku/tutorial/umts.pdf.

[95]   IEC (The International Engineering Consortium), Web ProForum
       Tutorials. *Wireless Short Message Service (SMS)*, 2007. Retrieved
       2012/04/30, from http://ipv6.ppk.itb.ac.id/~dikshie/buku/tutorial/
       wire_sms.pdf.

[96] informitiv. *informitiv - Glossary*, 2012. Retrieved 2012/04/30, from
http://informitv.com/resources/glossary/.

[97] InteractiveMedia. *InteractiveMedia - Online - Werbeformen*, 2012.
Retrieved 2012/04/30, from http://www.interactivemedia.net/de/
onlinewerbeformen/.

[98] INVIDI Technologies Corporation. *Audience Classifiers*, 2011. Retrieved
2012/04/30, from http://invidi.com/itc_tech_class.html.

[99] IP Deutschland. *Übersicht Werbeformen im Fernsehen*, 2012. Retrieved
2012/04/30, from http://www.ip-deutschland.de/ipd/basics/werbeformen/
fernsehen.cfm.

[100] ISC (Internet Systems Consortium). *Internet host count history*, 2012.
Retrieved 2012/04/30, from http://www.isc.org/solutions/survey/history/.

[101] ITU-T (International Telecommunication Union, Telecommunication
Standardization Sector), Focus Group IPTV. *IPTV Focus Group
Proceedings*, 2008. Retrieved 2012/04/30, from http://www.itu.int/pub/T-
PROC-IPTVFG-2008/en/.

[102] ITU-T (International Telecommunication Union, Telecommunication
Standardization Sector). *ITU-T Newslog - IPTV*, 2012. Retrieved
2012/04/30, from http://www.itu.int/ITU-T/newslog/CategoryView,
category,IPTV.aspx.

[103] iTV Dictionary. *The Interactive Television and Internet TV Dictionary*,
2012. Retrieved 2012/04/30, from http://www.itvdictionary.com/
dictionary.html.

[104] I. Jacobson. *Object-oriented software engineering : a use case driven
approach*. ACM Press, Wokingham, England, 4th edition, 1993.

[105] A. Josang and S. Pope. User Centric Identity Management. *Proceedings of
AusCERT*, Gold Coast, Australia, 2005.

[106] A. Josang, M. A. Zomai, et al. Usability and privacy in identity
management architectures. *Proceedings of the fifth Australasian*

symposium on ACSW frontiers - Volume 68, Ballarat, Australia, Australian Computer Society, Inc., 2007.

[107] Kantara Initiative. *WG - Telecommunications Identity*, 2012. Retrieved 2012/04/30, from http://kantarainitiative.org/confluence/display/telcoid/.

[108] P. Kelly and G. Ragoonanan, Analysys Mason. *Policy Management and Deep Packet Inspection*. Research Report, 2010.

[109] M. Kessler. *teltarif.de - Relaunch: Neues Gettings bietet lokale Einzelhandels-Angebote*, 2010. Retrieved 2012/04/30, from http://www.teltarif.de/gettings-e-plus-relaunch-einzelhandel-angebote-stationaerer-handel/news/40543.html.

[110] J. Kincaid. *Google Acquires AdMob For $750 Million - TechCrunch*, 2009. Retrieved 2012/04/30, from http://techcrunch.com/2009/11/09/google-acquires-admob/.

[111] A. Kishore, Heavy Reading. *Monetizing IPTV: The Next-Gen Video Advertising Opportunity*, 2007.

[112] A. Kishore, Heavy Reading. *Mobile Advertising: The Service Provider Revenue Opportunity*, 2008.

[113] A. Klahold. *Empfehlungssysteme: Recommender systems - Grundlagen, Konzepte und Lösungen*. Vieweg + Teubner, Wiesbaden, 1st edition, 2009.

[114] Kontakter. *Umsätze mit Video-Ads steigen um 400 Prozent*, 2008. Retrieved 2012/04/30, from http://www.wuv.de/kontakter/international/new_media/umsaetze_mit_video_ads_steigen_um_400_prozent.

[115] S. Krempl. *heise online - EU-Datenschützer begrüßt neue Regeln für Cookies und Infos über Sicherheitspannen*, 2009. Retrieved 2012/04/30, from http://www.heise.de/newsticker/meldung/EU-Datenschuetzer-begruesst-neue-Regeln-fuer-Cookies-und-Infos-ueber-Sicherheitspannen-856786.html.

[116] C. Larman. *Applying UML and patterns : an introduction to object-oriented analysis and design and iterative development*. Prentice Hall, Upper Saddle River, NJ, 3rd edition, 2005.

[117] R. Leenes, S. Poetzsch, et al., FIDIS (Future of Identity in the Information
       Society), FIDIS Deliverables. *D3.12: Federated Identity Management –
       what's in it for the citizen/customer?*, 2009. Retrieved 2012/04/30, from
       http://www.fidis.net/fileadmin/fidis/deliverables/new_deliverables/fidis-
       wp3-del3.12.Federated_Identity_Management.pdf.

[118] Y. Li and C. C. J. Kuo. Detecting commercial breaks in real TV programs
       based on audiovisual information. *Proceedings of SPIE*, Boston, MA,
       USA, SPIE, 2000.

[119] Liberty Alliance. *Liberty Specs Tutorial*, 2003. Retrieved 2012/04/30,
       from   http://www.projectliberty.org/liberty/content/download/423/2832/
       file/tutorialv2.pdf.

[120] Liberty Alliance. *Liberty ID-FF Architecture Overview*. Standards
       Specification,   2005.   Retrieved   2012/04/30,   from
       http://www.projectliberty.org/resource_center/specifications/liberty_allian
       ce_id_ff_1_2_specifications/.

[121] Liberty Alliance. *Liberty Alliance Project Whitepaper: Personal Identity*
       2006. Retrieved 2012/04/30, from http://www.projectliberty.org/liberty/
       content/download/395/2744/file/Personal_Identity.pdf.

[122] Liberty Alliance. *Digital Identity Management. A Critical Link to Service
       Success: A Public Network Perspective. A Telecompetition Group Market
       Study   Report   2007.   Retrieved   2012/04/30,   from
       http://www.projectliberty.org/liberty/content/download/2708/18249/file/T
       elecompetition%20Liberty%20Market%20Study%20Final%205%20Jan%
       2007.pdf.

[123] Liberty Alliance. *Liberty ID-WSF Advanced Client Implementation and
       Deployment guidelines for SIM/UICC Card environment*. Standards
       Specification,   2007.   Retrieved   2012/04/30,   from
       http://www.projectliberty.org/liberty/content/download/4655/31840/file/li
       berty-guide-adv-client-SIM-v1.0.pdf.

[124] Liberty Alliance. *Deutsche Telekom AG 2008 IDDY Award Winner Case
       Study*.   Case   Study,   2008.   Retrieved   2012/04/30,   from
       http://www.projectliberty.org/liberty/content/download/4421/29639/file/D
       eutsche%20FINAL9.08.pdf.

[125] Liberty Alliance. *Bridging IMS and Internet Identity*, 2009. Retrieved 2012/04/30, from http://www.projectliberty.org/liberty/content/download/ 4315/28869/file/WP-BridgingIMS_AndInternetIdentity_V1.0.pdf.

[126] Liberty Alliance. *Telecommunications SIG - The Project Liberty Wiki*, 2009. Retrieved 2012/04/30, from http://wiki.projectliberty.org/index.php/ TelecommunicationsSIG.

[127] G. Linden, B. Smith, et al. Amazon.com Recommendations - Item-to-Item Collaborative Filtering. *IEEE Internet Computing*, 7(1): 76-80, 2003.

[128] M. Mack. *3 trials new mobile TV technology*, 2007. Retrieved 2012/04/30, from http://www.voiceanddata.com.au/news/9033-3-trials-new-mobile-TV-technology.

[129] D. Maierhöfer, Nokia Siemens Networks GmbH & Co. KG. *Targeted Advertising*. Guided Interview (see Appendix), Munich, 2009.

[130] H. O. Mayer. *Interview und schriftliche Befragung : Entwicklung, Durchführung und Auswertung*. Oldenbourg, München, 5th edition, 2009.

[131] T. McElligot. *Alcatel-Lucent Getting an E-Plus for Advertising*, 2009. Retrieved 2012/04/30, from http://www.billingworld.com/news/briefs/ alcatel-lucent-getting-an-e-plus-for-advertis.html.

[132] B. Mehta, C. Niederee, et al. An architecture for recommendation based service mediation, Springer, Berlin, 2004.

[133] M. Meints and H. Zwingelberg, FIDIS (Future of Identity in the Information Society), FIDIS Deliverables. *D3.17: Identity Management Systems – recent developments*, 2009. Retrieved 2012/04/30, from http://www.fidis.net/fileadmin/fidis/deliverables/new_deliverables/fidis-wp3-del3.17_Identity_Management_Systems-recent_developments-final.pdf.

[134] D. M. Meyer. *heise mobil - Breitband-Mobilfunk. LTE setzt neue Maßstäbe*, 2011. Retrieved 2012/04/30, from http://www.heise.de/mobil/ artikel/LTE-setzt-neue-Massstaebe-1165055.html.

[135] E. Mikoczy, D. Sivchenko, et al. IMS based IPTV services: architecture and implementation. *Proceedings of the 3rd international conference on Mobile multimedia communications*, Nafpaktos, Greece, ICST (Institute for Computer Sciences, Social-Informatics and Telecommunications Engineering), 2007.

[136] MMA (Mobile Marketing Association). *Off Portal - An Introduction to the Market Opportunity*, 2007. Retrieved 2012/04/30, from http://mmaglobal.com/offportal.pdf.

[137] MMA (Mobile Marketing Association). *Mobile Advertising Overview*. Education Paper, 2009. Retrieved 2012/04/30, from http://mmaglobal.com/mobileadoverview.pdf.

[138] MMA (Mobile Marketing Association). *Mobile Advertising Guidelines*. Guidelines, 2011. Retrieved 2012/04/30, from http://www.mmaglobal.com/files/mmaglobal.com/file/mobileadvertising.pdf.

[139] MMA (Mobile Marketing Association). *MMA Glossary*, 2012. Retrieved 2012/04/30, from http://www.mmaglobal.com/wiki/mma-glossary.

[140] MMA (Mobile Marketing Association). *Universal Mobile Ad Package - UMAP - v.2.0*. Guidelines, 2012. Retrieved 2012/04/30, from http://mmaglobal.com/whitepaper-get2/TU1BVW5pdmVyc2FsTW9iaWxlQWRQYWNrYWdlRGVjMjAxMS5wZGY%3D.

[141] mobiForge. *Adding location to a non GPS phone: introducing CellID*, 2008. Retrieved 2012/04/30, from http://mobiforge.com/developing/story/adding-location-a-non-gps-phone-introducing-cellid/.

[142] MortarBlog. *How many ads do we see every day?*, 2006. Retrieved 2012/04/30, from http://www.mortarblog.com/2006/07/average_america.html.

[143] B. Negelmann. *E-CRM Reloaded. Trendthema Behavioral Targeting*, 2006. Retrieved 2012/04/30, from http://www.internetworld.de/Heftarchiv/2006/Ausgabe-20/Trendthema-Behavioral-Targeting.

[144] O. Neuwirt, J. D. Silva, et al. Towards a New User Experience in IPTV: Convergence Services and Simpler E-commerce on IMS-based IPTV. *NEC Technical Journal*, 3(4): 103-105, 2008.

[145] Nokia Developer Wiki. *How to get IMEI in Java ME*, 2009. Retrieved 2012/04/30, from http://www.developer.nokia.com/Community/Wiki/ How_to_get_IMEI_in_Java_ME.

[146] OASIS, OASIS Security Services TC. *Security Assertion Markup Language (SAML) V2.0 Technical Overview*. Standards Specification, 2008. Retrieved 2012/04/30, from http://docs.oasis-open.org/security/ saml/Post2.0/sstc-saml-tech-overview-2.0.pdf.

[147] OIPF (Open IPTV Forum). *Specifications Release 2*, 2011. Retrieved 2012/04/30, from http://www.oipf.tv/specifications-release-2.

[148] OMA (Open Mobile Alliance). *WAG UAProf*, 2001. Retrieved 2012/04/30, from http://www.openmobilealliance.org/tech/affiliates/wap/ wap-248-uaprof-20011020-a.pdf.

[149] OMA (Open Mobile Alliance). *White Paper on Mobile Advertising - Framework, Scope and Initiatives-*. White Paper, 2007. Retrieved 2012/04/30, from http://member.openmobilealliance.org/ftp/Public_ documents/TP/MobAd_BOF/Permanent_documents/OMA-WP-MobAd_ Framework_Scope_Initiatives-20070515-A.zip.

[150] OMA (Open Mobile Alliance). *Mobile Broadcast Services*. Standards Specification, 2009. Retrieved 2012/04/30, from http://www.openmobilealliance.org/Technical/release_program/docs/BCA ST/V1_0-20090212-A/OMA-TS-BCAST_Services-V1_0-20090212- A.pdf.

[151] OMA (Open Mobile Alliance). *Mobile Advertising Architecture*. Architecture Documentation, 2012. Retrieved 2012/04/30, from http://www.openmobilealliance.org/Technical/release_program/docs/Mob Ad/V1_0-20120320-A/OMA-AD-Mobile_Advertising-V1_0-20120320- A.pdf.

[152] OMA (Open Mobile Alliance). *Mobile Advertising Requirements*. Requirements Document, 2012. Retrieved 2012/04/30, from

http://www.openmobilealliance.org/Technical/release_program/docs/Mob
Ad/V1_0-20120320-A/OMA-RD-Mobile-Advertising-V1_0-20120320-
A.pdf.

[153] OpenTV. *Interactive Advertising Whitepaper*. White Paper, 2005.
Retrieved 2012/04/30, from http://www.broadbandbananas.com/images/
stories/OpenTV_Interactive_Advertising_White_Paper_April_2005.pdf.

[154] Orange. *Orange newsroom - Blyk continues its move from MVNO to
operator partnership*, 2009. Retrieved 2012/04/30, from http://newsroom.
orange.co.uk/2009/07/27/blyk-continues-its-move-from-mvno-to-operator-
partnership/.

[155] OVK (Online-Vermarkterkreis), BVDW (Bundesverband Digitale
Wirtschaft), Arbeitskreis Targeting. *Targeting - Begriffe & Definitionen*,
2009. Retrieved 2012/04/30, from http://www.bvdw.org/mybvdw/media/
download/bvdw-ak-targeting-defintionen-20090922.pdf?file=1137.

[156] OVK (Online-Vermarkterkreis), BVDW (Bundesverband Digitale
Wirtschaft), Arbeitskreis Targeting. *Was ist Targeting?*, 2009. Retrieved
2012/04/30, from http://www.bvdw.org/mybvdw/media/download/bvdw--
was-ist-targeting-dmexco-20090923.pdf?file=752.

[157] OVK (Online-Vermarkterkreis), BVDW (Bundesverband Digitale
Wirtschaft). *Werbeformen*, 2012. Retrieved 2012/04/30, from
http://www.werbeformen.de/.

[158] N. Özay and B. Sankur. Automatic TV Logo Detection and Classification
in Broadcast Videos. *17th European Signal Processing Conference
(EUSIPCO 2009)* Glasgow, Scotland, 2009.

[159] Packet Vision. *Advanced IPTV Advertising - Solution Overview*. White
Paper, 2009. Retrieved 2012/04/30, from http://www.slideshare.net/
RockyS11/advanced-iptv-advertising.

[160] G. Pfennig. Reformbedarf beim Kabelweitersenderecht? *Zeitschrift für
Urheber- und Medienrecht (ZUM)*, 52(5): 363-371, 2008.

[161]   A. Pichelin and A. Gordon. Advanced Identity Management in a Telco
        Environment. Challenges of Multi-play Identity Convergence. *Digital ID
        World - September 2007*, San Francisco, 2007.

[162]   M. Poikselkä and G. Mayer. *The IMS : IP multimedia concepts and
        services*, Chichester, U.K., 3rd edition, 2009.

[163]   V. Pronk, J. Korst, et al. Personal TV Channels: Simply Zapping through
        Your PVR Content. *Recommender-based Industrial Applications
        Workshop at The 3rd ACM Conference on Recommender Systems*, New
        York, USA, 2009.

[164]   C. Rack, S. Arbanowski, et al. A Generic Multipurpose recommender
        System for Contextual Recommendations. *Proceedings of the Eighth
        International Symposium on Autonomous Decentralized Systems*, IEEE
        Computer Society, 2007.

[165]   B. Ray. *Blyk goes bye-bye - The Register*, 2009. Retrieved 2012/04/30,
        from http://www.theregister.co.uk/2009/07/27/bye_bye_blyk/.

[166]   P. Resnick and H. R. Varian. Recommender systems. *Commun. ACM*,
        40(3): 56-58, 1997.

[167]   RGB Networks. *RGB Solutions - IP Video Delivery*, 2012. Retrieved
        2012/04/30, from http://www.rgbnetworks.com/solutions/iptv-video-over-
        ip.php.

[168]   T. Ritchey. *General Morphological Analysis. A general method for non-
        quantified   modelling*,   2011.   Retrieved   2012/04/30,   from
        http://www.swemorph.com/ma.html.

[169]   J.-C. Rochet and J. Tirole, IDEI (Institut d'Economie Industrielle). *Two-
        Sided Markets : A Progress Report*, 2005. Retrieved 2012/04/30, from
        http://idei.fr/doc/wp/2005/2sided_markets.pdf.

[170]   L. Rokach, A. Meisels, et al. Anytime AHP Method for Preferences
        Elicitation in Stereotype-Based Recommender System. *ICEIS 2008 -
        Proceedings of the Tenth International Conference on Enterprise
        Information Systems, Volume AIDSS, Barcelona, Spain, June 12-16, 2008*,
        2008.

[171] D. Rowe. *Unified Communications Client API Terminology*, 2008. Retrieved 2012/04/30, from http://servusinc.org/myblog/?p=58.

[172] W. W. Royce. Managing the development of large software systems: concepts and techniques. *ICSE '87: Proceedings of the 9th international conference on Software Engineering*, Monterey, California, United States, IEEE Computer Society Press, 1987.

[173] N. Ryan, J. Pascoe, et al. *Enhanced Reality Fieldwork: the Context-Aware Archaeological Assistant*. Computer Applications in Archaeology. V. Gaffney, M. van Leusen and S. Exxon. Tempus Reparatum, Oxford, UK, 1997.

[174] T. L. Saaty. A Scaling Method for Priorities in Hierarchical Structures. *Journal of Mathematical Psychology*, (15): 234-281, 1977.

[175] T. L. Saaty. *The analytic hierarchy process : planning, priority setting, resource allocation*. McGraw-Hill, New York, USA, 1980.

[176] D. A. Sadlier, S. Marlow, et al. Automatic TV Advertisement Detection from MPEG Bitstream. *Proceedings of the 1st International Workshop on Pattern Recognition in Information Systems: In conjunction with ICEIS 2001*, ICEIS Press, 2001.

[177] A. R. d. Santos and H. Y. Kim. Real-Time Opaque and Semi-Transparent TV Logos Detection. *Proceedings of the 5th International Information and Telecommunication Technologies Symposium (I2TS)*, Cuiabá, Brasilia, 2006.

[178] A. Sarma, A. Matos, et al. Virtual Identity Framework for Telecom Infrastructures. *Wireless Personal Communications*, 45(4): 521-543, 2008.

[179] B. Sarwar, G. Karypis, et al. Item-based collaborative filtering recommendation algorithms. *Proceedings of the 10th international conference on World Wide Web*, Hong Kong, Hong Kong, ACM, 2001.

[180] B. Satterwhite and O. Marques. Automatic detection of TV commercials. *Potentials, IEEE*, 23(2): 9-12, 2004.

[181] B. N. Schilit and M. M. Theimer. Disseminating Active Map Information to Mobile Hosts. *IEEE Network*, 8(5): 22-32, 1994.

[182] J. H. Schiller. *Mobile communications*. Addison-Wesley, London, 2nd edition, 2003.

[183] J. H. Schiller. *Mobile Communications - Course Material. Chapter 4: Wireless Telecommunication Systems*, 2012. Retrieved 2012/04/30, from http://www.inf.fu-berlin.de/groups/ag-tech/teaching/resources/Mobile_Communications/course_Material/C04-Wireless_Telecommunication_Systems.pdf.

[184] SCTE (Society of Cable Telecommunications Engineers). *ANSI/SCTE 30 2009 - Digital Program Insertion Splicing API*. Standards Specification, 2009. Retrieved 2012/04/30, from http://www.scte.org/documents/pdf/Standards/ANSI_SCTE%2030%202009.pdf.

[185] SCTE (Society of Cable Telecommunications Engineers). *ANSI/SCTE 35 2011 - Digital Program Insertion Cueing Message for Cable*. Standards Specification, 2011. Retrieved 2012/04/30, from http://www.scte.org/documents/pdf/Standards/ANSI_SCTE_35_2011.pdf.

[186] SeaChange. *SeaChange AdPulse On Demand Advertising System*, 2012. Retrieved 2012/04/30, from http://www.schange.com/Collateral/Advertising/Brochures/AdPulse_Brochure_3-14_2012.aspx.

[187] SeaChange. *SeaChange Spot - The Standard for Local Ad Insertion*, 2012. Retrieved 2012/04/30, from http://www.schange.com/Collateral/Advertising/Brochures/Spot_Brochure_3-16_2012.aspx.

[188] SevenOne Media. *SevenOne Media Showroom*, 2012. Retrieved 2012/04/30, from http://sevenonemedia.contentserv.com/ShowRoom/showroom_de.html.

[189] G. Shani, L. Rokach, et al. A Stereotypes-Based Hybrid Recommender System for Media Items. *The 22nd AAAI Conference on Artificial Intelligence (AAAI-07), Vancouver, Canada, July 22-26, 2007*, 2007.

[190] Sky Media. *Interactive Advertising*, 2012. Retrieved 2012/04/30, from http://skymedia.co.uk/Advertising/TV/introduction.aspx.

[191] S. Slone, The Open Group. *Identity Management*. White Paper, 2004. Retrieved 2012/04/30, from http://www.opengroup.org/projects/idm/uploads/40/9784/idm_wp.pdf.

[192] R. M. Smith. *The Web Bug FAQ*, 1999. Retrieved 2012/04/30, from http://w2.eff.org/Privacy/Marketing/web_bug.html.

[193] D. A. J. Sokolov. *heise mobil - DVB-H auch in Österreich gescheitert*, 2010. Retrieved 2012/04/30, from http://www.heise.de/mobil/meldung/DVB-H-auch-in-Oesterreich-gescheitert-1108096.html.

[194] I. Sommerville. *Software Engineering*. Addison-Wesley, Harlow, England ; New York, 8th edition, 2007.

[195] A. Soylu, P. D. Causmaecker, et al. Context and Adaptivity in Pervasive Computing Environments: Links with Software Engineering and Ontological Engineering. *Journal of Software*, 4(9): 992-1013, 2009.

[196] S. Steiniger, M. Neun, et al., CartouCHe - Lecture Notes on LBS, V. 1.0. *Foundations of Location Based Services - Lesson1*, 2007. Retrieved 2012/04/30, from http://www.e-cartouche.ch/content_reg/cartouche/LBSbasics/en/.

[197] STL Partners. *What is the Telco 2.0 Initiative?*, 2009. Retrieved 2012/04/30, from http://www.stlpartners.com/telco2_index.php.

[198] H. Störrle. *UML 2 für Studenten : [mit UML-Syntax-Poster]*. Pearson Studium, München, 2005.

[199] L. Story. *The Evolution of Facebook's Beacon - NYTimes.com*, 2007. Retrieved 2012/04/30, from http://bits.blogs.nytimes.com/2007/11/29/the-evolution-of-facebooks-beacon/.

[200] S. Suriadi, E. Foo, et al. A user-centric federated single sign-on system. *Journal of Network and Computer Applications*, 32(2): 388-401, 2009.

[201] TEKELEC. *Mobile Advertising - Creating New Revenue Opportunities with SMS-based Advertising*, 2009. Retrieved 2012/04/30, from http://connectedplanetonline.com/whitepapers/forms/wp062008-tklc-1.

[202] TeliaSonera MediaLab. *Mobile Broadcast/Multicast Service (MBMS)*. White Paper, 2004. Retrieved 2012/04/30, from http://www.medialab. sonera.fi/workspace/MBMSWhitePaper.pdf.

[203] S. Thiele, Deutsche Telekom AG, Products & Innovation. *Targeted Advertising & IPTV*. Guided Interview (see Appendix), Darmstadt, 2009.

[204] A. S. Tom. Targeted Advertising: The Opportunity And Delivery Architecture. *Broadcast Asia 2008*, RGB Networks, 2008.

[205] A. S. Tom, J. Tyre, et al. Stepping Beyond the 30-Second Spot Ad with Digital Overlays: Applying Intelligent Video Processing in the Cable Network to Deliver Advanced Advertising. *SCTE 2008 Conference on Emerging Technologies*, RGB Networks, 2008.

[206] T. Topaloglu, Deutsche Telekom AG, T-Home. *Targeting Technologies*. Guided Interview (see Appendix), Darmstadt, 2009.

[207] J. Tyre. Digital Ad Overlays - Double Ad Avails, Grow Revenue. *Communications Technology - Profitable Engineering for Voice, Video and Data*, 25(5), 2008.

[208] ULD (Unabhängiges Landeszentrum für Datenschutz Schleswig-Holstein). *Kurzgutachten wunderloop Integrated Targeting Platform*, 2010. Retrieved 2012/04/30, from http://www.datenschutzzentrum.de/ guetesiegel/kurzgutachten/g080502/.

[209] UMTS Forum. *Mobile TV Advertising - 3rd White Paper*, 2009. Retrieved 2012/04/30, from http://www.umts-forum.org/component/option,com_ docman/task,doc_download/gid,2090/.

[210] UMTSlink.at. *3G-Forum*, 2012. Retrieved 2012/04/30, from http://www.umtslink.at/.

[211] VG Media (Gesellschaft zur Verwertung der Urheber- und Leistungsschutzrechte von Medienunternehmen). *Tarif Weitersendung - Für die Weitersendung von Hörfunk- und Fernsehprogrammen*, 2012. Retrieved 2012/04/30, from http://www.vgmedia.de/de/weitersendung-tarif.html.

[212] G. Voulgaris and A. Constantinou, VisionMobile's Industry Atlas. *Active Idle Screen: 2009-2011. Who will own the screen?*, 2009. Retrieved 2012/04/30, from http://www.visionmobile.com/blog/2009/07/who-will-own-the-screen-an-analysis-of-the-active-idle-screen-market-2009-2011/.

[213] B. Wallace. *Post TelcoTV: Advertising Beat Goes On*, 2008. Retrieved 2012/04/30, from http://www.vision2mobile.com/news/2008/11/post-telcotv-advertising-beat-goes-on.aspx.

[214] A.-A. Wandtke and W. Bullinger. *Praxiskommentar zum Urheberrecht.* Verlag C. H. Beck, München, 3rd edition, 2009.

[215] D. Waters. *BBC News - BT advert trials were "illegal"*, 2008. Retrieved 2012/04/30, from http://news.bbc.co.uk/2/hi/technology/7325451.stm.

[216] J. Weber and T. Newberry. *IPTV crash course*. McGraw-Hill, New York, 2007.

[217] Y. Z. Wei, L. Moreau, et al. A market-based approach to recommender systems. *ACM Trans. Inf. Syst.*, 23(3): 227-266, 2005.

[218] J. Weihs, SeaChange International, Inc. *Targeted Advertising.* Guided Interview (see Appendix), Phone Call, 2009.

[219] R. Weisser and M. Höppener. Kabelweitersendung und urheberrechtlicher Kontrahierungszwang. *Zeitschrift für Urheber- und Medienrecht (ZUM)*, 47(8/9): 597-610, 2003.

[220] Werben & Verkaufen. *Es ist offiziell: AudienceScience übernimmt Wunderloop*, 2010. Retrieved 2012/04/30, from http://www.wuv.de/nachrichten/digital/es_ist_offiziell_audiencescience_uebernimmt_wunderloop.

[221] P. Whoriskey. Every Click You Make - The Washington Post. *The Washington Post*, 2008. Retrieved 2012/04/30, from http://www.washingtonpost.com/wp-dyn/content/article/2008/04/03/AR2008040304052.html.

[222] Wikipedia. *Contextual Advertising.* Retrieved 2012/04/30, from http://en.wikipedia.org/wiki/Contextual_advertising.

[223] F. Winkler, M. Schmidt, et al. Identity Management for IMS-Based IPTV. *Global Telecommunications Conference, 2008. IEEE GLOBECOM 2008. IEEE*, 2008.

[224] C. Wölbert. *heise mobil - Handy-TV lohnt sich in Korea für Betreiber nicht*, 2009. Retrieved 2012/04/30, from http://www.heise.de/mobil/meldung/Handy-TV-lohnt-sich-in-Korea-fuer-Betreiber-nicht-196258.html.

[225] Wunderloop. *Behavioral Targeting System*. White Paper, 2006. Retrieved 2012/04/30, from http://searchcio.techtarget.it/whitepaper_library/wunderLoop_behavioural_targeting.pdf.

[226] ZenithOptimedia. *Ad Spend Forecasts*, 2011. Retrieved 2012/04/30, from http://www.zenithoptimedia.com/zenith/wp-content/uploads/2012/02/Adspend-forecasts-October-2011.pdf.

[227] J. Zoric, T. H. Johannessen, et al. Identity management enabling AAA services in evolving telecom platforms – Strategic technological and business recommendations. *EURESCOM Summit 2005 - Ubiquitous Services and Applications, Exploiting the Potential - Conference Proceedings*, Heidelberg, VDE Verlag, 2005.

[228] F. Zwicky, A. G. Wilson, et al. *New methods of thought and procedure. Contributions to the Symposium on Methodologies, Pasadena, California, May 22-24, 1967*. Springer-Verlag, Berlin, Heidelberg, New York, 1967.

Appendix

Vendor Interviews

Questionnaire Structure

A. Introduction

1. What are your activities and solutions concerning TA? In which channels do you offer TA solutions?

2. On which devices will your TA solutions probably be most successful (PCs, mobile phones, STB, gaming consoles)?

B. Use Cases of Targeted Advertising

3. Which ad formats are supported by your TA solution (e.g. banner, overlay, pop up, wallpaper, splitscreen, pre-/post-/mid-roll)? Which ones do you consider to be most promising?

4. Based on these ad formats: What are the most interesting TA use cases in your business? Could you please give a brief description? Which use cases are imaginable in the future?

5. What direction will the development of your TA products take in the future?

C. Technical Platform

6. Could you please depict the technical architecture of your solution?

7. Which use cases are covered by your technical solution?

8. Could you depict a model of the underlying TA process of the use cases from a technical point of view?

9. Could you elaborate on your technical USPs in the area of TA?

10. What are the main issues/challenges (platform or device limitations)?

11. What are from your perspective the major technical possibilities and features in your area of TA near/ mid-term/ long-term?

D. Data Privacy & Security

12. What is your opinion concerning data privacy in the context of TA?

13. Which processes in your system are of a special relevance concerning data privacy? How do you ensure data privacy (e.g. anonymization/separation of user data from IP address)?

E. Standardization of Targeted Advertising

14. Which standardization efforts are you aware of? Which gaps do you see in the standardization in your area of TA?

15. Which TA standards are met by your solutions?

16. Are you involved in standardization efforts? Committees? Did you file any proposals?

F. Targeted Advertising Market

17. Which companies are you partnering with and who are your main competitors?

18. In your opinion, what are the most successful implementations of TA today? Could you name the most interesting/important players in your area of the TA business?

G. Conclusion

19. Are there any important topics/aspects of TA that should be additionally covered by my thesis?

Questionnaire Answers
Dietmar Maierhöfer, Nokia Siemens Networks GmbH & Co. KG

A. Introduction

1. What are your activities and solutions concerning TA? In which channels do you offer TA solutions?

   · Talks to media agencies since about two years
   · Technology Vendor A offers targeting solutions for the IPTV and mobile environment

   Business Approach for targeted advertising:
   · Make service cheaper
   · Goal of increasing usage of a service through advertising is mostly not successful
   · High usage is a necessary condition for advertising!
   · Question to be asked: In which services is the targeted advertising promising, examples could be: prepaid account status SMS, voicemail, advertising in the context of a video call

2. On which devices will your TA solutions probably be most successful (PCs, mobile phones, STB, gaming consoles)?

   Current conditions for targeted advertising:
   · Web portal advertising is common, but not yet widespread in the mobile world
   · The Internet/Web is state-of-the-art for targeted advertising, high user numbers, established medium
   · Mobile device will play predominant role in future, interesting playfield being much in motion
   · Mobile is THE personal device and therefore predestined for targeting
   · Technology Vendor A's vision: The mobile is a device the user always carries with her

   Situation in mobile vs. IPTV:
   · Targeted advertising is currently more successful in the mobile environment. Market penetration and growth are much higher than in IPTV increasing the relevance of ads. Critical mass is reached
   · IPTV still focuses more on basic services

   Mobile:
   · Necessary device capabilities are only given since the emergence of the iPhone and its followers (e.g. Nokia N97, Android phones)
   · Users must be enthusiastic about the usage of such devices and advanced services

· Technological opportunities are an essential driver

IPTV:

· Technological capabilities are already given for a longer time, e.g. STB-based overlay technology
· Problem in IPTV is rather to make IPTV a mass market
· Low user numbers: no target group definitions possible, critical mass required for targeting
· Added value of advanced IPTV services must be communicated to win more users
· Currently, users only recognize time shift, interactivity is not advertised enough

B. Use Cases of Targeted Advertising

3. Which ad formats are supported by your TA solution (e.g. banner, overlay, pop up, wallpaper, splitscreen, pre-/post-/mid-roll)? Which ones do you consider to be most promising?

· Overlay advertising in IPTV is complex if realized in the network, STB-based can for example be implemented using Flash Light
· But generally most ad formats do not pose a big challenge in terms of technology
· Most promising: Formats with good cost-benefit ratio
· Banner advertising is still important
· In video: pre-/post-roll has great potential, mid-roll unclear

4. Based on these ad formats: What are the most interesting TA use cases in your business? Could you please give a brief description? Which use cases are imaginable in the future?

· Targeted advertising is not yet a mass product, unclear if chasm is already crossed? No cash cow use cases so far
· Driving questions: Which service? Is the required technology for the desired application available?

Voice use case example:

· Users calls service hotline on her (mobile/fixed line) phone and listens to advertising
· She answers some ad related questions, in order to make sure that she has listened to the ad
· She receives free minutes
· Advertising is the only purpose of the call
· Opt-in necessary! Subscription is the only data source for targeting in this case

Top 3 use cases:
1. Subsidized browsing
   · Subsidized browsing is very interesting due to current mobile Internet boom
   · Possible scenario: Browsing free of charge with ads in a header/banner ad
   · Important: Additional services and features e.g. privacy services (anonymization proxy), identity management services (Single Sign-On (SSO)/auto sign-in for Twitter)
2. Push messaging
   · Highest potential in mobile advertising
   · Example: Blyk (MVNO using the network of Orange in the UK) offered mobile services completely funded by targeted advertising. The Blyk model had high acceptance and click-rates, but did not work out as MVNO with advertising as only source of revenues. Can however be an additional revenues source for operators (e.g. E-Plus "Gettings")
3. Person-to-person subsidization
   · User A sends SMS/MMS for free, User V receives message including ads
   · Problem: User A benefits while User B gets the ads. Therefore also imaginable to send an ad message back to User A, which would also have advantages in terms of targeting, as subscriber data is available.

5. What direction will the development of your TA products take in the future?
   · Technology Vendor A understands itself as a solution house not a product house
   · Targeted advertising development will therefore take place in each ICT channel on a solution basis
   · No classic roadmap for products, rather: identify the paint points and find a solution
   · Observe technological and media developments and identify the one's with the largest impacts and business opportunities
   · Determining factor: Less technical capabilities, but create customer acceptance through transparency
   · Technology Vendor A's customer are mostly Communication Service Providers (CSPs)
   · Service orientation: Which services exist? Do they fit with advertising?
   · For example: Web portal advertising is not so relevant for them, as CSP portals typically do not belong to the top ten pages in the Web.

C. Technical Platform

6. Could you please depict the technical architecture of your solution?

   Technology components:
   - Central ad controlling unit including targeting and recommendation technology
   - Profiling unit built on a data warehouse solution. Track e.g. the location of a user and separates anonymized users into segments e.g. "International Business Traveler"
   - Service provisioning through a browsing gateway/publishing service
   - Short Message Service Center (SMSC), Multimedia Messaging Service Center (MMSC)
   - No own products for ad server, ad Management, campaign management. Collaboration with partners e.g. ad networks. Often several ad networks combined in one solution.

7. Which use cases are covered by your technical solution?

   Use cases covered in IPTV:
   - Banner advertising
   - EPG portal advertising
   - Recommendation apps
   - Media related advertising: pre-roll, ad breaks

   Use cases covered in the mobile environment:
   - Banner and other portal advertising
   - Different kinds of video advertising
   - Messaging
   - Voice

8. Could you depict a model of the underlying TA process of the use cases from a technical point of view?

   Not discussed.

9. Could you elaborate on your technical USPs in the area of TA?

   Not discussed.

10. What are the main issues/challenges (platform or device limitations)?

   Main issues:
   - Attractive services
   - Good design, high usability
   - Reasonable cost structure, acceptable data plans
   - New technological aspects/opportunities must be observed and adopted

· Example: XHTML/XML first in the Internet and now driver in the mobile Web

11. What are from your perspective the major technical possibilities and features in your area of TA near/mid-term/long-term?

Location-Based Services (LBS):
· First hype ten years ago, expected growth rates could not be achieved
· High existing potential, but not clear when it breaks through. Acceptance?
· Attractive use cases: e.g. message (SMS/MMS) advertising of a business/shop if someone passes by, the mobile networks allows locating the subscriber
· Requires opt-in for privacy reasons and also to distinguish the service from SPAM

D. Data Privacy & Security

12. What is your opinion concerning data privacy in the context of TA?
· Transparency is very important to convince users
· Good example: Google's interest-based targeting model, where users can check personal data stored about them and activate/deactivate single attributes/properties
· Privacy is not only important for ethic and legal reasons. Business success requires transparency, compare BT/Phorm example

13. Which processes in your system are of a special relevance concerning data privacy? How do you ensure data privacy (e.g. anonymization/separation of user data from IP address)?
· Ad controlling unit incorporates anonymization/pseudonymization functionality
· Paradigm: user data not to be distributed over multiple systems
· Profile data are encrypted by default
· Personal data that can be used to identify the customer is never stored together with profiling data
· Opt-in/-out portal available across all channels in which Technology Vendor A's solutions operate

E. Standardization of Targeted Advertising

14. Which standardization efforts are you aware of? Which gaps do you see in the standardization in your area of TA?
· So far only few technology-driven standards, lack of spread and acceptance in existing standards
· Development is less driven by classic standardization organizations

Some standards stemming form the U.S. cable TV sector have been adopted for IPTV:

- The Society of Cable Telecommunications Engineers (SCTE) specifies different standards in the context of ad insertion (linear TV and VoD)
- SCTE 130: Interface between publishing channel/service provider and campaign management/ad marketer, seller and buyer, open interface!

Apart from that de facto standards from the Internet drive the development:

- Browser embedded Flash support
- Banner advertising in Web-based EPGs enabled through XML can be considered as de facto standard
- Cost Per Mille (CPM) and Click-Through Rate (CTR) are common standards for ad metrics and performance indication adopted from the Internet world

Gaps that require standardization:

- Targeted advertising in videos is difficult due to many different codecs and interfaces
- Heterogeneity of devices
- No open standards, e.g. STBs are bound to proprietary middleware systems

15. Which TA standards are met by your solutions?
- Flash as a de facto standard is used for Web video applications
- Example: Collaboration with Google for a pre-roll advertising in YouTube

16. Are you involved in standardization efforts? Committees? Did you file any proposals?
- Open Mobile Alliance (OMA), context: client-side metrics analysis and methods
- Mobile Marketing Association (MMA)

F. Targeted Advertising Market

17. Which companies are you partnering with and who are your main competitors?
- Competition is a technology driver!
- Competition question is market importance question: Who can reach for the small advertising budgets
- Competitors in CSP/mobile: Ericsson, Alcatel-Lucent
- Competitors in IPTV: Microsoft, Ericsson

- Competitors in the Internet environment: Google, but also seen as partner in order to leverage synergies, e.g. collaboration in YouTube video advertising (pre-roll clips)
- Big problem in the Telco environment: Web competitors degrading CSPs to bit pipes!

18. In your opinion, what are the most successful implementations of TA today? Could you name the most interesting/important players in your area of the TA business?

Interesting market activities:
- Discussion concerning LBS is exciting: Can Telcos find assure their position in the mobile communication market and gain a hold in the mobile advertising value chain?
- Operator knows the location of users through the Home Location Register (HLR): Can he manage top exploit this asset. A combined solution of cell ID and GPS data is most promising as the result of the location finding process has to be delivered quickly.

Important players:
- Blyk, E-Plus "Gettings": very cutting-edge concepts!
- Telia Sonera Surf Open (Scandinavia): very sophisticated in mobile advertising
- Alcatel-Lucent: Advanced service on demand concepts, services are made available through cloud-like concepts and are not located ate the operator's site anymore

Important players in ad management/ad marketing/ad serving:
- Open X: Open Source Ad Server
- Ad networks are region- and channel-specific, most important players include AdMob, Gruner + Jahr, YOC-Gruppe (Germany), Doubleclick (international)

G. Conclusion

19. Are there any important topics/aspects of TA that should be additionally covered by my thesis?
- Targeted advertising is a paradigm change, away from single paid services towards full ad funding

Questionnaire Answers
Joseph "Yossi" Weihs, SeaChange International, Inc.

A. Introduction

1. What are your activities and solutions concerning TA? In which channels do you offer TA solutions?
   - Mobile video subsidary in UK
   - Linear TV (zone-based, household-based) and VoD ad insertion solutions
   - Company was founded on legacy cable ad insertion product

2. On which devices will your TA solutions probably be most successful (PCs, mobile phones, STB, gaming consoles)?
   - Devices: STB

B. Use Cases of Targeted Advertising

3. Which ad formats are supported by your TA solution (e.g. banner, overlay, pop up, wallpaper, splitscreen, pre-/post-/mid-roll)? Which ones do you consider to be most promising?

   Ad formats IPTV:
   - Pre-/post-/mid-roll
   - Overlay: RGB Networks

   Ad formats mobile:
   - Banner ads

   - Linear splicing: local linear TV, merging of content & ad
   - Splicing process can also take place in the STB
   - Focus on U.S. (30s spots), fixed slots, Q-tone (data about fixed slots)

   - Legal aspects/problem in Germany: "do not touch the stream", at least in ARD/ZDF
   - Transcoding: same problem in U.S. with untouchable ad streams

4. Based on these ad formats: What are the most interesting TA use cases in your business? Could you please give a brief description? Which use cases are imaginable in the future?
   - Around 30s or shorter spots
   - 2 variants of targeting:
     - Cable company owns targeting data
     - Other companies measure media about who's watching, audience research companies/companies with infos on consumers, example Coca

   Cola ad: Aquafax/Transunion (research company owning data), cable
   company (deliver user info/STB-IDs)
- Splitting channels
- Targeted in terms of content basically

- Interesting developments are not really in technical infrastructure
- TV is going to benefit from Internet developments, successful models will
  get leveraged in TV
- "UpFront" (Meeting for selling and buying commercial airtime in U.S.),
  takes place every may before television season starts, volume: $70B, since
  30-40 years, make new contacts. Cancelled in 2009 for the first time due
  to developments in Internet/Web advertising business

More use case scenarios:
- "Snow birds" (people that live in Florida during winter), problem: STB is
  turned on and STILL on while they are away, problem to solve in terms of
  gaining statistics about usage
- Google TV: analyzing feature about how many people change channels
  during ad, feedback about success when changing spots, data on STB level
- Technology Vendor B's mobile subsidiary in the UK enables mobile video
  content sponsoring by advertiser through specific banner targeting, pre-roll
  and post-roll, shorter spots
- Generally do not distinguish between linear TV and VoD user in terms of
  profiling and targeting, aggregate over all audiences
- Time-based targeting: replace ads dependent on time, but challenge on the
  business side. Must have ability to sell slot. Question: Can the advertiser
  show different ads/commercials (cost of production,...)?

5. What direction will the development of your TA products take in the future?
   Not discussed.

C. Technical Platform

6. Could you please depict the technical architecture of your solution?

7. Which use cases are covered by your technical solution?

8. Could you depict a model of the underlying TA process of the use cases from
   a technical point of view?

9. Could you elaborate on your technical USPs in the area of TA?
   Technical platform details were not discussed. Interview was conducted on
   phone, hence no good opportunity for depicting the technology architecture.

However, SeaChange provides a series of whitepapers that were sent to the author by email.

10. What are the main issues/challenges (platform or device limitations)?
    Not discussed.

11. What are from your perspective the major technical possibilities and features in your area of TA near/mid-term/long-term?

    Challenges:
    · Companies in TV advertising business are very conservative, much more in TV than in mobile/Internet
    · "sit-and-wait" mentality

    Technical point of view:
    · Cable: bandwidth, running out of capacity, hybrid fiber network
    · TA needs bandwidth!
    · Decision to be made: better sell more broadband Internet or do TA on TV?
    · Business optimization problem: "money per GHz"

D. Data Privacy & Security

12. What is your opinion concerning data privacy in the context of TA?
    · Former TA trial technically worked out, but ran into legal issues: serious topic!

13. Which processes in your system are of a special relevance concerning data privacy? How do you ensure data privacy (e.g. anonymization/separation of user data from IP address)?
    Not discussed.

E. Standardization of Targeted Advertising

14. Which standardization efforts are you aware of? Which gaps do you see in the standardization in your area of TA?
    · Number of standards in the cable industry
    · SCTE 130: has not been deployed yet
    · SCTE 30 + 35
    · "Canoe" initiative: business standards
    · CableLabs: "Advanced Advertising" and interactive services

15. Which TA standards are met by your solutions?
    · Technology Vendor B claims to have currently the only SCTE 130 compliant product that is getting close to being deployed.

16. Are you involved in standardization efforts? Committees? Did you file any proposals?

Not discussed.

F. Targeted Advertising Market

17. Which companies are you partnering with and who are your main competitors?

Not discussed.

18. In your opinion, what are the most successful implementations of TA today? Could you name the most interesting/important players in your area of the TA business?

Competitors in IPTV:
- Visible World
- Invidi
- Big Band, Alcatel-Lucent, Cisco (actually almost all companies with VoD solutions)

G. Conclusion

19. Are there any important topics/aspects of TA that should be additionally covered by my thesis?
- Big issue: data collection as only anonymous use unproblematic

Questionnaire Answers
Taras Bugir, Sun Microsystems, Inc.

A. Introduction

1. What are your activities and solutions concerning TA? In which channels do you offer TA solutions?

   Activities on 2 levels:
   · Partnering
   · Developing TA technologies

   · Customer-driven approach
   · Lot of talk about TA, but no one is doing it in large scale/as mass infrastructure, except e.g. Disk Networks, ITV (UK)
   · Reason:
       · A lot more power for broadcast, on has to have CPM multiplier
       · There is no easy way to buy TA, problem: TV advertising value chain!

   Realization chances of TA in IPTV:
   · Technically: can already be done
   · Business point of view: not easy to buy TA in IPTV, in Web much easier. IPTV first has to reach the "tipping point" (economics)

   Realization chances of TA in the mobile environment:
   · New, fast growing medium, is taking advantage of TA

2. On which devices will your TA solutions probably be most successful (PCs, mobile phones, STB, gaming consoles)?
   · Mobile space
   · IPTV: companies are going to retool their infrastructure; technology change is chance for TA!

   · Move to IP world will drive TA, most devices will have browsers, sophisticated formats can be leveraged

B. Use Cases of Targeted Advertising

3. Which ad formats are supported by your TA solution (e.g. banner, overlay, pop up, wallpaper, splitscreen, pre-/post-/mid-roll)? Which ones do you consider to be most promising?
   · Ads formats are emerging
   · Some ad formats apply better to some channel, e.g. no mid-roll in premium content
   · There will be a certain kind of ads for each channel

Ad formats for IPTV:
· Banner/overlay
· Most interesting: inline advertising/linear ad splicing

4. Based on these ad formats: What are the most interesting TA use cases in your business? Could you please give a brief description? Which use cases are imaginable in the future?
· Most interesting use case (hard to realize!): inline advertising video
· Challenge: computing power for live ad insertion
· Inline has to be synchronized (in headend, not in STB,...)

Interactive advertising and ad telescoping:
· Promising use case scenarios
· Problem: Tow users away from TV "forever", they don't come back
· Big issue for TV networks!

Joint infrastructure (convergence) provides interesting opportunities:
· Watch on mobile, pause, go home, continue watching at home
· TA implications: are you the same person? Mobile is personal, but at home? Then targeted on family, requires: identity management!
· Different STBs in different rooms require management of multiple personalities, affects money you can take for ad space
· Figure out who uses STB: company Invidi analyzes RC usage, can already detect, e.g. 10-year-old girl from her zapping behavior. Problem again: access/connection vs. person

5. What direction will the development of your TA products take in the future?

Research shows:
· People watch more and more TV
· TV watching is changing: 80% of hours are being watched in the lounge room

Focus on:
· Personalized devices
· Lounge devices
· Products: core technology
· No application company, but technology company

C. Technical Platform

6. Could you please depict the technical architecture of your solution?

7. Which use cases are covered by your technical solution?

8. Could you depict a model of the underlying TA process of the use cases from a technical point of view?

9. Could you elaborate on your technical USPs in the area of TA?

Technical platform details were not discussed. Interview was conducted on phone, hence no good opportunity for depicting the technology architecture. However, Technology Vendor C provides a series of whitepapers that were sent to the author by email.

10. What are the main issues/challenges (platform or device limitations)?
   - Infrastructure for unicast streaming, which is necessary for TA
   - Distinguish: TA and personalized advertising! Personalization (1-2-1) is tough, aggregation to groups afterwards is easy

Main issues/challenges:
   - Personalizing the content
   - Afterwards be able to make sure that content is delivered to right person, requires BW, storage for all content, content management!
   - What is the cost of transaction? TA is expensive!
      - Need lots, lots, lots of ads, each expensive
      - More expensive, more can go wrong/risk compared to traditional TV campaign
      - Good automation is necessary!
      - Balance of: value and cost of TA, business equation has to be found!
   - Buying the stuff is difficult: across all these mediums, formats, rules, placement systems,… Makes it difficult to justify multimedia campaign!

11. What are from your perspective the major technical possibilities and features in your area of TA near/mid-term/long-term?

Not discussed.

D. Data Privacy & Security

12. What is your opinion concerning data privacy in the context of TA?

Two facts about privacy:
   - Privacy is important
   - But many companies aggregate already personal data

   - Privacy is already gone anyway! Just accept that fact…
   - The question is more: how to prevent people from abuse?!!
   - Create mechanisms to anonymize data is important!

User perspective:
- 1-2-1-marketing: if you're interested in something, you will let know your data = opt-in (sort of)
- Balance: I go looking = I am prepared to give away information

Requirements:
- Data must generally be anonymized when aggregated in DB
- Offer customer possibility to give opt-in!

13. Which processes in your system are of a special relevance concerning data privacy? How do you ensure data privacy (e.g. anonymization/separation of user data from IP address)?

Not discussed.

E. Standardization of Targeted Advertising

14. Which standardization efforts are you aware of? Which gaps do you see in the standardization in your area of TA?
- Project "Canoe"
- Tru2way: Java interactive TV framework
- SCTE 30, 35 (technical standards, ad insertion)
- More non-ad related technical standards: MPEG,...

- Not many top-level-standards; there exist more standards in the context of ad formats, buying, and transaction

15. Which TA standards are met by your solutions?

Not discussed.

16. Are you involved in standardization efforts? Committees? Did you file any proposals?

Not discussed.

F. Targeted Advertising Market

17. Which companies are you partnering with and who are your main competitors?

Partners:
- Invidi: cable space, RC company
- BSkyB: uses Think Analytics "profiling technologies", originally from defense technology, distributed architecture, Java
- Bunch of companies in digital asset management
- Video splicing: Inuk (UK), university companies

18. In your opinion, what are the most successful implementations of TA today? Could you name the most interesting/important players in your area of the TA business?

   Not that many out there:
   · "TV Anywhere": installed base, go to market; but not really existing business model
   · Cisco
   · Alcatel-Lucent
   · Ericsson (IMS)
   · Google TV Ads

G. Conclusion

19. Are there any important topics/aspects of TA that should be additionally covered by my thesis?
   · Important question in IPTV value chain context: how to connect buyer and seller?
   · Buying/selling community

Interview Targeting Platform Operator

Questionnaire Structure

1. Welche Bedeutung hat Targeted Advertising im Werbegeschäft?

2. Welche Bedeutung hat TA für Telcos? Welche Rolle werden Telcos im Zusammenhang mit TA künftig einnehmen?

3. Wie ist der Trend in den letzten Jahren? Gibt es entscheidende Entwicklungen/Veränderungen am Markt bzw. technologische Entwicklungen, die TA zum Durchbruch verhelfen (können)?

4. Wie positioniert sich TA im Vergleich zu traditioneller Werbung?

5. Welche Kanäle bieten sich Ihrer Meinung nach besonders für TA an? In welchem Umfeld/bei welchen Anwendungen ist TA am viel versprechendsten (Portale, Spiele, Social Networks, Video)?

6. Welche strategischen und technischen Möglichkeiten bieten sich in den für Sie relevanten Kanälen (Online, Mobile, IPTV)? Können Sie einen Ausblick geben?

7. Auf welchen Devices wird TA künftig besonders erfolgreich sein (PCs, mobile phones, STB, gaming consoles)? Wo sehen Sie diesbezüglich Probleme/Herausforderungen (Limitationen bei Plattformen, devices,...)?

8. Welche Use Cases (möglicherweise aus Projekten, an denen Sie beteiligt waren) finden Sie besonders spannend? Können Sie diese kurz beschreiben? Welche künftigen/anderen interessanten Use Cases sind vorstellbar?

9. Auf welchen Webseiten/Portalen des Konzerns (German Telco) wird bereits TA eingesetzt? Gibt es dort einheitliche TA-Plattform?

10. Welche Technologien werden eingesetzt (Eigenentwicklungen/ Fremdhersteller)?

11. Welche sind die wichtigsten/interessantesten Targeting-Lösungen bzw. andere relevante Projekte/Aktivitäten im Web? Welche Anbieter sollte man sich näher anschauen?

12. Welche Aktivitäten anderer Telcos sind Ihnen bekannt?

13. Was passiert beim Profiling/TA mit den persönlichen Daten der Nutzer? Welche datenschutzrechtlich relevanten Abläufe gibt es?

14. Welche datenschutzrechtlich relevanten Abläufe gibt es speziell bei Ihrer Profiling/TA-Lösung? Welche Maßnahmen zum Datenschutz werden getroffen (Anonymisierung/Trennung der Profilinformationen von der IP-Adresse)?

15. Werden in Ihrer Lösung spezielle TA-Standards umgesetzt?

16. Sind Ihnen Standardisierungsmaßnahmen/Standards im Bereich des TA bekannt? Wo vermissen Sie ggf. eine Standardisierung?

17. Sind Sie diesbezüglich in Standardisierungsgremien aktiv? Haben Sie Vorschläge eingereicht? Welche?

18. Gibt es Aspekte des TA, über die wir noch nicht gesprochen haben, die sie besonders interessant finden bzw. die es wert sind genauer untersucht zu werden?

Questionnaire Answers
Torsten Topaloglu, Deutsche Telekom AG, T-Home

1. Welche Bedeutung hat Targeted Advertising im Werbegeschäft?
   - TA ist seit einigen Jahren Thema
   - Wie groß Verwendung? Jeder meint: Zukunft
   - Frage von enormer Bedeutung: Zahlungsbereitschaft? Nachvollziehbar, ob Geld wert?

2. Welche Bedeutung hat TA für Telcos? Welche Rolle werden Telcos im Zusammenhang mit TA künftig einnehmen?
   - Wichtiges Thema für den Konzern: schon lange angewandt, bevor darüber gesprochen

3. Wie ist der Trend in den letzten Jahren? Gibt es entscheidende Entwicklungen/Veränderungen am Markt bzw. technologische Entwicklungen, die TA zum Durchbruch verhelfen (können)?
   - Leistungsfähigkeit der Hardware: Finanzierbarkeit jetzt gegeben
   - Nutzerzahlen waren im Web nicht das Problem, hier ist eher die technische Entwicklung eines DER Kriterien
   - Finanzkrise: Budgets für Marketing klein, Streuverluste vermeiden. Die ist durch Targeting möglich.

4. Wie positioniert sich TA im Vergleich zu traditioneller Werbung?
   - Noch dominiert traditionelle Werbung im Online-Bereich
   - TA ist auch Marketingkriterium für Anbieter: Zeichen dafür, dass man die neueste Technologien zur Verfügung hat

5. Welche Kanäle bieten sich Ihrer Meinung nach besonders für TA an? In welchem Umfeld/bei welchen Anwendungen ist TA am viel versprechendsten (Portale, Spiele, Social Networks, Video)?
   - Prinzipiell keine Beschränkung auf einen Kanal
   - Voraussetzung für die Anwendbarkeit: Man muss den Nutzer identifizieren können
   - Möglichkeiten sind grundsätzlich in allen Kanälen gegeben

6. Welche strategischen und technischen Möglichkeiten bieten sich in den für Sie relevanten Kanälen (Online, Mobile, IPTV)? Können Sie einen Ausblick geben?
   - Alle Kanäle gleich für Kampagnenaussteuerung verwenden: Rückkanal notwendig!
   - Bei Mobile ist Endgerät die Beschränkung: Browser!

- Bei IPTV schwierig: oft keine Cookie-Unterstützung!
- Man muss gedanklich vor Bannern wegkommen
- Personalisierung immer möglich, nicht nur auf Werbung beschränken
- Begriff „Targeting" nicht nur auf Werbung beziehen. Dies ist gerade für Telcos wichtig.
- Beispiel für Personalisierung: Erkennen, ob Kunde/Nicht-Kunde, Kunden-Lebenszyklus erkennen, Kundenbindung! Upselling-Möglichkeiten!

7. Auf welchen Devices wird TA künftig besonders erfolgreich sein (PCs, mobile phones, STB, gaming consoles)? Wo sehen Sie diesbezüglich Probleme/Herausforderungen (Limitationen bei Plattformen, devices,...)?
   - Neue Möglichkeiten durch iPhone usw. Browser ist aber wichtig.
   - Problem der Identifizierung: Nicht alle mobilen Engeräte/Browser unterstützen Cookies.

8. Welche Use Cases (möglicherweise aus Projekten, an denen Sie beteiligt waren) finden Sie besonders spannend? Können Sie diese kurz beschreiben? Welche künftigen/anderen interessanten Use Cases sind vorstellbar?

Aus Abteilungssicht (Targeting/Marketing):
- Alles spannend, wo man etwas messen/monitoren kann: ohne Targeting/mit Targeting im Vergleich
- Vorhandenes Inventar so gut monetarisieren wie möglich: CTR, Conversion-Rate-Erhöhung
- Egal, ob Access-Produkt von Operator oder bspw. Reiseanbieter

Aus Telco-Sicht:
- Vor allem Kundenbindung!

Interessante Use Cases:
- Im Web Banner + mehr
- Idealerweise konvergente Plattformen
- Technisch auch bereits möglich, Problem: alle an einen Tisch kriegen

Targeting vs. Empfehlungssystem:
- Von der Idee her keinen Unterschied zwischen Rec. + TA
- Oft zweigliedrige Realisierung, Synergien nutzen!

9. Auf welchen Webseiten/Portalen des Konzerns (German Telco) wird bereits TA eingesetzt? Gibt es dort einheitliche TA-Plattform?
   - Früher „aktive Personalisierung" mit eindeutiger Nutzeridentifikation, jetzt zunehmend „passive Personalisierung" = Targeting, seit 7 Jahren mit Wunderloop

- Targeting aktuell auf allen Web Portalen die vom konzerneigenen Ad Marketer vermarktet werden, sowie generell auf allen Portalen des Konzerns
- Unterscheidung: Auslieferung (Ad Marketer) vs. Tracking (Targeting Platform Operator)
- Ziel: das gesamte Konzern-Netzwerk tracken!

10. Welche Technologien werden eingesetzt (Eigenentwicklungen/ Fremdhersteller)?

- Eigenentwicklungen + Fremdleistung
- Fremdleistung steht Inhouse, kein ASP mit Modifikation, Wunderloop einziger Dienstleister
- Tracking-Komponente auf hauseigenen Servern

- Ad Server von AdTech eingekauft
- Targeting Platform Operator stellt Cookie-Werte für Ad Marketer zur Verfügung
- Bsp.: Targeting Platform Operator gibt Cookie für Sport an Ad Marketer weiter, Ablauf:
1. Nutzer bekommt ID
2. Welche Inhalte sieht der Nutzer sich an?
3. Nur Inhalt, nicht die Seite selbst. Wie viele Seiten mit welchem Inhalt
4. Info wird in Cookie geschrieben
5. Info wird von Ad Server des Ad Markerters ausgelesen

11. Welche sind die wichtigsten/interessantesten Targeting-Lösungen bzw. andere relevante Projekte/Aktivitäten im Web? Welche Anbieter sollte man sich näher anschauen?

- YooChoose – Personal Media Recommendations
- Nugg.ad, Wunderloop, 1&1

12. Welche Aktivitäten anderer Telcos sind Ihnen bekannt?
Nicht diskutiert.

13. Was passiert beim Profiling/TA mit den persönlichen Daten der Nutzer? Welche datenschutzrechtlich relevanten Abläufe gibt es?
Nicht diskutiert.

14. Welche datenschutzrechtlich relevanten Abläufe gibt es speziell bei Ihrer
    Profiling/TA-Lösung? Welche Maßnahmen zum Datenschutz werden getrof-
    fen (Anonymisierung/Trennung der Profilinformationen von der IP-Adresse)?

    · Wunderloop besitzt „EuroPrice" Gütesiegel (EU)
    · Unabhängiges Landeszentrum für Datenschutz (ULD) in Deutschland
      (Schleswig-Holstein)
    · Problem: Man kann mit der Technik auch Missbrauch betreiben, obwohl
      die Technik zertifiziert ist!

15. Werden in Ihrer Lösung spezielle TA-Standards umgesetzt?

    Nicht diskutiert.

16. Sind Ihnen Standardisierungsmaßnahmen/Standards im Bereich des TA be-
    kannt? Wo vermissen Sie ggf. eine Standardisierung?

    · TA bezogene Standards gibt es kaum, teilweise herrscht sogar Unklarheit
      bezüglich der Begrifflichkeiten, z.b. genaue Bedeutung von „behavioral
      targeting"
    · Bundesverband digitaler Wirtschaft (BVDW) und seine Fachgruppe Onli-
      nevermarkterkreis (OVK), Zusammenschluss von Unternehmen der Onli-
      ne-Werbeindustrie
    · Beschäftigen sich mit der Standardisierung von Online-Werbeformaten
    · Definitionen zu Begriffen, auch Gruppe zu Targeting
    · Einschätzung: Einheitliche Standards sind für die weitere Entwicklung und
      Verbreitung von TA wichtig und werden sich durchsetzen.

17. Sind Sie diesbezüglich in Standardisierungsgremien aktiv? Haben Sie Vor-
    schläge eingereicht? Welche?

    · Konzern ist über seinen Ad Marketer im BVDW/OVK vertreten

18. Gibt es Aspekte des TA, über die wir noch nicht gesprochen haben, die sie
    besonders interessant finden bzw. die es wert sind genauer untersucht zu wer-
    den?

    · DMEXCO (Messe für Online-Vermarkter) besuchen, 2009 liegt der Fokus
      unter anderem auf TA

Interview IPTV Operator

Questionnaire Structure

1. Welche Bedeutung hat TA für Telcos? Welche Rolle werden Telcos im Zusammenhang mit TA künftig einnehmen?

2. Wie ist der Trend in den letzten Jahren? Gibt es entscheidende Entwicklungen/Veränderungen am Markt bzw. technologische Entwicklungen, die TA zum Durchbruch verhelfen (können)?

3. Welche strategischen und technischen Möglichkeiten bieten sich in den für Sie relevanten Kanälen (Online, Mobile, IPTV)? Können Sie einen Ausblick geben?

4. Auf welchen Devices wird TA künftig besonders erfolgreich sein (PCs, mobile phones, STB, gaming consoles)? Wo sehen Sie diesbezüglich Probleme/Herausforderungen (Limitationen bei Plattformen, devices,...)?

5. Welche Werbeformate werden von Ihrer TA Lösung unterstützt (Banner, Overlay, Pop up, Wallpaper, Splitcreen, Pre-/Post-/Mid-Roll)? Welche sind am viel versprechendsten?

6. Welche Use Cases (möglicherweise aus Projekten, an denen Sie beteiligt waren) finden Sie besonders spannend? Können Sie diese kurz beschreiben? Welche künftigen/anderen interessanten Use Cases sind vorstellbar?

7. Welche Technologien werden verwendet (Eigenentwicklungen/Hersteller)? Wie sieht die Roadmap bezüglich TA im IPTV aus? Ist TA vorgesehen?

8. Gab es weitere TA Projekte, an denen Sie beteiligt waren? Wurden diese Projekte erfolgreich umgesetzt? Welche Probleme haben sich ergeben? Lösungen?

9. Sind Ihnen Projekte zur Konvergenz der verschiedenen Kanäle (Online, IPTV, Mobile) unter dem Aspekt des TA bekannt? Wie wichtig ist eine konzernweite TA-Plattform?

10. Wie schätzen sie den Status Quo des Konzerns hinsichtlich der Einführung/Umsetzung von TA-Maßnahmen im Vergleich zu anderen Telcos ein?

11. Welche Aktivitäten anderer Telcos sind Ihnen bekannt?

12. Was passiert beim Profiling/TA mit den persönlichen Daten der Nutzer? Welche datenschutzrechtlich relevanten Abläufe gibt es?

13. Welche datenschutzrechtlich relevanten Abläufe gibt es speziell bei Ihrer Profiling/TA-Lösung? Welche Maßnahmen zum Datenschutz werden getroffen (Anonymisierung/Trennung der Profilinformationen von der IP-Adresse)?

14. Werden in Ihrer Lösung spezielle TA-Standards umgesetzt?

15. Sind Ihnen Standardisierungsmaßnahmen/Standards im Bereich des TA bekannt? Wo vermissen Sie ggf. eine Standardisierung?

16. Sind Sie diesbezüglich in Standardisierungsgremien aktiv? Haben Sie Vorschläge eingereicht? Welche?

17. Gibt es Aspekte des TA, über die wir noch nicht gesprochen haben, die sie besonders interessant finden bzw. die es wert sind genauer untersucht zu werden?

Questionnaire Answers
Sebastian Thiele, Deutsche Telekom AG, Products & Innovation

1. Welche Bedeutung hat TA für Telcos? Welche Rolle werden Telcos im Zusammenhang mit TA künftig einnehmen?

   · Feasibility-Analyse anhand von Use Cases und Marktstudie in 2008
   · Technische Machbarkeit abhängig von Weiterentwicklung der im Konzern verwendeten Microsoft IPTV-Lösung (Microsoft Mediaroom)
   · Business insights: Kommerzieller Erfolg in naher Zukunft noch fraglich

2. Wie ist der Trend in den letzten Jahren? Gibt es entscheidende Entwicklungen/Veränderungen am Markt bzw. technologische Entwicklungen, die TA zum Durchbruch verhelfen (können)?

   Einstieg in die Werbevermarktung im TV-Bereich ist schwierig:
   · Konzerneigener Ad Vermarkter bisher nur im Web-, Mobile-, und Out-of-Home-Bereich tätig
   · Problem bei IPTV: Content gehört Broadcastern!
   · strategische Interessen, vor allem der „Privaten"
   · Vorbehalte gegenüber Revenue Shares
   · Ein IPTV Operator wäre neues Glied in der Wertschöpfungskette, da Sender bereits eigene Vermarkter haben: RTL/IP Deutschland, Pro Sieben-Sat.1/ProSiebenSat.1 Media
   · Telcos werden eher als Dienstleister in der Technik gesehen: Strategie: Technical Enabler vs. Full Service Provider?
   · Für ein mögliches Projekt muss definiert werden: Welche Use Cases?
   · Wie sieht der Business Case genau aus: Revenue Sharing Konzept?
   · Definition einer Markteintrittstrategie: Kombination mit Lead-Sender für Proof-of-concept
   · Problem: Werbebranche ingesamt sehr konservativ!

3. Welche strategischen und technischen Möglichkeiten bieten sich in den für Sie relevanten Kanälen (Online, Mobile, IPTV)? Können Sie einen Ausblick geben?

   Grundsätzliche Relevanz von TA für TV-Bereich:
   · Targeting: jeder Vendor hat seine eigene Lösung
   · Strategische Frage für Telco: Ist TA derzeit ein „must-have" oder eher relevant für Phase 2-3?
   · Fernsehwerbung ist grundsätzlich nicht auf Targeting ausgelegt sondern auf „Eyeballs"

- Eher Umfeld-abhängig: wichtiger für Fernsehbranche als personengenaue Ansprache auf Plattformseite, Targeting durch Umfeldgruppen ist schon recht stark!
- Vorsicht: Man kann mit TA auch viel „kaputt" machen, z.b. bei wenigen Kunden/kleiner Nutzerbasis, Anzahl ist das Problem (im Vergleich zum Internet noch sehr gering).

4. Auf welchen Devices wird TA künftig besonders erfolgreich sein (PCs, mobile phones, STB, gaming consoles)? Wo sehen Sie diesbezüglich Probleme/Herausforderungen (Limitationen bei Plattformen, devices,...)? Nicht diskutiert.

5. Welche Werbeformate werden von Ihrer TA Lösung unterstützt (Banner, Overlay, Pop up, Wallpaper, Splitscreen, Pre-/Post-/Mid-Roll)? Welche sind am viel versprechendsten?

Fernsehwerbeformate im klassischen Linear TV:
- 30s Spot
- Sponsorships (7s)
- Splitscreen (30 countdown)
- Platzierungen vor und nach Werbeblock
- Banner-Formate noch relativ neu

Format-Kategorien im IPTV:
1. Pre-/mid-/post-roll
- Relevant für VoD Dienste und TV-Archiv
2. Banner (Display) Advertising
- Technisches Problem, Banner mit bisheriger Lösung anzubieten
- Niedriges Potential
3. Interaktive Fernsehwerbung
Einfache Interaktivität:
- „Request-for-info" (RFI), Overlay mit Möglichkeit Info abzurufen, nicht Bildschirm füllend, im „lower third" des Bildschirms
- Red Button drücken, z.B. Barilla-Werbung, Button liefert Rezept
- Opt-in: Registrierungsmöglichkeit schaffen
- Bsp.: Sky „Red Button", „Impulse Response" = Gewinnspiel mit Texteingabemöglichkeit
Komplexere Formate:
- „Dedicated Advertiser Location" (DAL), komplexere Markenwelten, Gewinnspiele (mit Integration von Impulse Response)
- „Mini DAL", fließender Übergang von DAL, Werbeseite 3/4 des Bildschirms, Interaktionsmöglichkeiten: Seiten, Bilder, Video-Inhalte

- Microsite, interaktive (Bildschirm füllende) Applikation, 2-3 Seiten zur Auswahl, Zusatzinfos zu Werbeprodukt, mit Farbtasten hin und her springen

4. Mischformate: Advertainment
- Elemente aus allen Formaten, Bsp.: Branded Channels wie Bahn TV (vertragsrechtliche Fragen zu beachten), Apps mit gerankten Werbespots (Vorbild: YouTube)

5. Ad Splicing
- Austausch einzelner Werbespots innerhalb von Werbeblöcken
- Teilweise Haushalts(mitglied) genau
- Personalisierte Werbung, konzeptueller Unterschied zu normalem Fernsehen: nicht so viele wie möglich erreichen
- Problematik: Spot-Austauschung geht wieder in Werbevermarktungsrichtung, dauert vermutlich noch 5-10 Jahre in Deutschland

- Theoretisch Verknüpfung der beschriebenen Formate interessant: „Mix-and-match"

6. Welche Use Cases (möglicherweise aus Projekten, an denen Sie beteiligt waren) finden Sie besonders spannend? Können Sie diese kurz beschreiben? Welche künftigen/anderen interessanten Use Cases sind vorstellbar?

Interessante Use Cases:

1. VoD Advertising:
- Aus strategischen Gründen interessant, etwa Refinanzierung im TV-Archiv
- Bsp.: iPlayer (BBC) UK/USA, Sky On Demand, Virgin Cable
- On Demand Werbung erst dieses Jahr bei der Gesellschaft für Konsumforschung (GFK) erfasst, daher noch kaum Statistiken über Erfolg verfügbar
- Pre-/post-roll haushaltsgenau
- Interessant: personalisierte Bereitstellung für einzelne Personen im Haushalt
  Bsp.: User wählt Format aus, 1-2 Pre/Post-rolls à 10-15s (Targeted Spots)

2. Display Advertising:
- Mehr interaktive Inhalte sind Voraussetzung für Erfolg
- Denkbar: Einbindung v. Facebook/UGC (YouTube)
- Internet-Targeting-Ansätze aus Online übernehmen, aber zunächst ohne Flash (Performance-Gründe Mediaroom-Lösung + STB)

Ansatzpunkte für Targeting-Arten:
- Geographical targeting
  Bsp.: BMW Spot unterschiedlich (etwa Händlerinfo), je nachdem ob User in München oder Hamburg
- Problematik: Fernsehmarkt in Deutschland ist nicht so lokal wie in USA, daher fraglich als Einstiegsszenario
- Demographisch:
  Technisch heute zu realisieren, aber vertragsrechtlich problematisch

7. Welche Technologien werden verwendet (Eigenentwicklungen/Hersteller)? Wie sieht die Roadmap bezüglich TA im IPTV aus? Ist TA vorgesehen?

   Status Quo TA im IPTV im Konzern:
   - Bisher gar kein Advertising möglich
   - Seit Anfang 2009 Microsoft Advertising Platform im Mediaroom verfügbar
   - Erste Realisierungen wohl erst in 2011

8. Gab es weitere TA Projekte, an denen Sie beteiligt waren? Wurden diese Projekte erfolgreich umgesetzt? Welche Probleme haben sich ergeben? Lösungen?
   - Erster Targeted VoD Advertising Showcase auf IFA 2009 mit RTL
   - Bildet zwei Profilgruppen nach, technisch nachvollzogen/implementiert

9. Sind Ihnen Projekte zur Konvergenz der verschiedenen Kanäle (Online, IPTV, Mobile) unter dem Aspekt des TA bekannt? Wie wichtig ist eine konzernweite TA-Plattform?
   - Eine Plattform wäre sinnvoll, um existierende Operator Assets (Nutzerdaten, Nutzerverhalten von mehreren Kanälen) effektiver auszunutzen
   - Möglichkeit einer Cross Plattform mit Kampagnenmöglichkeit über konzerneigenen Ad Marketer, Nähe zu Internet erforderlich!
   - Ziel: Eine Kampagne mit Targeting über alle Kanäle aussteuern

10. Wie schätzen sie den Status Quo des Konzerns hinsichtlich der Einführung/Umsetzung von TA-Maßnahmen im Vergleich zu anderen Telcos ein?
    Nicht diskutiert.

11. Welche Aktivitäten anderer Telcos sind Ihnen bekannt?
    Nicht diskutiert.

12. Was passiert beim Profiling/TA mit den persönlichen Daten der Nutzer? Welche datenschutzrechtlich relevanten Abläufe gibt es?
    Nicht diskutiert.

13. Welche datenschutzrechtlich relevanten Abläufe gibt es speziell bei Ihrer Profiling/TA-Lösung? Welche Maßnahmen zum Datenschutz werden getroffen (Anonymisierung/Trennung der Profilinformationen von der IP-Adresse)? Nicht diskutiert.

14. Werden in Ihrer Lösung spezielle TA-Standards umgesetzt? Nicht diskutiert.

15. Sind Ihnen Standardisierungsmaßnahmen/Standards im Bereich des TA bekannt? Wo vermissen Sie ggf. eine Standardisierung? Nicht diskutiert.

16. Sind Sie diesbezüglich in Standardisierungsgremien aktiv? Haben Sie Vorschläge eingereicht? Welche? Nicht diskutiert.

17. Gibt es Aspekte des TA, über die wir noch nicht gesprochen haben, die sie besonders interessant finden bzw. die es wert sind genauer untersucht zu werden? Nicht diskutiert.

Note: This interview had a very strong focus on relevant ad formats, use cases, and the general market situation for targeted advertising in IPTV. As the interviewee's input concerning these topics was very valuable for use case development, the author decided to omit some of the other questions.